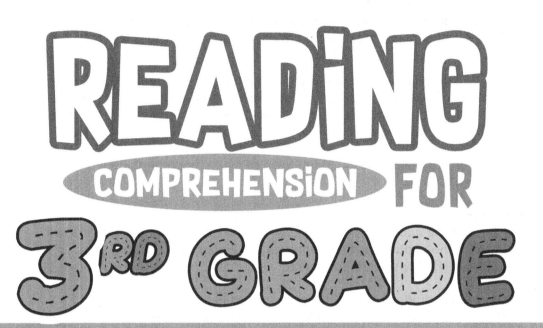

READING COMPREHENSION FOR 3RD GRADE

100 ACTIVITIES - THIRD GRADE READING COMPREHENSION WORKBOOK

Patrick N. Peerson

Reading Comprehension Grade 3
100 Activities

Third grade reading comprehension workbook

Reading comprehension grade 3 improve reading comprehension skills for the third grade through the fun learning activities inside this 3rd grade reading books. Good comprehension is vital, the reading should have a purpose, and a reader should engage with and learn from a text. This is one of the recommended books for 3rd grade classroom must haves because the reading comprehension skill is one of the most important skills, which is the ability to read text, process it, and understand its meaning.

This 3rd grade reading comprehension workbook contains 100 awesome skill-building practicing lessons by answering the questions of fun stories, crossword games, word search, fill-in-the-blanks to complete the sentences, choosing the meaning of Vocabulary.

Learn with fun Activities through the Reading comprehension workbooks for 3rd graders:

Features :
• Answer the questions – In this section, the questions and answers are relevant to the context in which they read. It would help children learn to understand the context of the story.

• Answer with Word search – Find the word in the puzzle and circle.
In this part, children would learn to know more Vocabulary through understanding the context.

• Crossword – Read the clues and write the answers in the crossword puzzle. In this part, children would learn to spell more new Vocabulary and understand the meaning through reading the context.

•Choosing the meaning of Vocabulary – In this part, this activity would help children learn how to explain and describe the meaning of words.

•• Complete the Sentence – In this part, this activity would help children understand the main idea of the article.

Help your kids to improve their reading comprehension skills with this third grade workbook.

Patrick N. Peerson
Funny Learn Play

The Roller Coaster

Adam and his family woke up very early. They were going to an amusement park today! They had to drive three hours to get there, so they wanted to get an early start.
"You can sleep in the car, Adam," said his mom, "if you are still sleepy."
"I am too excited to be sleepy!" exclaimed Adam.
When they arrived at the amusement park, Adam was surprised by all the rides!
It was like nothing he had ever seen before in his life! Adam felt as if he were on another planet! There was a carousel with colorful figures of horses that people could ride on! There was a Ferris Wheel that took riders way up high where they could see the whole park from above!
There was a ride where people rode in little boats and got splashed with water!
But the ride that Adam was most excited to see was the roller coaster. The roller coaster was the tallest and fastest of all the rides. Adam watched as people rode the roller coaster, and he heard them as they shouted with excitement.
The roller coaster looked thrilling, but it also looked really scary.
Adam was not sure he wanted to go on it.
"Adam, which ride do you want to go on first?" asked his dad.
"Let's try the carousel," Adam said. They rode on the carousel.
"Which should we ride on next?" asked his mom.
"Let's go on the boat ride," Adam said. They rode on the boat ride.
"Well," said Adam's dad, "are you ready for the roller coaster?"
Adam looked up at the roller coaster.
He felt so nervous! But he also felt very excited! "Okay!" he said. "Let's do it!"
They got in line for the roller coaster. It was finally their turn. Adam held onto the safety bar of the roller coaster car very tightly!
The ride began and started out slowly; the car moved up, up, up into the air. Then suddenly the car stopped moving up, and— whoosh! —the car raced downward and all around the roller coaster track! Adam yelled out in delight!
He loved riding on this roller coaster! What a thrill!

1. How long did it take to get to the amusement park?

   _____

2. Which ride had colorful figures of horses to ride?

   _____

3. Which ride did Adam go on second?
   a. the roller coaster
   b. the carousel
   c. the Ferris Wheel
   d. the boat ride

4. How did Adam feel about the roller coaster at the end of the story?

   _____

Peter's Lucky Pebble

Peter and his older brother, Christopher, liked to run. They would run around in their backyard, and they would run at the park. They would run whenever they could! They were always racing to see who was faster, Peter or Christopher. Christopher, who had longer legs, usually won.

One day while the brothers were at the beach, they decided to have a race to the top of the biggest sand dune.

"This will be a hard race," said Peter. "It is a big sand dune!"

"Yes," said Christopher, "but we can do it!"

The sand was very hot, so they put on their shoes. They did not want to burn their feet while running!

The race began, and Christopher was in the lead. Peter was trying his best but was still falling further behind. Just when he thought he was going to lose again, he felt something in the shoe on his left foot. There was something in his shoe rubbing against his toes. It did not feel good!

"Should I stop?" thought Peter. "There must be a pebble in my shoe. Should I quit the race to shake the pebble out of my shoe?"

Peter kept going. In fact, he started running faster. He wanted to finish the race so he could take his shoe off! Peter ran faster than he ever ran before. He passed Christopher! He won the race to the top of the dune!

"Wow!" exclaimed Christopher. "How did you do that? How did you run so fast?"

Peter sat down and took his left shoe off. He shook the shoe, and out came a little brown pebble. He held the pebble up for Christopher to see.

"This little pebble helped me to win!" said Peter, laughing.

Christopher laughed too. "That is your lucky pebble. Are you going to always race with it in your shoe?"

"I will always race with it," said Peter, "but I think I will keep it in my pocket instead of my shoe!" The brothers ran back down the sand dune with Peter's lucky pebble!

1. Which brother was older?

_____

2. What helped Christopher to usually win the races?
    a. He had shorter hair.
    b. He had longer arms.
    c. He had longer legs.
    d. He had stronger muscles.

3. Why did they put their shoes on for the race at the beach?

_____

4. How did the pebble help Peter to win the race?

_____

The Most Amazing Tree

Evelyn felt very happy because she was going to her grandparents' house. Their house was located deep in the woods. It was a special, very peaceful place to visit. There were all kinds of interesting things to see inside of their house. Evelyn loved to look at all of the old photographs and to read the old books that they had. She loved the cookies that her grandmother baked for her!

But what Evelyn loved the most were the woods outside of her grandparents' house—she thought those woods were magical!

"Grandfather, please, let's go for a walk in the woods!" Evelyn said.

Her grandfather smiled and put on his hiking boots. Evelyn put on her boots too.

"Today, I will show you the most amazing tree in the woods! It is the oldest tree, even older than me!" said her grandfather.

Together they walked on the trail. Evelyn saw little flowers growing beneath the branches of big trees. She saw birds making nests and squirrels chasing one another through the leaves. She even saw a mouse hiding under a pile of sticks. "Where is the most amazing tree, Grandfather?" Evelyn asked. "We are almost there," her grandfather answered. "You will soon see." They walked a little further, and then Evelyn's grandfather stopped in front of the tallest, widest, oldest tree Evelyn had ever seen. "This is the tree! Isn't it amazing?" said her grandfather.

Evelyn looked way up high into the branches of the old tree. She walked all around the trunk of the tree. She touched the bark of the tree. She picked up a leaf that had fallen off of the tree.

"Yes, Grandfather, this is the most amazing tree I have ever seen. I think it is the grandfather of these woods!" said Evelyn. "Thank you for showing it to me." Evelyn gave her grandfather a big hug.

Evelyn and her grandfather walked back to the house. There, her grandmother had just finished baking cookies. While they ate the cookies, Evelyn told her grandmother all about the tree. Evelyn had a wonderful time seeing the amazing tree and seeing her amazing grandparents!

1. Where was Evelyn's grandparents' house?

_____

2. Name four things that Evelyn saw while walking in the woods.

_____

3. Why did Evelyn call the tree the "grandfather of these woods?"

_____

_____

4. What did Evelyn's grandmother bake?
   - a. cookies
   - b. cakes
   - c. pies
   - d. spaghetti

Carly's New Friend

"Come on, Carly!" called her mom. "We are going to be late!"
It was Thursday afternoon, and every Thursday afternoon Carly and her mom volunteered at the animal shelter. The animal shelter was filled with dogs and cats that did not have a home.
Carly did not feel like going to volunteer today. Helping at the animal shelter was a lot of work—and it usually smelled bad there! She had to clean out cages, feed the animals, and fill their water bowls. Carly wanted to stay home and watch TV today. But she knew her mom would never allow that! "I'm coming, Mom!" Carly said, and she hurried to the car.
When Carly and her mom arrived at the animal shelter, the director asked her to do a new job. Carly was asked to walk the dogs on leashes around the yard outside. She was to help them to get some exercise.
The first dog Carly walked was a big shaggy black dog named Max. It was very strong and pulled Carly along as they walked around the yard.
The second dog was a small white dog named Rizzo, who barked the whole time. He barked at everything he saw!
The third dog was a medium-sized brown dog who had no name, as he was new to the animal shelter. This dog was very shy and did not want to come out of his cage. Carly had to encourage him to come out by petting him and speaking to him in a calming voice.
When this dog finally came out, he would not leave Carly's side. Carly did not mind. In fact, she really liked this dog! The director said, "Wow! This dog really likes you! I think you made a new friend! Maybe you can help to think of a name for him?"
Carly said, "I know the perfect name for this dog—Buddy!"
"Then his name will be Buddy!" said the director.
The next Thursday, Carly couldn't wait to get to the animal shelter to volunteer. She couldn't wait to see Buddy again. Carly's mom asked if she would want to adopt Buddy and bring him home to live with them. Carly was so happy to have her new friend become a part of their family!

1. Which day of the week did Carly volunteer at the animal shelter?

_____

2. With whom did Carly go to the animal shelter?
    a. her brother
    b. her best friend
    c. her aunt
    d. her mom

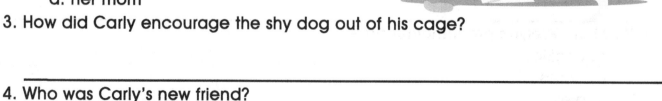

3. How did Carly encourage the shy dog out of his cage?

_____

4. Who was Carly's new friend?

_____

Ronnie and the Chess Tournament

When Ronnie was only five years old, his father taught him to play the game of chess. Ronnie learned very quickly how to move the different pieces, and he learned how to capture the pieces of his opponent.

Over the next four years, Ronnie got even better at the game. He loved playing chess with his family and friends. They all knew that he would usually win, even though he was so young.

One day, when Ronnie was nine years old, his father saw a sign at the library advertising for a chess tournament. The sign said that all ages were welcome to play in the tournament.

"Ronnie, would you like to play in a chess tournament?" asked his father. "You would get to play chess with lots of other people who love to play the game."

"Yes!" exclaimed Ronnie. "I want to play in the tournament!"

Ronnie's father signed him up for the tournament. It was going to take place on Saturday at the library.

Saturday morning, Ronnie woke up early. He and his father walked to the library. There were a lot of tables and chess boards set up. The man in charge told Ronnie where to go.

Ronnie sat down, and so did a man who looked very old. He even looked older than Ronnie's father! The man was surprised he was going to play chess with a little boy. They started their chess match, and Ronnie thought very carefully about each move. He won the game!

"Congratulations," said the man. "You played a great game of chess!" The man shook hands with Ronnie.

The tournament continued, and Ronnie played six more games, and he won every one of them! He was declared the champion of the tournament! Ronnie walked home with his father after the tournament, proudly carrying a giant golden trophy.

"Thank you," Ronnie said to his father. "Thank you for teaching me how to play chess!"

1. How old was Ronnie when he learned how to play chess?

_____

2. Where was the chess tournament?

    a. at the school

    b. at the park

    c. at the book store

    d. at the library

3. Why was the man surprised that he was going to play chess with Ronnie?

_____

4. What did Ronnie receive after winning the tournament?

_____

Name:_____

Washing Dishes with Grandma

Helen was on vacation from school. She had an entire week to do anything she wanted—and she wanted to go to her grandma's house!

Helen and her grandma loved to do many things together. They would sometimes go shopping together. They would sometimes go to the movies together. They would sometimes play card games together.

But Helen's favorite thing to do with her grandma was to help her wash the dishes! At Helen's house, there was a dishwasher to do this chore, but not at her grandma's house! So, this was a special job that she only got to do while at her grandma's house.

Whenever there were dirty dishes in the sink, Helen and her grandma would have a fun time washing them together. "Today, let's sing songs while we wash the dishes," said Helen one day. "Lovely idea!" her grandma responded. Together they sang their favorite songs while washing all the dishes. The next day Helen said, "Today, let's tell each other jokes while we wash the dishes!"

"Fabulous idea!" her grandma responded. Together they giggled at the funny jokes they told to each other while washing all the dishes. Every day they found something fun to do while washing dishes—they told scary ghost stories, they made up silly rhymes, they even quizzed each other on math problems!

On the last day of Helen's vacation, she was feeling sad that she would have to leave her grandma's house.

"I have an idea," said her grandma. "Today, let's be grateful for all the fun things that we did together this week!"

"Wonderful idea!" Helen responded. Together they remembered all the activities that they did during Helen's vacation and planned new ones for the next time they would be together.

"Let's not forget the activity I am most grateful for..." Helen said, "...washing dishes with you!" Helen's grandma gave her a big, soapy hug!

1. Where did Helen want to go on her vacation?

_____

2. Why didn't Helen wash dishes at her own house?

_____

3. How was Helen feeling on the last day of her vacation?

_____

4. What was one thing Helen and her grandma did not do while washing the dishes?

     a. tell jokes

     b. read books

     c. sing songs

     d. tell ghost stories

The Baby

Johnny was feeling very nervous. His mom and dad were coming home today
from the hospital. His mom had a baby! The baby was coming home too.
Johnny was not sure what it would be like to have a new baby in the family.
"Johnny, you will love your new baby brother," said his grandmother.
"You will help to take care of him."
But Johnny was not sure about that. He did not know how to take care of a baby!
How could he help?
When his parents came home, they gave him a big hug and introduced him to
the baby, who was sleeping. The baby's name was Timmy. Johnny was not sure
what to think about this new baby.
"Johnny, would you like to hold the baby?" asked his mother. "Come and sit on the
couch next to me. I will show you how to safely hold the baby."
"I don't think I can," said Johnny. "I am afraid I won't do it right."
"Let's try," said his mom. "I think you can do it!"
Johnny went to the couch with his mom. She showed him how to hold Timmy.
Johnny could not believe that he was actually holding a baby!
He could not believe this little baby was his new brother!
Timmy opened his eyes. He started to cry a little bit. Johnny started to get worried
again. "Mom, please take the baby from me. He is crying!"
"Don't worry, Johnny. Timmy is just hungry. Would you like to help feed him?"
asked his mom.
"I don't think I can," said Johnny. "I am afraid I won't do it right."
"Let's try," said his mom. "I think you can do it!"
Johnny's mom brought him a bottle filled with special milk for the baby. She
showed him how to hold the bottle so Timmy could take a drink from it.
Timmy stopped crying and started drinking the milk. Johnny could not believe
he was feeding the baby!
"You are a wonderful big brother, Johnny," said his mom. Johnny smiled.
He loved being able to help, and he loved his baby brother!

1. Where did Johnny's mom go to have the baby?

    a. to the library

    b. to the police station

    c. to the hospital

    d. to the restaurant

2. What was the baby's name?

_____

3. How did Johnny feel at the beginning of the story?

_____

4. Johnny's mom showed him how to hold the baby. What else did she show him?

_____

Cloud Stories

Sarah was so excited! She was spending the day with her cousin Beth and her Aunt Linda. Together they were going on a picnic.

Aunt Linda drove them to a park with lots of green grass, where they spread out a big blanket. Beth brought a basket filled with sandwiches, carrot sticks, fruits, and cookies. Sarah brought bottles of cold lemonade.

"This is the best picnic ever!" Sarah said. They had eaten all of the delicious food and were now sipping on the lemonade.

"Yes," agreed Beth,

"even the fluffy clouds look happy up in the beautiful blue sky."

"Today is the perfect day to tell cloud stories!" exclaimed Aunt Linda.

"What is a cloud story?" asked Sarah.

"A cloud story is when you look up at the clouds and find images within the shapes they make. Then you use your imagination to create a story about those images!" answered Aunt Linda.

"Oh! Let me try!" said Beth. "Let's see…that cloud looks like a polar bear! I think the polar bear is making an ice cream sundae…with a cherry on top!" They all giggled at Beth's polar bear cloud story!

Next, Aunt Linda thought of a cloud story. She pointed up towards a cloud and said, "That cloud looks like a horse! I think that horse was running in a race and just won first place!"

"It is your turn, Sarah!" said Beth. "What do you see? Tell us a cloud story!" Sarah looked up at the clouds and tried to see an image. She was having trouble finding an image to tell a story about. But then a breeze shifted the clouds in the sky, and suddenly one of them seemed to look just like a bunny rabbit!

While pointing up at the cloud, Sarah said, "That bunny rabbit over there just finished munching on a carrot stick that he took from our picnic basket!"

They all laughed! What a perfect day for cloud stories!

1. How was Beth related to Sarah?

_____

2. What was in Beth's basket?

_____

3. Who told a cloud story about a horse?
    a. Aunt Linda
    b. Beth
    c. Sarah
    d. Uncle Frank

4. What was Sarah's cloud story about?

_____

Lauren's Loose Tooth

Everyone else in Lauren's class at school had already lost at least one baby tooth. Richard had already lost two baby teeth. Lauren's best friend Grace had already lost four baby teeth! Lauren still had not lost even one baby tooth. She was feeling very frustrated!

"Don't worry," her mother told her,

"your baby teeth will fall out when they are ready."

"But I'm ready now!" Lauren complained. She didn't want to wait any longer! She wasn't a baby anymore; why'd she still have her baby teeth?

"Are any of your teeth wiggly?" asked her older brother, Matthew.

Lauren tried wiggling each tooth in her mouth. One of them was wiggly!

"Try eating something crunchy," advised Matthew. "That will help get the tooth looser."

Lauren went to the kitchen for some crunchy food. First, she tried a big red apple. She chomped on the apple, but the tooth still didn't come out.

Next, Lauren tried a bright orange carrot. She bit down on the crunchy carrot, but her tooth still did not come out.

Then, Lauren tried some little brown peanuts. She chewed the crunchy peanuts, but her tooth still did not come out.

"Don't worry," her mother said, "perhaps tomorrow your tooth will be ready to come out."

Lauren went to school feeling a bit sad the next day. She could feel the wiggly tooth moving back and forth in her mouth, but why wouldn't it fall out? Would she have her baby teeth forever?

At lunchtime, Lauren sat next to her friend, Grace. While she was eating her sandwich, something felt funny in her mouth…her tooth fell out!

"Your tooth!" exclaimed Grace. "Let's go to see the school nurse. She will help you." The nurse helped Lauren to rinse her mouth with water and then gave her a special little bag in which she put the tooth.

Lauren felt very proud to have lost her first baby tooth! She smiled widely for everyone to see!

1. Who had already lost four baby teeth?
   - a. Lauren
   - b. Richard
   - c. Bernie
   - d. Grace

2. How did Matthew advise Lauren?

_____

3. Which three crunchy foods did Lauren eat to try to loosen her tooth?

_____

4. Who gave Lauren a special little bag for her tooth?

_____

Name: _____

Teddy's New Bicycle

"Today is the day!" declared Teddy's father.
"Today, we are going to try out your new bicycle!"
Teddy looked up from his cereal bowl with a worried look on his face. His new bicycle was really big. It only had two wheels instead of three, like his old tricycle. Teddy wasn't sure that he'd be able to ride his new bicycle.
"I like my tricycle," he said. "I can save my new bicycle for next summer."
"I think you will like your new bicycle better," his father said.
"You are taller now, so a bigger bicycle is what you need. Come on, let's take it to the park to try it out."
The park by their house had many trails where people liked to go for walks, to go for jogs, and to ride bicycles. Teddy and his father brought the new bicycle to one of the trails.
His father held onto the back of the bicycle as Teddy tried to sit and balance on it. He had to stretch his legs out in order to reach the pedals with his feet. Teddy felt very nervous.
"You can do it!" his father exclaimed. They started moving on the trail.
Teddy held on tightly to the handlebars and moved the pedals with his feet. His father ran along behind him, still holding onto the bicycle.
"Don't let go!" Teddy shouted. "I don't want to fall!"
"You are doing a great job! You can do this all by yourself. If you fall, we can try again," encouraged Teddy's father.
Teddy kept pedaling and steering with the handlebars. He was starting to enjoy his new bicycle! As he was moving along, his father let go.
Soon Teddy lost his balance, and the bicycle fell over.
Teddy looked at his scraped knees and dirty hands. He looked at the bicycle, which was on the ground next to him. He didn't like falling, but it really didn't hurt too much. "I can do this!" he thought.
Teddy's father ran up to him and helped him to his feet.
"Are you okay?" he asked. Teddy nodded.
"Let's try again!" Teddy said with a smile. "Today is the day!"

1. How many wheels did the new bicycle have?

_____

2. What didn't people do on the trails at the park?
    a. go for a walk
    b. go for a swim
    c. ride bicycles
    d. go for a jog

3. How did Teddy's father help to get him started on the bicycle?

_____

4. Teddy felt more confident at the end of the story. How do you know?

_____

Playing in the Band

Andrea felt very excited. She was going to the high school, where her older sister Chloe was a student. Chloe was a clarinet player in the band at the high school, and they were having a concert! "Mom, can I wear my new blue dress to the concert?" Andrea asked. "Sure, that dress will be perfect for tonight's concert!" said her mom. Chloe had a special band uniform that she was wearing. After Andrea put the dress on, her mom braided her hair. Her mom braided Chloe's hair too. Andrea and her family were finally all ready to go to the concert.

When they arrived at the high school, Chloe went to warm-up with the other musicians. "Good luck, Chloe!" Andrea said. She gave her sister a hug before she went.

Andrea and her parents found seats in the school auditorium. The auditorium was such a big place! On the stage there were many seats set up for the band.

Soon the band members started to come onto the stage and sit in their seats. Andrea saw Chloe carrying her clarinet! She also saw many other students with flutes, trumpets, oboes, trombones, and saxophones. There were some students standing in the very back with percussion instruments.

Then a man carrying a short stick in his hand came out and stood in front of the band. "Who is that? Why is he holding a stick?" Andrea whispered quietly to her dad. "He is the conductor of the band. That stick is called a baton and he uses it to direct the band," her dad answered.

The band started playing and Andrea heard the most beautiful music she had ever heard in all her life. She thought the band was wonderful! When it was over, she clapped her hands and felt so proud that her sister was one of the musicians.

"I cannot wait until I am in high school!" Andrea exclaimed. "I also want to be in the band!" That night when Andrea went to sleep, she dreamed that she had a clarinet of her own and was playing in the band!

1. Did Andrea enjoy the band concert?

   _____

2. What is a baton?

   _____

3. What color was Andrea's new dress? _____

4. Which instrument does Chloe play?

   a. flute

   b. clarinet

   c. tuba

   d. oboe

The Time Machine

A big brown box had arrived at Ellie's house. Inside the box was the new washing machine that her parents had ordered. Ellie was not interested in the new washing machine, but she was interested in the big brown box!

It was big enough for her to sit inside—big enough for her and a friend!

"Can I please have this box?" Ellie asked her mom.

"Sure," said Ellie's mom. "Why do you want this big empty box?"

"You'll see!" replied Ellie. Ellie took the big box outside to the yard. Her best friend, Oscar, came over from his house next door.

"Wow! Cool box!" said Oscar. "What should we do with it?"

"Let's make a Time Machine!" exclaimed Ellie.

Ellie and Oscar used markers, paint, crayons, colored paper, and glue to decorate the inside and outside of the box. They made dials, switches, buttons, and colorful designs. Now it looked like a Time Machine!

The two friends sat inside the Time Machine. They were ready to go!

"Where in time should we travel?" asked Oscar.

"Hmmm…" thought Ellie. "I have an idea!" She ran inside the house and returned with a book about dinosaurs.

"Let's go back in time to see the dinosaurs!" said Ellie.

"That will be awesome!" said Oscar. They pushed their buttons, turned their dials, and counted to ten, and, using their imaginations, traveled to the time of the dinosaurs!

Ellie and Oscar imagined being surrounded by huge dinosaurs. They looked in the book to learn the names of the dinosaurs that they imagined were walking all around their Time Machine. It was amazing!

"Where should we go next?" Ellie asked. "I have an idea," said Oscar. He ran home and returned with a book about knights and castles. "Let's go!" exclaimed Ellie. They said goodbye to the dinosaurs and set the dials for the Middle Ages!

1. Why had a big brown box arrived at Ellie's house?

_____

2. What did the friends use to decorate the box?

_____

3. What kind of book did Ellie get from her house?_____

4. Where did Oscar live?

a. next door to Ellie

b. on a boat

c. in a different city

d. deep in the woods

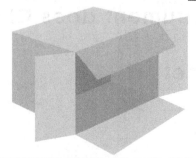

Julia and the Bird's Nest

Spring had finally arrived! Julia was happy to be able to open the windows of the house and let in the fresh air. It had felt like a long winter. Now that the cold, snowy days were over, Julia was excited to see signs of spring popping up all over the place! "Look, Mom!" exclaimed Julia. "I see a yellow flower in the yard!"

"That is a daffodil. Daffodils are one of the first flowers of springtime!" said Julia's mom.

"Look, Dad!" exclaimed Julia. "The leaves are growing on the trees!"

"The leaves come back in the springtime!" said Julia's dad. Julia noticed new signs of spring every day. One day while playing outside, she heard a chirping sound coming from a nearby tree. Julia walked over to the tree and saw a bird sitting in a nest! She quickly went and got her parents. She wanted to show them!

"That is a mother robin," said her dad. "You know it is springtime when the robins return!" The mother robin flew from the nest. Julia saw that there were three small blue eggs in the nest! "Eggs!" exclaimed Julia happily. "Three eggs!"

"There will be baby robins in this nest soon," said Julia's mom.

Over the next several weeks, Julia kept a close watch on the mother robin and the eggs. Most days the mother robin sat on the nest all day long.

"The mother robin is sitting on the eggs to keep the eggs warm," explained Julia's dad. One morning Julia went outside to see the mother robin. But the mother robin was not there. She peeked into the nest, and to her surprise, the eggs were not there either! Instead, there were three baby birds! Julia's mom and dad came out to see the baby birds too. They watched as the mother robin returned. She had a little worm in her beak that she was bringing to the baby birds to eat. "This bird's nest was the best sign of spring!" exclaimed Julia.

1. Which season has cold, snowy days?
    a. spring
    b. summer
    c. autumn
    d. winter

2. What color are daffodils?

    _____

3. Why did the mother robin sit on the eggs?

    _____

4. Who brought the baby birds a worm to eat?

    _____

Nina's Secret

Nina loved school. She especially loved math! But lately, that had changed. She was getting math problems wrong because she couldn't see the board clearly. "Nina, could you please come up to my desk?" her teacher asked. Nina walked slowly up to the teacher's desk. She knew why the teacher had called her up there—she had gotten all of her math problems wrong. "Nina, you are a very good math student," said her teacher. "But you copied the math problems down incorrectly from the board. I think you may need to visit the eye doctor."

The next week, Nina's mom brought her to the eye doctor. There she was fitted with eyeglasses to help her see things that were far away. Nina was amazed at how clear everything suddenly looked!

But now Nina had a new problem: she felt embarrassed about wearing her glasses. She wasn't sure what the other kids at school would say about them. She decided to keep her glasses a secret.

At school the next day, Nina carefully hid her eyeglasses in her backpack. "No one will ever know about my eyeglasses," thought Nina.

The teacher announced to the class that they were going to have a math contest! The students were divided into two teams, and whichever team got the most problems correct would get a prize—a candy bar!

The teams had to copy down math problems from the board and take turns answering them. It was very exciting! The score was tied, and it was the final problem. Nina felt very nervous. It was her turn, and she couldn't see the problem on the board! She did not want to let her team down.

"Wait a moment, please!" Nina said. She hurried to her backpack and took out her new eyeglasses. The students were all surprised to see Nina wearing them. Nina could now see the board clearly. She completed the math problem, and her team won the contest!

"Hooray for Nina!" the other students shouted! Nina felt very proud. She was so happy to have her new eyeglasses!

1. Why was Nina getting her math problems wrong?

_____

2. Who took Nina to the eye doctor?
    a. her teacher
    b. her dad
    c. her classmate
    d. her mom

3. Why did Nina want to keep her glasses a secret?

_____

4. What was the math contest prize?

_____

Ruthie and the Swim Class

Summer was coming soon. This summer was going to be the best ever—her family was getting a swimming pool! "Our swimming pool will be so awesome!" Ruthie said. "I cannot wait to jump into the cool water on a hot day!"

"Yes, having a swimming pool will be awesome," said her dad, "but you will not be jumping into it until you learn how to swim!"

"That is why we signed you up for a swim class," said Ruthie's mom, "so you will know how to be safe in our new pool. You start swim class tomorrow after school."

The next day Ruthie arrived at the swim class. Her mom sat on a bench to watch while Ruthie got into the pool with the instructor. The instructor showed Ruthie how to float. They practiced putting their heads under the water. They also practiced kicking their legs while holding onto the side of the pool. "Am I swimming yet?" asked Ruthie.

"Not yet," said the instructor. "You are first learning skills that will help you swim. Every week you will learn more skills to make you a strong swimmer."

Ruthie felt impatient! She wanted to learn how to swim now!

Each week Ruthie went to class and did exactly what the instructor taught her. She was motivated to become a very strong swimmer so she would be allowed to jump into her family's new pool!

After many classes with the swim instructor, Ruthie could swim on her back and her front. She enjoyed learning how to swim!

"You are becoming a very good swimmer," the instructor said, "but remember that no matter how well you swim, an adult must always be watching while you are in the pool." "I will always remember that rule," said Ruthie.

When summer came, the new pool at Ruthie's house was installed. Ruthie's parents went over all the rules with her about using the pool safely. Then finally, Ruthie got to jump into the pool with a big splash!

1. When was Ruthie's family's getting swimming pool?

_____

2. What does Ruthie want to do on a hot day?

_____

3. Name one of the skills that the instructor taught Ruthie.

_____

_____

4. An important rule the instructor told Ruthie was:
   a. Always swim alone.
   b. Always swim with your shoes on.
   c. An adult must always be watching while you are in the pool.
   d. Only swim on your back.

The Haircut

Deena had very long hair. It was so long that it hung all the way down her back! Her mother often braided her hair into two beautiful thick braids.

Deena's cousin Kara had long hair too. Whenever they visited one another, they would take turns brushing each other's long hair and pretend that they worked in a hair salon! It was such fun!

Today Kara was coming to Deena's house for a visit, and Deena was so excited to see her. Kara had told her that she had a big surprise to show her. Deena wondered what the surprise could be!

"Kara is here!" Deena's mom said. Deena came running to the front door to greet her cousin. When Deena saw Kara, she could not believe her eyes! Kara had gotten a haircut! Kara's hair was now very short!

"What do you think of my surprise?" asked Kara. "Don't I look grown-up?"

Deena thought that Kara did look very grown-up with her new haircut. Deena suddenly felt like a baby with her own long hair in braids.

"We can still play hair salon," said Kara. Deena didn't think playing hair salon would be much fun with Kara's short hair—but then she got an idea.

"I want to look grown-up too," said Deena. "Do you think you can give me a haircut in our hair salon? A haircut like yours?"

"Sure!" said Kara. "I will cut your hair just like mine!"

Deena found scissors in her mom's sewing kit and quietly snuck them into her bedroom. She wanted her new haircut to be a surprise for her mom!

"Okay," said Kara, "you sit in this chair and I will be the hair stylist." Kara had the scissors and was about to cut off one of Deena's long braids when Deena's mom came into the room.

"Girls!" exclaimed Deena's mom. "What are you doing?"

"I'm getting a haircut," said Deena. "I want to look grown-up too!"

Deena's mom took the scissors. She told Deena that if she wanted a haircut, they could go to a real salon. Deena decided that she still liked her long hair. Maybe she would get her hair cut some day—but not today!

1. What did Deena and Kara like to pretend?

    a. that they were famous singers

    b. that they worked in a restaurant

    c. that they were movie stars

    d. that they worked in a hair salon

2. What was Kara's big surprise?

_____

3. Why did Deena feel like a baby?

_____

4. What did Kara plan to do with the scissors?

_____

Fireworks!

It was the day of the annual Summer Fun Festival, and Danny felt very excited. The festival helped to raise money for the local school. His family went to the festival every year and always had a wonderful time!

"Is it time to go yet?" Danny asked his mother. The festival was in a park which was a short drive from Danny's home.

"Almost," she said, "I just have to finish icing this cake."

Danny's mother liked to help with the Cake Walk at the festival. She would bake cakes, cookies, and pies to donate to the Cake Walk. Many people would try to win his mother's delicious desserts!

"I'm ready to go! I've been practicing my aim!" said Danny's brother.

Danny's brother liked to play the Ring Toss game. It was his favorite because one year, he won a bouncy red ball while playing it. He was going to try to win another ball this year! "And I am hungry!" said Danny's father with a wink.

Danny's father liked to sample all of the food vendors' dishes. He liked the burgers, tacos, hot dogs, and pizzas that were sold at the festival. Yum!

But Danny's favorite part of the festival was at the very end of the day after the sun went down and the sky grew dark. That was when the fireworks display began!

Danny's family arrived at the festival and enjoyed a wonderful day. All of his mother's desserts were won, his brother played the Ring Toss game three times, and his father tried every food available!

Finally, the sun started to set, and the sky grew dim. Danny and his family made their way to the grassy area of the park and laid down a blanket to sit on while they relaxed and watched the display. The fireworks were amazing! Bright colors decorated the sky and seemed to rain down from high above. Loud booms, exciting pops, and surprising whistles filled the air. Danny loved watching the fireworks with his family! "This is my favorite part of the Summer Fun Festival!" Danny exclaimed happily. "I really love fireworks!"

1. For what did the Summer Fun Festival raise money?

_____

2. How did Danny's mother help with the festival?

_____

3. What game did Danny's brother like to play at the festival?
   - a. the Cake Walk
   - b. the Ring Toss
   - c. the Cake Toss
   - d. basketball

4. Which part of the festival did Danny like the best?

_____

Logan's Hiccups

It was Logan's turn to read aloud during class. He had been practicing at home, so he felt confident about all of the new vocabulary words in the story. Just as he started reading, a hiccup jumped out of his mouth! Logan felt embarrassed. The other boys and girls laughed.

"Excuse me," he said. He started again. Another hiccup jumped out!

"Oh dear," said Ms. Zayner, his teacher. "Why don't you go get a drink of water to help your hiccups go away."

Logan quickly went to the drinking fountain in the hallway. He took a long sip of water and then returned to the classroom.

"Let's try again," said Ms. Zayner. Logan started to read, but then all of a sudden—"Hiccup!" Another hiccup jumped out of his mouth!

"Hmmm…why don't we give Anna a turn reading until your hiccups go away," said Ms. Zayner.

Soon it was lunchtime, and all the students went to the cafeteria. Logan still had the hiccups! His best friend, Zachary, tried to help him.

"Boo!" shouted Zachary as he snuck up behind Logan in the lunch line.

"Hey!" said Logan, startled. "Why did you do that? I almost dropped my lunch tray!" The other kids around him all giggled.

"Haven't you heard? Scaring someone is the best way to get rid of the hiccups!" said Zachary. "I'm just trying to help!"

"Hiccup! Well, it doesn't seem to have helped," said Logan sadly.

Logan's hiccups continued all afternoon. When he arrived home, his mother asked, "Why do you look so sad?"

"I have had the hiccups all day!" replied Logan. "I didn't get to have my turn reading in class, and the other kids laughed at me."

"Oh, I'm sorry," said his mother. "Let's see…I remember my grandmother had a cure for the hiccups…try this spoonful of honey mixed in water."

Logan slowly sipped on the spoonful of honey in water. His great-grandmother was right! His hiccups went away! Finally!

1. Who is Ms. Zayner?

_____

2. What happened to Logan when he started to read aloud?

_____

3. How did Zachary try to help Logan?

_____

4. What was Logan's great grandmother's cure for hiccups?
   a. sipping on a spoonful of honey mixed in water
   b. eating an egg
   c. scaring the hiccups away
   d. reading a scary story

Stanley Builds a Treehouse

Stanley enjoyed being outside. He would much rather be out in the fresh air than inside the house. He didn't mind the cold weather or even the rainy weather! He just always preferred to be outside!

"Stanley," called his mom, "it is time for you to come in. You must do your homework!"

"I can do it out here!" said Stanley. He ran in to get his backpack and brought it back outside with him. He sat in the sunshine and worked on his homework.

The next several days, Stanley continued to do his homework outside. He did math outside, he read his science book outside, and he wrote his history report outside. He was so pleased that he could stay outside!

But then the weather changed. The sunshine that had filled the sky disappeared behind heavy clouds. The rain started falling, and his books started to get wet.

"Uh-oh," thought Stanley, "I don't mind the rain, but my books do! I need to go in." Stanley stared gloomily out the window. He always felt so much better when he was surrounded by fresh air, but he could not let his books and papers get wet. Then he had an idea—he would build a treehouse!

Stanley told his mom and dad about his idea and asked if they would allow him to build a treehouse. They decided to help him build a treehouse! On Saturday, they went to the hardware store to buy the supplies. Stanley and his parents found a good spot in a tree in their backyard for the treehouse.

"This is going to be the best treehouse ever!" Stanley said. They worked for two days building the treehouse together. It had a strong floor to sit on and a roof to keep Stanley dry. It was perfect!

"Thank you!" said Stanley to his parents. They were all very proud of the treehouse that they had built together. The next day, Stanley could not wait to bring his homework outside and work on it in his new treehouse!

1. What does Stanley like about being outside?
    a. Stanley likes to watch TV outside.
    b. Stanley likes only warm weather outside.
    c. Stanley likes the fresh air outside.
    d. Stanley likes bringing his radio outside.
2. What problem did Stanley have while doing his homework outside?

_____

3. Who helped Stanley to build the treehouse?

_____

4. Where is Stanley's treehouse located?

_____

Renee's First Sleepover

Friday night was coming soon, and Renee felt worried. She had been invited to a sleepover at her friend Henrietta's house. Renee was worried because she had never slept at someone else's house before.

"You will have a fun time," her mother reassured her. "You have played at Henrietta's house before."

"But I have never slept there," replied Renee. "What if I get scared in the dark? What if I have a bad dream? What if I want to come home?"

"I have an idea," said her mother. "Let's get your things ready.
We will pack useful items. You will be prepared for anything!"

Renee and her mother started to gather items she would need for the sleepover. They put pajamas, slippers, a toothbrush, and clothes for the next day in her backpack. They rolled up her sleeping bag and a pillow.

"Now," said Renee's mother, "you are worried about the dark?"

"Yes," said Renee. "I have a nightlight at home.
What if Henrietta does not have a nightlight? What if her room is very dark?"

"Why don't you pack this small flashlight in your backpack. If Henrietta doesn't have a nightlight, and it gets too dark, you can use this flashlight!"

"Oh, that's a good idea!" said Renee smiling. She packed the flashlight.

"Next, you're worried about having a bad dream?" said Renee's mother.

"Yes," said Renee. "What if I dream about monsters or snakes?"

"Well," said Renee's mother, "your teddy bear usually helps you to sleep soundly here at home. Why don't you bring him with you?"

"I can bring him with me?" asked Renee excitedly.

"Of course!" her mother answered. "And if you still want to come home, call me, and I will come to pick you up, even if it is late."

Friday night arrived, and Renee went to the sleepover. The girls had so much fun! They watched movies and played games. They ate pizza and popcorn.
Renee forgot all about being worried! She had a wonderful time and never had to call her mother to pick her up!

1. Who invited Renee to a sleepover?

   _____

2. What items does Renee pack?

   a. pajamas and roller skates

   b. a sleeping bag and a tent

   c. pajamas and a toothbrush

   d. a pillow and a book

3. What helpful item does Renee's mother suggest she pack in case it is too dark?

   _____

4. What did the girls eat at the sleepover?

   _____

Harry's Newspaper

The houses in Harry's neighborhood all looked pretty similar. They were built from stucco and were painted white. Harry was interested in learning more about the people who lived inside of these similar-looking houses.

He saw many of his neighbors coming and going, but they all felt like strangers who didn't say hello or wave to one another.

"I'd like to know the people who live in our neighborhood," Harry said.

"I bet they would like to know you too!" said his mom.

Harry thought for a while and then came up with a plan. "I'm going to start a neighborhood newspaper!" Harry used his computer to type up an article all about himself and his family. He wrote another one about his pet bird, another about his favorite sports teams, and another about what music he liked. He also requested to interview anyone who'd be willing to be featured in a future edition of his newspaper.

Harry printed out his newspaper and made enough copies for every house in his neighborhood. The next morning, he woke up very early and delivered a copy of his newspaper to each house in his neighborhood.

By the next day, Harry had received many calls from people who were willing to be interviewed! Harry took a notebook and a pen and headed out to start his interviews. The first person he interviewed was an older adult who lived three houses from Harry's. The man, Mr. Kubin, was a fascinating person. He had worked his whole life in a paper factory. He also had been in the army. Mr. Kubin was now retired and had a small pet dog. Harry wrote it all down.

Next, he interviewed the Ayala family that had moved to the neighborhood from Mexico. They knew how to speak Spanish and taught Harry a few words, like "hola" and "amigo." Harry wrote it all down.

Harry felt so good learning about the people in his neighborhood. He would spend lots more time interviewing the rest of the neighbors and printing out many more newspapers! In time, the neighbors did not feel like strangers to one another. The neighbors all loved reading Harry's newspaper and loved getting to know one another!

1. What did the houses in Harry's neighborhood look like?

_____

2. Harry has a pet _____ .
    a. cat
    b. bird
    c. dog
    d. turtle

3. Where had Mr. Kubin worked?

_____

4. How did Harry help his neighbors get to know one another?

_____

Name:_____

Oliver the Artist

The morning school bell rang, and Miss Anderson gathered the excited students onto the bus. Today they would not be sitting at their desks to study. Today they were going on a field trip to the Art Museum! Oliver and his friends, Joshua and Connor, were excited about having a field trip but not very happy that it was to the Art Museum. They did not like art. They thought art was boring and wanted to go on a field trip to somewhere more exciting, like to the Space Museum.

"I don't want to go look at old paintings all day!" complained Oliver.

"At least at the Space Museum, we could see cool stuff," said Joshua.

"Yeah, I will probably fall asleep during the boring tour," laughed Connor.

When they arrived at the Art Museum, Miss Anderson introduced the class to their guide, a young man named Justin. He said he had just graduated from college.

Oliver was surprised that Justin would want to work at the boring Art Museum. He seemed like a cool guy; why would he work here?

Justin walked them all around the museum, where they saw artwork from painters, sculptors, and even artists who created figures out of glass! Some of the artwork was very old, some of it more modern, but none of it was boring.

Oliver started to think that he was wrong about this field trip!

"So, do you kids want to check out my favorite room of the museum?" asked Justin.

"Follow me!" Justin took them to a room filled with paints of every color and lots of paintbrushes. There were lots of easels around the room with blank paper hanging on them. "This is where you get to become an artist! Have fun making your own masterpiece!"

Oliver and his classmates each got to paint a picture. Then their artwork was displayed on a huge bulletin board in the museum.

"Now when other people visit the museum, they will admire your work too! You are all artists!" said Justin. Oliver felt very proud of his painting.

On the bus ride back to school, Oliver, Joshua, and Connor agreed that the Art Museum was much cooler than what they expected. Oliver wondered how many people would see his painting when they visited the museum. He liked being Oliver the Artist!

1. Where did Oliver's class go on their field trip?

_____

2. At first, what did Oliver and his friends think about the Art Museum?

_____

3. Who was the guide at the Art Museum?
   a. Joshua
   b. Connor
   c. Oliver
   d. Justin

4. Where was Oliver's artwork displayed?

_____

Kyle Plays Tennis

Kyle's school had many sports teams. There was a football team, a soccer team, a basketball team, a track team, and a volleyball team. There was even a golf team and a swim team. But Kyle could not find a sports team that he wanted to join.
One day there was an announcement that a new sports team was forming.
The school was going to have its first-ever tennis team. Kyle had never played tennis before, but he was interested in finding out about it. He signed up to go to the informational meeting being held after school.
At the meeting, there were lots of other boys and girls.
The teacher in charge was Mr. Heintz. "Welcome to the tennis team informational meeting!" said Mr. Heintz. "I think we are going to have a great school tennis team!"
He explained when the practice sessions would be and when they would have tennis matches against other schools. Kyle hurried home with all the information on paper.
He excitedly showed it to his dad and mom. "Can I join?" asked Kyle.
"Mr. Heintz said that the school would provide all of the equipment!"
"Of course!" said his parents. "Tennis is a really fun sport!"
At the first practice, Kyle felt nervous. Would he be any good at playing tennis?
He wasn't even sure how the game was played.
Mr. Heintz explained to the students the rules of tennis and the complicated scoring system. He gave each student a racket and a bright yellow tennis ball.
They all walked onto the tennis courts and were assigned a partner. They were to practice hitting the ball back and forth.
Kyle served the ball, and it went right over the net! He was so pleased!
He and his partner continued to practice hitting the ball to one another. Kyle was having so much fun! Mr. Heintz came over to watch them.
"Kyle, you are very good at playing tennis!
I cannot believe this is your first time!" said Mr. Heintz. Kyle felt very proud of himself!
Kyle continued to attend all of the tennis team practices. He did very well in the tennis matches. Kyle became the school's star tennis player!

1. What sports teams did Kyle's school have? Name at least three.

_____

2. Who was the teacher in charge of the tennis team?

_____

3. What did Mr. Heintz give to the students at the first practice?

    a. a racket and a uniform

    b. a book about tennis and a bright yellow ball

    c. a racket and a shoe

    d. a racket and a bright yellow ball

4. How did Kyle feel at the end of the story?

_____

The Haunted Attic

Gabriel and Claudia always enjoyed visiting their grandma and grandpa's house. It was a big old house with lots of rooms to explore. The rooms were filled with all kinds of interesting items like old books, games, and antiques. They would spend hours looking at all the cool old stuff.

One day while playing at their grandparents' house, Gabriel said, "There is one place in this house that we have never explored—the attic!"

"The attic!" exclaimed Claudia. "I don't think we should go up there!"

"Why not?" asked Gabriel. "Grandma said we could go anywhere."

"Hmm," said Claudia thoughtfully, "I suppose we could go take a peek."

Gabriel and Claudia found the staircase to the attic and slowly walked up the creaky old stairs. It was quite dark, as there were very few lights in the attic. Gabriel brought a flashlight, and he turned it on.

"Oh wow! Look at all this stuff!" Gabriel exclaimed. There were old chairs, boxes of fancy old clothes, a broken mirror, a dusty trumpet, an antique dollhouse, a large clock...so much stuff! Suddenly they heard a strange squeaky sound coming from the corner. Both Gabriel and Claudia got so startled that they screamed in fright and ran down the stairs. They were sure there was a ghost in the attic!

"Grandma! Grandpa!" they yelled. "The attic is haunted!"

"Haunted?" asked Grandma calmly. "Hmmm...there are many things in that attic, but I don't think a ghost is one of them!"

"Why don't we all go up together and see if we can figure out what really scared you, kids," said Grandpa.

Together they all went back up into the attic. Gabriel pointed to the corner where the strange sound came from. Grandpa bravely walked to the corner with a flashlight. He lifted up an old sheet that was on the floor, and underneath, they saw a family of mice living there! They all started laughing! Gabriel and Claudia felt relieved.

"I guess this attic isn't haunted," said Gabriel, "just home to a family of spooky, squeaky mice!"

1. Which place in the house had the children not yet explored?

_____

2. Why did they need a flashlight to look around in the attic?

_____

3. Why did the children think the attic was haunted?

_____

4. What was living in the attic?
  a. a ghost
  b. a monster
  c. a family of mice
  d. a family of birds

Maizy Moves Away

Maizy and Rachel had been neighbors since they were tiny babies. They spent time together almost every day. They went to the same school and played on the same soccer team. They were best friends.

One day Maizy's mom had some news to share. "Maizy's dad got a new job. It is in a different state, and our family will be moving there."

Maizy and Rachel both felt very sad about this news. Together they cried.

"This is awful news," said Rachel. "I will miss you so much. Who will I play soccer with? Who will I walk to school with? I don't want you to go!"

"I think it is awful too," said Maizy. "I don't want to go to a new school. I don't want a new house. I wish my dad didn't have a new job!"

The girls spent many hours feeling sad and worried. They cried many tears.

Rachel's mom said, "Let's find on a map where Maizy's new house will be."

She got out a big map and together they found the new state. They saw that Maizy's new house would be only two hours away.

Maizy's mom said, "We would love for Rachel to come to visit—we can have a sleepover! And there is a beach near our new house—we could all go spend time together at the beach! Won't that be fun?"

Maizy and Rachel agreed that a sleepover and the beach did sound like fun. They stopped crying and started to make plans.

Over the next several weeks, Rachel helped Maizy to pack up her things. They sometimes cried a little more, but they also shared lots of laughs!

"The moving truck is all ready," Maizy said sadly to Rachel on the day of the move. They looked out to the street and saw a gigantic truck waiting to go.

They gave each other a big hug and didn't want to let go.

"Girls, I have a present for each of you!" said Rachel's mom. She handed them small boxes wrapped with matching pink satin bows. Inside the boxes were pretty stationery, matching envelopes, and new pens.

"We can write letters to each other," said Rachel. "And send pictures!"

"I may be moving away, but we will always be best friends!" said Maizy.

1. How long have Maizy and Rachel known one another?

    a. since yesterday

    b. since they were tiny babies

    c. since last year

    d. since they were grown ups

2. What sport do the girls like to play?

_____

3. Why is Maizy moving?

_____

4. What can the girls do with their new stationery?

_____

Name:_____

Nora's Nickname

Nora wanted a nickname. She thought it would make her feel special if people called her by a special name. But the name "Nora" didn't seem to have a nickname to go along with it.

"How about we call you 'Nory?'" her little sister Becky suggested.

"No," said Nora, "that doesn't sound quite right. It is not special."

"Maybe we can call you Nor-Nor," said her brother Jimmy.

"No," said Nora, "that sounds silly, not special."

"Why don't we call you Ra-Ra?" asked her cousin Lizzie.

"No," said Nora, "that isn't special either."

Nora felt jealous. Her name wasn't special without a nickname. Becky was a nickname for Rebecca, Jimmy was a nickname for James, and Lizzie was a nickname for Elizabeth. She was the only one without a special name. Nora went out to sit by herself in her favorite place, the garden.

Nora's mother went outside to pick vegetables from the garden and noticed Nora sitting there looking sad. "What's wrong, Nora?" she asked.

"My name isn't special! Why didn't I get a special name?" Nora said.

"Nora, do you like this garden of ours?" asked her mother.

"Of course, I do! You know that it's my favorite place. We have the loveliest vegetables, fruits, and flowers growing here," said Nora.

"Well, this garden was started many years ago, by your great-grandmother. She also loved to work in this garden, and she grew many of these same kinds of vegetables, fruits, and flowers. Your great-grandmother taught me how to take care of a garden," she said. "Her name was Nora."

Nora's eyes grew wide.

"You were named after your great-grandmother. I wanted to honor the woman who was most special in my life," explained her mother.

Nora hugged her mother tightly and said,

"Thank you for giving me the most special name of all!"

1. Why didn't Nora think her name was special?

_____

2. What did Becky suggest they call Nora?
     a. Nory
     b. Nor-Nor
     c. Ra-Ra
     d. Aron

3. Where was Nora's favorite place?

_____

4. What was special about Nora's name?

_____

Victor's Robot

Victor had so many chores to do. His mom had made a list of chores he had to do every day. Victor was not allowed to play with his friends until his chores were done. He did not like this rule!

"Victor, want to come to play video games?" asked his friend Leland.

"I wish I could," said Victor, "but I need to do my chores." Victor felt sad that he couldn't go play with Leland. He wished someone else would do his chores for him. He wished he had a robot!

"Yes, a robot would be awesome," thought Victor. "I would never have to make my bed, take out the trash, mow the lawn, feed the cat, fold the laundry...I would be able to play video games all day!"

Victor lay on his unmade bed and thought about how cool a robot would be to have in his house. He wondered if he would be able to build one.

Then he heard a noise outside of his bedroom. He got up and opened the door—and there stood a robot! It was very tall and made of silver metal and had bright blue lights for eyes. It had wheels instead of feet and an antenna on top of its head. It was looked amazing!

"Hello, Victor. I am Marvin. I am your robot. I will do anything you tell me to do," said the robot in a funny-sounding voice. "Shall I make your bed? Take out the trash? Feed the cat?"

Victor couldn't believe his eyes! This was great! Now he could go play video games with Leland while the robot did all of his chores for him!

The robot started to make his bed, but instead of straightening out the blanket, he ripped it to shreds! The robot then took the trash out—by throwing it out the window! Then he headed to the cat...

"No!" shouted Victor, "Wait! Stop, Marvin! I'll take care of the cat!" Victor was terrified at what the robot might do to his cat!

Suddenly Victor felt someone shaking him.

"Wake up, Victor! You are having a bad dream! Who is Marvin?" said his mom.

Victor opened his eyes. He had fallen asleep!

This was all a dream! He laughed and told his mom about Marvin the robot. She laughed too, and together they made his bed.

1. What did Leland want to play with Victor?

    a. soccer

    b. chess

    c. tennis

    d. video games

2. Why couldn't Victor play with Leland?

_____

3. How did Marvin take out the trash?

_____

4. Was Marvin the robot real?

_____

The Cat Who Liked to Read

Summertime in Dolton, Missouri, was very hot. Miss Gish, the librarian at the Dolton Public Library, was very grateful that the library had air conditioning to help keep it cool. Many people would come into the library to read, relax, and escape from the outdoor summer heat.

One summer day, Miss Gish heard a meowing sound coming from behind a bookshelf. She peeked behind it and was surprised to see a gray striped cat sitting there! The thin cat appeared to be very hungry and thirsty.

"Oh my!" said Miss Gish. "Where did you come from, little kitty?" The cat did not have a collar or any sort of identification tags on her.

Miss Gish got a small bowl and put some water into it and set it in front of the cat. The cat quickly started to lap up the water. She purred happily.

After the cat finished the water, Miss Gish said, "Okay, kitty, I think your owner may be looking for you. You are such a pretty little kitty!" Miss Gish put the cat back outside to find her way home.

The next day Miss Gish was putting some books away onto the library shelves when she felt something furry rub up against her leg. "Oh my!" said Miss Gish in surprise. "How did you get back in here?"

The cat went and sat on a pile of books. Several people in the library came over to see what was going on. They all smiled, seeing a cat sitting atop the books!

"That cat must like to read!" said Mr. Norris, a man who often came to the library. Mr. Norris looked closely at the cat. "I recognize this cat! This cat is a stray who wanders around the streets. She has no home."

"The poor kitty must have been so hot outside in this heat," said Miss Gish.

"I think this cat snuck into the library when the door was open. I think this cat wanted to cool down in your air conditioning!" said Mr. Norris.

Miss Gish gave the cat some more water. She decided that this stray cat needed a home, and she decided that the library needed a cat!

Miss Gish adopted the cat and named her Paige. Everyone who visited the library loved to see Paige, the cat who liked to read!

1. **Where did Miss Gish work?**
    a. Dolton Public Zoo
    b. Dolton Public Animal Shelter
    c. Dolton Public Library
    d. Dolton Public Park

2. **How was the weather in Dolton, Missouri, in the summertime?**

_____

3. **Why did Mr. Norris say that the cat must like to read?**

_____

4. **What name did Miss Gish give to the cat?**

_____

Uncle Arthur's Camera

Jane and her brother, Brian, were traveling from Pennsylvania to California to visit their Uncle Arthur. She and Brian were excited to go! They had never been to California before!

"Welcome to California!" exclaimed Uncle Arthur when they arrived.
"Are you ready to do some sightseeing?"

"Yes!" both Jane and Brian shouted. "Where are we going first?"

"Sequoia National Park!" said Uncle Arthur. They got into Uncle Arthur's car, and he drove them to Sequoia National Park. It was amazing there—Jane and Brian saw trees so big and tall that they felt like little ants standing next to them.

"Smile!" said Uncle Arthur as he took a picture of them with his camera in front of the huge trees. Jane and Brian smiled widely at the picture.

The next day they went to see the Golden Gate Bridge. It was so cool to see! Jane and Brian could not believe their eyes.

There were no bridges like this in Pennsylvania!

"Smile!" said Uncle Arthur as he took a picture of them by the bridge.

The following days they visited many more interesting places, such as Santa Monica Pier, Hollywood, and even Alcatraz Island! Uncle Arthur brought his camera to each place and took lots of pictures.

"Goodbye," Jane said as she gave her Uncle Arthur a big hug. "We will miss you—and we will miss California!"

"We loved sightseeing with you!" said Brian. "We will miss you and your camera!"

Two weeks after Jane and Brian had returned home, a package arrived.

"What could this be?" wondered Brian. They quickly opened up the box.

Inside was a beautiful photo album. It was filled with pictures that Uncle Arthur had taken of them while they were in California! They were able to remember all the fun places they had visited by looking at the pictures!

Jane and Brian were very grateful to Uncle Arthur for the photo album and for his wonderful camera!

1. **Where do Jane and Brian live?**

_____

2. **Why are Jane and Brian going to California?**

_____

3. **Which was the first place they went sightseeing?**
   a. Alcatraz Island
   b. Hollywood
   c. Golden Gate Bridge
   d. Sequoia National Park

4. **What helped Jane and Brian to remember all of the places they had visited in California?**

Cousin Camp

Jackson had a big family—he had five sisters! He loved his sisters all very much, but he was the only boy in the family, and sometimes he wished he had a brother. Especially when his sisters all left to go to Girl Scout Camp in the summer, and he was left home without them.

One day his mom came into his room and said, "Jackson, how would you like to go to visit your cousins this summer?" Jackson had three older cousins: Tristan, Gavin, and Adrian. They lived in a town about an hour away.

They were so much fun! They knew how to do so many things!

"Yes!" exclaimed Jackson. "I would love to visit them!"

So, when Jackson's sisters were all going to Girl Scout Camp, Jackson went to stay with his cousins for a week. They called it Cousin Camp!

Jackson was so excited to be surrounded by other boys all week! He went for nature hikes with them, he rode bicycles with them, he watched movies with them, and he played video games with them!

One day Tristan said, "Jackson, would you like to learn a magic trick?"

"Sure!" replied Jackson. Tristan taught Jackson a magic trick using a coin.

Another day Gavin taught Jackson how to play chess.

"You are really good at chess!" Gavin said. Jackson felt so proud!

"Do you know how to play ping pong, Jackson?" asked Adrian.

Jackson had never played ping pong before, so Adrian taught him.

When the week of Cousin Camp was over, Jackson's mom came to pick him up. He showed her the magic trick and challenged her to games of chess and ping pong!

"Wow, Jackson! You have learned a lot this week!" said his mom.

"Cousin Camp was the best! Can I come again next summer?" asked Jackson.

"I think so," said his mom, "as long as your cousins would like that."

Tristan, Gavin, and Adrian all agreed that Cousin Camp should be an annual event. Jackson was so happy to have these boy cousins!

1. How many sisters did Jackson have?

_____

2. Where did his sisters go in the summer?

_____

3. Who taught Jackson how to do a magic trick?
    a. Tristan
    b. Gavin
    c. Adrian
    d. His mom

4. What two games did Jackson learn from his cousins?

_____

Clouds

Have you ever looked up into the sky and admired the beautiful white puffs floating up there? Or have you ever looked outside to a darkened sky, knowing that it was going to rain soon? You are seeing clouds!

Clouds are actually large groups of very tiny water droplets that are visible in the air. Some clouds look white because they reflect light from the sun, others; look gray because they are filled with so many water droplets that they no longer reflect the sun's light.

Scientists have identified three main types of clouds: stratus, cumulus, and cirrus. These three types of clouds have different characteristics, and they help scientists to know what kind of weather is happening. You can learn to tell the different types of clouds apart.

Stratus clouds hang low in the sky and are gray in color.

They mean snow or rain is coming!

Cumulus clouds are the largely white, fluffy clouds seen on days when the sky is clear and blue. They often appear on warm, sunny days.

Cirrus clouds are found high in the sky. They are small and wispy. A cirrus cloud often means there will be a change in the weather.

The next time you are outside, take a look up in the sky.

What kind of clouds do you see?

Find the words in the puzzle and circle.

CLOUD   CUMULUS   DROPLET   REFLECT   WEATHER

S	H	Z	C	I	O	O	P	A	V	K	Q	V	L
P	E	O	L	F	K	Z	C	U	M	U	L	U	S
L	B	M	O	R	E	F	L	E	C	T	D	V	E
W	A	K	U	E	Q	X	O	E	K	I	S	F	L
Z	H	X	E	Q	K	Q	U	A	H	M	E	S	D
W	E	A	T	H	E	R	D	R	O	P	L	E	T

The Water Cycle

Water is necessary for all living things. Plants, trees, animals, and people all need water to survive. On our Earth, water is found in three states of matter: solid, liquid, and gas. Solid water, called ice, is found in glaciers and snow. It is most commonly found in places where it is very cold, such as the North Pole and the South Pole.

Liquid water is found in oceans, lakes, and rivers. It can even be found in soil and underground. Water vapor, a gas, is found in the atmosphere around the Earth. Water can change from one state of matter to another by following the path of the water cycle. Solid water and ice can change into a liquid when it gets warm. This process is called melting. Melting ice flows in the Earth's oceans, lakes, and rivers.

The heat from the sun causes water to evaporate from oceans, lakes, and rivers. When liquid water evaporates, it turns into water vapor. The water vapor enters the atmosphere and can form clouds.

As the water vapor in the clouds cools down, it becomes liquid again. This process is called condensation. Condensation is the opposite of evaporation.

When a cloud becomes full of liquid water, it falls from the sky like rain or snow. This is called precipitation. The rain and snow fill the oceans, lakes, and rivers, and the water cycle starts all over again.

It is important for us to learn about the water cycle and to keep our water clean!

Find the words in the puzzle and circle.

ATMOSPHERE   CONDENSATION   EVAPORATION   OCEANS   HEAT

C	O	N	D	E	N	S	A	T	I	O	N	P	E
F	L	K	E	O	K	P	E	O	L	C	M	O	H
P	A	T	M	O	S	P	H	E	R	E	O	E	E
C	O	N	F	L	V	L	B	M	O	A	C	A	A
E	V	A	P	O	R	A	T	I	O	N	E	C	T
P	A	A	H	M	E	S	D	V	B	S	S	H	Z

The Cloud Race

Martin liked to look out the windows of the car while his father drove him to school in the mornings. He would often notice things in the sky, such as birds, airplanes, and clouds.

Clouds were his favorite thing to see. If they were the large, fluffy white clouds he could look for shapes in them! Sometimes he could see clouds shaped like dragons with giant wings. Other times he saw turtles crawling slowly along. Once he even saw a huge whale swimming through the sky!

"Dad, today is a perfect day to see cloud shapes!" Martin said one morning. The sky was blue and the white clouds were high overhead.

"Tell me if you see any cool shapes!" His dad said as he started the car.

Martin pressed his face against the window and looked up towards the sky. He looked and looked for a shape, but couldn't see anything special. They were almost to his school when he noticed a cloud shaped exactly like a horse!

"Dad! There is a beautiful horse! And he is going to win a race!" said Martin. His dad parked the car at the school. They got out, and Martin pointed up to where he saw the horse shape in the sky.

"That does look like a fast horse, but I think you are faster! Let's get on the grass and see if you can beat him in the race!" said his dad.

Martin hurried over to the grass and started running along, imagining that he was racing the horse! It was a great day to see cloud shapes!

Read the clues and write the answer in a crossword puzzle:

1. Tiny water droplets gathered together in the air

2. A lawn, usually kept trimmed and free of weeds

3. Time of day when you first wake up

4. Push up against

5. Formation

Name:_____

The Wright Brothers

Have you ever flown in an airplane? If so, you have the Wright brothers to thank! Orville and Wilbur Wright invented the first airplane. They spent years experimenting with the design and technology and finally made the first flight on December 17, 1903.

Wilbur was older than Orville by four years. They also had five other siblings! They were American and grew up in the states of Indiana and Ohio, as their family moved to different houses a few times.

The brothers loved to invent things and became interested in flying when their dad gave them a toy helicopter. When they were young, they loved to build kites and fly them for fun. They also were very interested in how bicycles worked, and when they were young men, they opened a bicycle shop.

They decided to try out their first plane in Kitty Hawk, North Carolina. They chose Kitty Hawk because it had strong breezes to help the plane and soft sand below in case it crashed. The first flight only lasted 12 seconds!

Orville and Wilbur Wright were very courageous to attempt such an invention and very smart to figure out how to make it work! They are known as the Fathers of Modern Aviation, and you can see their original airplane on display at the Smithsonian Air and Space Museum in Washington D.C.

Find the words in the puzzle and circle.

AVIATION   EXPERIMENT   INVENT   HELICOPTER   TECHNOLOGY

H	E	L	E	X	P	E	R	I	M	E	N	T	L
S	H	Z	A	T	E	C	H	N	O	L	O	G	Y
F	L	V	L	B	M	O	A	V	I	C	O	N	F
H	E	L	I	C	O	P	T	E	R	K	E	M	E
T	E	C	P	A	E	M	E	N	T	P	E	O	A
E	X	P	E	A	V	I	A	T	I	O	N	C	C

Nicholas and his Brother

Nicholas loved doing things with his younger brother. Today they were playing on the swings in the park. Nicholas was very good at swinging—he could go so high that he felt like he was flying!

"I'm flying!" Nicholas shouted happily as his mother gently pushed his younger brother on the baby swing nearby.

"Are you flying like a bird?" asked his mother with a smile.

"No," said Nicholas, "I'm flying like an airplane! I love airplanes!"

Before they returned home, they stopped by the library. There Nicholas and his mother found a book about airplanes. They checked the book out and brought it home. While his brother was taking a nap, Nicholas and his mother read the book. It had lots of colorful photographs of airplanes and lots of interesting information about how they were invented.

"Wow! I didn't know that two brothers invented the airplane!" exclaimed Nicholas. He looked closely at the photograph in the book that showed Orville and Wilbur Wright. "Yes," said his mother. "The Wright brothers worked hard to figure out how to design and build a new type of machine."

Nicholas looked over at his brother, who was still napping in his crib.

"Maybe we will invent something together someday, brother," he whispered quietly. "Just like the Wright brothers!"

Read the clues and write the answer in a crossword puzzle:

1. Knowledge that you could get from a picture or a book

2. A mechanical tool made to do something

3. The Wright Brothers' invention

4. A place to find great books

5. A short sleep

Penguins

Everyone seems to agree that the penguin is a cute animal! The way they waddle around in their black and white tuxedos is truly adorable! But did you know that the penguin is not only cute but one of the unique birds in the world? What makes it so unique?

The penguin is a flightless bird. This means it does not fly in the air. The penguin swims in the water instead! A penguin can spend at least half of its time swimming in the water. Their bodies are shaped in a streamlined way to help them to be able to dive deep into the water, and their sleek shape helps them to be very fast swimmers! Penguins can swim comfortably in very cold water because they have a thick layer of blubber under their skin. Blubber is a special type of fat that helps to insulate their bodies and keep them warm.

And while their black and white feathers are fun to look at, they also serve an important purpose—they help to camouflage the penguins from predators while swimming. The black feathers on their backs are hard to see from above, and the white feathers on their fronts look like the sun reflecting off the surface of the water when seen from below! These special adaptations help to make the penguin quite a unique, remarkable bird—and cute too!

Find the words in the puzzle and circle.

ADORABLE   CAMOUFLAGE   FEATHERS   INSULATE   UNIQUE

U	C	A	M	O	U	F	L	A	G	E	P	E	R
N	A	D	O	R	N	E	X	P	E	I	N	O	N
I	H	E	L	I	I	N	S	U	L	A	T	E	A
F	E	A	T	E	Q	T	I	O	N	C	M	E	N
I	N	A	V	I	U	A	D	O	R	A	B	L	E
C	A	M	N	F	E	A	T	H	E	R	S	G	Y

Penelope Goes to the Zoo

Penelope had an exciting day planned—she was going to see lions, monkeys, and gorillas. She was going to see zebras, giraffes, and elephants. She was going to the zoo! Penelope's dad made sure they brought their sunhats and sunblock, as it was a hot, sunny day. Penelope's mom prepared a bag with water bottles and snacks. Penelope had her camera to take pictures.

When they arrived, Penelope got a zoo map showing where the different animals were located. They decided to see the giraffes first. At the giraffe habitat, it was hard to see the giraffes because they were standing far from the visitors in the shade of a tree.

"It is so hot outside. The giraffes are not feeling friendly," said Penelope's dad. Penelope felt a bit disappointed.

They went next to see the lions. They were just lying in the grass, swatting flies with their tails. Penelope could not see them well enough to get a picture. She felt even more disappointed.

"I have an idea," said her mom. "Let's go to one of the indoor exhibits, where it will not be so hot. Perhaps those animals will be easier to see."

They went to a building that had various birds in it. There Penelope saw a type of bird she had never seen before—a penguin! The penguins were happily swimming around in their cool watery habitat, and Penelope got lots of cute photographs!

"These penguins are my favorites!" exclaimed Penelope. "I love the zoo!"

Read the clues and write the answer in a crossword puzzle:

1. Feeling unhappy about the results of something

2. People who come for a short amount of time

3. Place where specific animals live best

4. Paper that shows where things are

5. Within a building

The Pyramids

Randy and Mary are students at Grandacre Elementary School. One morning, Mary sees Randy reading a large book called About the Egyptians.

"That looks like a very interesting book, Randy!" says Mary. "Can you tell me about it?"

"Sure," says Randy, turning to a different page. "Here's an interesting part of the book. It's all about the Egyptian pyramids! Listen to this: the first pyramid was built in 2680 BC! This pyramid does not look like the famous pyramids. It is called a step pyramid since it was built by stacking smaller and smaller layers on top of each other. The sides of this pyramid look like a staircase."

"Wow!" said Mary. "I thought all the pyramids looked the same.
Who built this strange pyramid?"

Randy shows Mary the page. "A man named Imhotep built the pyramid for Djoser, an Egyptian pharaoh," he replies. "Pharaohs were rulers of ancient Egypt. Imhotep was Djoser's architect." Randy turns a few more pages and shows Mary another picture. "Here is the Great Pyramid of Giza. This pyramid had smooth sides. It is the largest Egyptian pyramid, over 450 feet tall! It was built as a tomb for a ruler named Khufu. In ancient Egyptian culture, it was important for powerful people to have great tombs constructed for them. It probably took over 20 years to build."

"That's amazing, Randy.
I learned so much about the pyramids!" says Mary.
"Thank you for sharing."

Find the words in the puzzle and circle.

ANCIENT   ARCHITECT   CONSTRUCT   PYRAMIDS   TOMB

C	O	N	F	L	K	O	A	N	C	I	E	N	T
P	A	R	C	H	I	T	E	C	T	S	H	Z	C
E	X	P	E	M	L	O	A	R	C	T	I	O	N
Q	S	P	Y	R	A	M	I	D	S	W	A	K	U
O	P	A	O	E	I	B	L	B	M	O	K	F	O
C	O	N	S	T	R	U	C	T	P	Y	R	A	E

Name:_____

Sir Isaac Newton

Sir Isaac Newton, born in England in 1643, is considered one of the most important scientists in history. Some people think he was the smartest person who ever lived! He made many scientific discoveries throughout his life, and he developed important inventions that are still used today.

One of Newton's most famous discoveries was the theory of gravity. This theory helped to explain the movements of the planets around the sun. It also explains how we stay on the earth instead of floating out into space!

Newton also invented a whole new type of mathematics which he called "fluxions." Today we call this type of math "calculus." It is an important type of math used in engineering and science.

The reflecting telescope, which uses mirrors to reflect light and form an image, was invented by Newton. Astronomers today still use telescopes based on Newton's original design. Newton wrote a book that is considered one of the most important science books ever written. It is called Philosophiae Naturalis Principia Mathematica, which means Mathematical Principals of Natural Philosophy.

We all have something in common with Sir Isaac Newton—he lived during a pandemic, just as we have done! Some of his greatest discoveries were made while he was staying at home during the Great Plague of 1665-1667. Later in his life, Newton was made an honorary knight by the Queen of England in 1705.

That is why he has the word "Sir" in front of his name!

Find the words in the puzzle and circle.

DISCOVERIES   GRAVITY   INVENTIONS
        PLAGUE   THEORY

G	R	A	V	I	N	V	E	N	T	I	O	N	S
T	D	I	S	E	X	P	E	M	H	C	O	N	F
H	O	P	A	P	L	A	G	U	E	H	X	E	Q
E	A	R	C	T	I	O	N	B	O	S	H	Z	C
O	P	D	I	S	C	O	V	E	R	I	E	S	U
F	K	Z	G	R	A	V	I	T	Y	P	Y	R	A

Name: _____

Ashley Sees the Stars

The car ride to Uncle Edgar's house was very long. He lived out in the rural countryside where there was nothing to look at but farm fields. Ashley was worried that she would be bored while visiting him.

"Cheer up, Ashley," said her mother. "We will have a great time visiting—my brother Edgar always has some interesting things to look at!" Ashley doubted that she would think anything out here in the countryside would be interesting to her.

When they finally arrived, Uncle Edgar was waiting for them on the porch. There he stood beside a strange piece of equipment. Ashley had no idea what it was, and she didn't really care. She figured it was probably something boring.

She carried her suitcase inside the house and stayed there while everyone else visited outside. Soon it became evening, and it was time for dinner.

"Ashley, come on out. We are going to eat outside at Uncle Edgar's picnic table," said her mother. While eating dinner, Ashley couldn't help but look up into the night sky. There she saw millions of twinkling stars! It was amazing how many she could see without the bright lights of the city interfering! Uncle Edgar noticed her looking at them.

"Ashley, would you like to take a closer look at those stars?" asked Uncle Edgar.

"A closer look? How?" asked Ashley.

Uncle Edgar showed her the strange piece of equipment that he had on the porch—a telescope! Through it, Ashley saw the most amazing stars!

Read the clues and write the answer in a crossword puzzle:

1. An instrument used for viewing far away objects

2. Luminous celestial bodies visible in the night sky

3. A tool used to do something

4. An outdoor part of a house

5. An area far from any city

Galileo

Galileo Galilei was an Italian astronomer born in 1564. He is famous for performing revolutionary experiments and challenging old ideas about science.

For example, Galileo once disproved old beliefs about gravity. In those days, people believed that heavier objects always fell faster than lighter objects. To test this, Galileo climbed to the top of the Leaning Tower of Pisa and dropped two balls of different weights at the same time. They fell and hit the ground together!

About ten years later, news of the telescope had reached Italy. Most of the people interested in this invention thought it would be a great tool in battle, but Galileo had other plans. Galileo modified the telescope so that it could be used to look up at the stars.

Galileo went on to discover many things with the telescope. First, he looked at Earth's moon up close, finding that its surface was rough and full of craters. Then he saw four odd spots traveling around Jupiter. At first, he thought they were stars, but then he realized that they were moons of Jupiter!

In those times, most people believed that the Earth was the center of the universe. However, Galileo learned about old ideas that the Earth and other planets actually revolved around the Sun. He supported these ideas and wrote about them. His books and ideas were widely rejected during his lifetime, but they are now famous!

Find the words in the puzzle and circle.

REVOLVED   TELESCOPE   UNIVERSE   PLANETS   DISCOVERY

A	S	D	K	E	F	R	E	V	O	L	V	E	D
V	F	U	N	I	V	E	R	S	E	Z	O	D	O
T	E	L	E	S	C	O	P	E	W	M	Q	S	O
L	H	B	E	Q	X	B	P	L	A	N	E	T	S
K	Q	V	F	L	H	B	Q	A	X	V	F	P	Z
F	L	K	O	K	D	I	S	C	O	V	E	R	Y

Name:_____

The Jigsaw Puzzle

Are you looking for an entertaining, inexpensive way to have fun with your family and friends? Consider doing a jigsaw puzzle! While attempting to solve a jigsaw puzzle, you will try to correctly arrange oddly shaped, interlocking pieces. Each piece has a portion of a picture printed onto it. When all pieces are arranged correctly, they create a complete, unified picture.

Does that sound easy? Well, some jigsaw puzzles are easy—if they only have a few pieces to arrange—but some jigsaw puzzles have thousands of pieces! Those are quite difficult! The first jigsaw puzzles were made in the 1760s by a mapmaker named John Spilsbury. He drew maps onto pieces of wood and then cut them into small pieces. He gave the puzzles to a local school to help the children there learn their geography lessons. These puzzles were a big success!

These days, you can find jigsaw puzzles with many different pictures on them, not just maps! Animals and nature images, cartoon characters, city skylines, and abstract colorful designs can all be found on jigsaw puzzles. You can even have a photograph of your own family made into a personalized jigsaw puzzle!

Scientists have even discovered that by regularly working on jigsaw puzzles, you can help your brain to stay healthy! Jigsaw puzzles make good gifts for your grandparents and friends, and they usually do not cost very much money.

So, turn off the television set and try out a jigsaw puzzle!
Your family, friends, and even your brain will thank you!

Find the words in the puzzle and circle.

HEALTHY   JIGSAW   ABSTRACT   ARRANGE   BRAIN

Q	O	L	H	M	E	A	B	S	T	R	A	C	T
L	F	V	Z	O	A	R	R	A	N	G	E	M	A
E	I	S	L	F	K	Z	A	P	W	M	Q	S	O
B	H	X	V	F	L	J	I	G	S	A	W	D	O
K	Q	V	F	L	H	B	N	A	X	V	F	P	Z
H	E	A	L	T	H	Y	A	S	D	K	E	Q	W

Mike's Puzzling Day

Mike didn't know what to do today. It was Saturday, so he didn't have school. He had finished his homework and chores.

"What are we going to do today?" he asked his dad.

"I'm sorry, Mike," said his dad. "I'm busy fixing the car today."

"Okay," said Mike, "I'll ask Mom what we're doing."

Mike found his mom in the kitchen. She was baking cookies. "I'm sorry, but I'm busy today baking cookies for the church bake sale."

Mike went to play with his sister, but she was still working on her homework. Mike felt upset that everyone else in his house was busy. He did not know what to do all by himself. Mike looked around his bedroom and found a box under his bed. It was a gift that he had gotten last year for his birthday. Mike had forgotten all about this gift—it was a jigsaw puzzle! Mike opened up the puzzle and spread the pieces out. The goal of the puzzle was to make a picture of a hot air balloon. Mike started working on it.

Soon his sister walked into the room. She had finished her homework and asked if she could help with the puzzle.

"Sure!" said Mike. Next his dad finished fixing the car. He asked if he could help too.

"Sure!" said Mike. Then his mom came into the room with a plate of cookies. "Would you like some of these extra cookies?" asked his mom.

"Sure!" they all said.

Together they all worked on the jigsaw puzzle and ate cookies!

Read the clues and write the answer in a crossword puzzle:

1. A special kind of puzzle with interlocking pieces

2. The date on which someone was born

3. Having many things to do

4. An activity that you try to solve

5. Small, sweet treats, usually circular

Name:_____

Hot Air Balloons

Have you ever looked up in the sky and seen a giant, colorful balloon floating by? Then you are really lucky, as it is not often that hot air balloons are out traveling around!

A hot air balloon is a type of flying machine. But it doesn't have an engine or use batteries…it uses fire to heat the air inside the huge balloon! The warmed-up air is lighter than the cool, unheated air outside of the balloon. The balloon, therefore, rises up once there is enough warm air inside of it!

Attached to the bottom of the balloon is a large basket that holds the mechanism from which the fire is controlled. This basket is also big enough to carry passengers for a ride!

Did you know that the very first hot air balloon passengers were a sheep, a duck, and a chicken? This ride took place in France in 1783. Soon after, people started taking rides in them—this makes it the oldest form of flying technology used by humans!

Hot air balloons can only be used on days when there is no rain. This is because the raindrops would get boiling hot when in contact with the inflated balloon and destroy the balloon's fabric.

So, on a dry, sunny day, be on the lookout for
a hot air balloon! Perhaps you will get to go for
a ride in one someday!

Find the words in the puzzle and circle.

BALLOONS   PASSENGERS   GIANT   BOILING   MACHINE

Z	G	K	Q	V	S	H	K	Q	O	L	H	M	E
L	I	B	A	S	D	K	M	A	C	H	I	N	E
P	A	S	S	E	N	G	E	R	S	E	Q	W	A
V	N	B	H	X	V	F	L	D	O	M	Q	S	O
F	T	B	O	I	L	I	N	G	F	L	H	P	Z
A	X	V	F	F	K	B	A	L	L	O	O	N	S

Computers

If you've ever read an email, played a video game, or searched for something online, you've used some kind of computer. Computers play many important roles in our lives today, but they weren't always so powerful.

The first computers were built in the 1930s. These computers were much different than the ones we use today; they were really just big calculators. These early computers couldn't do much more than mathematical calculations, and they were so big that they took up whole rooms!

The first computers were made for government workers. However, in the 1970s, the first PCs (personal computers) were released. These allowed typical people to have and use household computers.

An even greater invention came in the 1980s: the internet! With the internet, computers are able to communicate with one another. This is how you can send and receive emails, play online games, or visit websites.

At the same time, laptop computers were being popularized. Laptops are very convenient computers that can be carried around and used anywhere. They fold up when not in use and are usually very portable.

However, they aren't as portable as smartphones!

The smartphone was invented in the 1990s. Smartphones feature "touchscreen" displays, meaning you control them by touching their screens with your finger. These computers are very small compared to the early ones; they can fit right into your pocket!

Find the words in the puzzle and circle.

CALCULATOR   INFORMATION   SMARTPHONES   CONVENIENT   ONLINE

S	H	Z	S	M	A	R	T	P	H	O	N	E	S
E	Q	X	B	E	O	M	Q	S	O	N	L	W	A
K	Q	O	L	H	M	E	S	D	K	L	Z	O	M
L	B	A	V	C	O	N	V	E	N	I	E	N	T
I	N	F	O	R	M	A	T	I	O	N	H	P	Z
C	A	L	C	U	L	A	T	O	R	E	V	F	K

Grandma and the Computer

It was summer vacation and Rachel was visiting her grandma's house. Rachel was excited to be out of school for the summer, and she was happy to get to spend time with her grandma.

"How did you do in school this year?" asked her grandma.

"Oh, it was a great year!" replied Rachel. "I really liked my teacher, and I did well on my final report card. Would you like to see it?"

"Sure! Did you bring it with you?" asked her grandma.

"No, my report card is not printed on paper, it is on the computer! It is posted onto the school's website," Rachel explained.

"I do not really understand what that means," said her grandma. "I still do not know how to use the computer that your parents bought for me. It just sits on the desk—I do not even know how to turn it on!"

"Oh, Grandma! I can teach you! You will love it." Together Rachel and her grandma went into the room with the computer.

Rachel showed her how to turn the computer on, how to get onto the internet, and how to look up different websites. She showed her grandma her report card!

"How wonderful—both your report card and this computer!" exclaimed her grandma. "The computer is like a whole new world for me. Thank you, Rachel, for teaching me!"

"Today's lesson is just the beginning. Tomorrow I will teach you even more!" Rachel was so happy that her grandma could finally use the computer!

Read the clues and write the answer in a crossword puzzle:

1. The online community that computers connect to
2. A machine made for searching the internet
3. Last and most recent
4. The day after today
5. The day it is now

Name:_____

Polar Bears

Do you want to impress your family and friends with an amazing fun fact? Tell them that polar bears are not really white! This is true because their fur is actually made up of clear, hollow tubes that reflect the light, causing the bears to appear white. The skin beneath polar bears' fur is black!

The polar bear is the world's largest land predator; they hunt for and eat seals. Polar bears live in the countries that ring the Arctic Circle: Norway, Greenland, Canada, Russia, and the United States (Alaska). They live on sea ice, which is frozen ocean water. That is why you will not find a polar bear in warmer climates. But do not worry about the polar bears getting too cold while out in the snow and ice! They are insulated with two layers of fur and under the fur, a thick layer of fat. In fact, they have more problems with overheating than they do with getting too cold!

Polar bears are excellent swimmers. They can swim for long distances to get from one piece of sea ice to another. Their large paws are specially adapted for swimming, and they use them to paddle through the icy water.

As the world is going through a period of global warming, polar bears are at risk. Their sea ice is melting, and so they are losing their natural habitat. It is important to learn more about how to help protect polar bears and to save this unique species!

Find the words in the puzzle and circle.

FROZEN   POLAR   PREDATOR   SPECIES   ADAPTED

S	H	Z	O	M	Q	S	O	L	W	A	K	P	F
H	M	E	S	D	E	P	R	E	D	A	T	O	R
A	D	A	P	T	E	D	E	I	S	F	L	L	O
L	B	A	V	K	Q	V	L	E	Q	X	B	A	Z
P	Z	H	X	S	P	E	C	I	E	S	H	R	E
F	K	Z	O	M	E	Q	V	F	L	D	V	B	N

Brock Saves the Polar Bears

One day Brock was watching television and saw a show about global warming. The show explained how the Earth's temperature is rising and why that is a major problem—especially for the polar bears.

Polar bears thrive in areas where it is very cold. They live around the icy, frozen ocean waters of the Arctic Circle called sea ice. Brock learned that those icy areas are beginning to melt because the Earth's temperature is too warm to freeze the water. The polar bears' entire ecosystem is at risk because the sea ice is disappearing.

"This is terrible," said Brock. "I wish I could do something to help."

"Well, Brock," said his mom, "we could try to help. We can raise awareness about this problem. We can give people ideas of how changes in their daily behavior could reduce global warming."

"Yes! I want to help! I want to help save the polar bears!" exclaimed Brock.

Together they researched information about ways to help, such as planting trees, using the car less often, and using less electricity. Brock and his mom decided to form a club to spread this useful information. Brock named the club the Save the Polar Bears Club!

At the first meeting, Brock explained to the group what global warming is and the simple ways we could help. Then the club members all planted new trees in a nearby park. Brock felt proud that he was helping to save the polar bears!

Read the clues and write the answer in a crossword puzzle:

1. The way that someone acts

2. How hot or cold something is

3. Energy that powers machines

4. Huge, furry animals with large teeth

5. Natural environment in which plants and animals live

Name:_____

Antarctica

"I'm so excited!" said Noah, Timothy's best friend. "My dad is coming into class today!"
The bell rang, and Timothy was excited. Noah's father walked in through the door.
"Class, we have a guest today, so please give him your full attention," said Mrs. Kranz,
the teacher.
"Hello, everyone, my name is Mr. Casal. Today, I'm going to tell you about my job as a
glaciologist. A glaciologist is someone who studies glaciers! And I have just returned
from an amazing trip to a very interesting place: Antarctica."
The whole class gasped. Some kids started whispering.
Mr. Casal continued. "I learned so much about Antarctica during my trip. Did you know
that it's actually a desert?" This confused Timothy. What did he mean? Antarctica is full
of ice, not sand!
"It's true that Antarctica is cold and covered in ice," said Mr. Casal, "but it is considered
a desert because it has very little rain or snow. In fact, Antarctica is the driest continent
on the planet!"
"Did you see any penguins?" asked Suzie, one of Timothy's classmates.
"Well, I was quite busy, but I did see a few! They were beautiful in their natural habitat."
"How cold was it?" asked Josh, another student.
"On most days, it was far colder than the inside of your freezer! However, it was not as
cold on the coast."
"Could I ever go there?" asked Timothy.
Mr. Casal smiled. "If you study hard!"

Read the clues and write the answer in a crossword puzzle:

1. Flightless birds that can live in Antarctica

2. Quickly inhaled in surprise

3. Huge chunks of ice

4. Least wet or moist

5. Frozen water

Rainforests

Did you know that approximately 25% of all medicines come from the rainforest? Rainforests are full of unique plant species that have been proven to provide various health benefits.

Not all plants in the rainforest are used for medicine, though! Sugar, pineapples, and cinnamon originate from the rainforest, along with cocoa beans, which are used to make chocolate!

The rainforest is also home to many unique animals, including sloths, orangutans, poison dart frogs, and macaws. In fact, about 50% of the world's plant and animal species can be found somewhere in the rainforest!

Unfortunately, the world's rainforests are in trouble. A big problem called deforestation poses a threat to these amazing places. Deforestation is the gradual loss of forest area due mostly to people cutting down trees for lumber to create room for farms or buildings.

Over half of the world's rainforests have vanished since 1950 due to deforestation. At its current rate, at least 150 acres of rainforest are lost to deforestation every minute!

If we don't stop or dramatically slow down deforestation, millions of irreplaceable plant and animal species could be lost forever. It's very important that we make good decisions that positively affect the environment.

Find the words in the puzzle and circle.

MEDICINES   PLANT   RAINFORESTS   THREAT   UNIQUE

S	H	Z	P	I	O	O	D	A	V	K	Q	V	L
P	E	O	L	F	K	Z	O	M	E	Q	K	Q	O
L	B	R	A	I	N	F	O	R	E	S	T	S	E
W	A	K	N	E	Q	X	B	U	N	I	Q	U	E
Z	H	X	T	H	R	E	A	T	H	M	E	S	D
M	E	D	I	C	I	N	E	S	E	I	S	F	L

The Unexpected Artwork

Julia was excited to be starting her new job.
She was going to be the babysitter for a four-year-old boy named
Tyler. Julia gathered some supplies to bring with her: a box of crayons
and paper to color on and a few books that she thought Tyler might
like to read with her. She was all ready for her new job!
She arrived and showed Tyler her supplies.
"Would you like to read a book?" asked Julia.
"Yes! I love books!" said Tyler. Together they took out the books that Julia had brought.
Tyler picked up the book titled Diego. It was about the mural artist Diego Rivera. They
read it, and Tyler loved the book!
"Let's make some artwork too!" said Julia. She took out the crayons and paper. As she
was clearing off a table for them to work upon, Tyler quietly went into the other room.
When Julia turned around, she realized Tyler had gone—with the crayons!
"Tyler! Where are you?" she called.
"In here!" Tyler said happily. "I'm making my own mural! Just like Diego!"
Julia ran to the other room and saw Tyler coloring on the wall!
"Oh no!" she cried. "We are supposed to color on paper, not the wall!"
"But I want to be like Diego!" said Tyler.
"How about you help me clean up your mural, and we can color on paper and then
hang it on the wall?" suggested Julia.
Tyler agreed. Luckily, the crayon marks came off the wall with soapy water! Then they
got to work coloring new artwork—on paper this time!

Choose the correct meaning:

AGREED   ___ Accepted a suggestion   ___ Rejected a suggestion

COLORING   ___ Making art with paint   ___ Making art with crayons

CRAYONS   ___ Colored sticks of wax   ___ Pieces of paper

EXCITED   ___ Enthusiastic and eager   ___ Bored and tired

LOVED   ___ Really hated   ___ Really liked

MURAL   ___ Painting on a wall   ___ Drawing on paper

SOAPY   ___ Containing dirt and grime   ___ Containing soap

SUPPLIES   ___ Useful materials   ___ Useless items

WALL   ___ Horizontal structure you walk on

                  ___ Flat, vertical structure

Diego Rivera

Diego Rivera was born on December 8, 1886, in Guanajuanto, Mexico. People from all over the world have heard of him. Why? Because he helped to change the meaning of art.

Instead of making paintings to hang in museums and galleries, Diego Rivera painted murals in public spaces for everyone to see. For Diego, the public wall was the perfect place to express his deep respect both for the common people of Mexico and for the working-class people around the world.

Diego Rivera loved his Mexican heritage so much that he wanted to create an art form that was entirely Mexican. This is why he was asked to paint murals all over the country of Mexico. He painted murals in schools, palaces, and government buildings. Diego's reputation of being a talented artist stretched beyond his own country. He was also asked to paint murals in various states of the United States, such as California, Michigan, and New York.

People everywhere love seeing his colorful artwork! Other artists have been inspired by his murals and have painted murals of their own. This style of artwork brings cheer to a community and is often appreciated by visitors as well!

It has been estimated that in his lifetime Diego Rivera painted more than two and a half miles of murals! Those public walls are now so much more than simple brick and mortar!

Read the clues and write the answer in a crossword puzzle:

1. Liked and recognized

2. Set of cultural traditions

3. Admiration of someone

4. Distances of 5280 feet

5. Roughly guessed

Easter Island

In the Pacific Ocean, thousands of miles away from the nearest civilization lies Easter Island. It is a strange and mysterious place famous for what happened there many years before and the unique kind of evidence that has been left behind.

The island, called Rapa Nui in the local language, got its English-language name from Holland's Capitan Jacob Roggeveen, who landed there on Easter Sunday in 1722. Roggeveen found a strange culture on the island and even stranger statues called Moai.

The Moai are giant rocks, about 13-feet-tall and weighing more than 14-tons, shaped into faces. Scientists determined that they were made between 1400 and 1600 AD. They are found all along the coastlines as if guarding the island's people from intruders. To this day, no one knows who made them or how they did it.

In all, 887 Moai have been found, many still in stone quarries on the island. But how exactly did the islanders move the 14-ton moai? In those days, the powerful machinery that we have today did not exist. Historians believe the islanders may have used wooden logs as rollers, and ropes and ramps to help set them upright.

As for the people of Easter Island, they mostly died out, leaving their numbers only in the hundreds. Historians believe at the height of their civilization as many as 10,000 Rapa Nui people lived on the island. It is believed that the decline of their culture was caused by the deforestation of almost all the island's trees.

Today, the descendants of the Rapa Nui people work hard to preserve the island's culture and traditions—and to preserve the Moai!

Read the clues and write the answer in a crossword puzzle:

1. Unlike others, unexpected

2. Unknown, puzzling

3. Gradual worsening

4. Two thousand pounds

5. Unlike any other

Name:_____

Sophia's Tree

Sophia's family visited their cousins who live in Brazil near the Amazon rainforest. They had traveled all the way from the United States, so it was a very far trip!

"Wow! What a beautiful place this is!" Sophia exclaimed.

"I have never seen so many trees!"

"I wish you could have seen this area ten years ago," said her Uncle Rogelio. "There were many more trees then."

"Why are there fewer trees now?" asked Sophia.

"There are fewer trees because people are cutting them down. They want to use the land for other purposes, so they are taking the trees down. It is called deforestation."

"That makes me feel so sad. What happens to all of the animals who live in those trees? Where will they go?" asked Sophia.

"They usually have trouble finding new homes, and they may die. Also, fewer trees means more carbon dioxide in the atmosphere, which is contributing to global warming," replied Uncle Rogelio.

"Is there anything we could do to help? How can we stop deforestation?" asked Sophia.

"Reforestation is a great way to fight back. That means we should plant more trees and encourage other people to do the same. We should also write letters to our government officials to encourage them to make laws to protect the rainforests," said Uncle Rogelio.

When Sophia returned home, she and her family planted a tree in their yard. The tree always reminded Sophia of what she learned while in Brazil.

Read the clues and write the answer in a crossword puzzle:

1. Dense group of trees with lots of rainfall

2. Support someone by talking to them

3. Place, region

4. Traveling vacation

5. Reasons for using or

   doing something

Nelson Mandela

Our world is made up of people who have skin colors different from one another. Sadly, sometimes people are treated differently because of their skin color; this is called discrimination.

Nelson Mandela is someone you should know about because he helped to move us towards a world where everyone is treated fairly and equally. Even though there is still a lot of discrimination in the world today, Nelson Mandela's work made a positive difference in many people's lives.

Nelson Mandela, born in 1918, lived in the country of South Africa, where there are many different cultures and races of people. When he was growing up, there was a huge racial divide in the country.

White people ran the country, and they had all the good jobs, and the white children went to good schools. Most black people did not have access to good jobs or schools. They were not even allowed to vote in the elections.

Nelson Mandela felt that everyone deserved to be treated the same, no matter what their skin color was. He worked hard to change the laws of South Africa, so this could be a reality. He was even put into prison for trying to make this change. Eventually, Nelson Mandela's hard work gained support from people around the entire world. He even became South Africa's first black president! For his work towards equal rights in South Africa, Nelson Mandela won the Nobel Peace Prize in 1993.

Read the clues and write the answer in a crossword puzzle:

1. Events in which leaders are chosen by the people

2. Reward for your actions

3. Leader of a country

4. Make a choice in an election

5. Time without fighting or conflict

The Nobel Prize

The Nobel Prize is one of the most prestigious awards that you can receive. There are six given out every year, in six different subject areas. The areas are physics, chemistry, medicine, literature, economics, and peace. The Nobel Prize honors people from around the world who have done outstanding work in one of these areas.

The Nobel Prize winners receive a gold medal, a diploma, and some money. The prizes are given out at a very fancy banquet in Stockholm, Sweden, every year on December 10th, which is the birthday of Alfred Nobel.

Alfred Nobel was a Swedish scientist who invented an explosive called dynamite. Dynamite was used for mining, construction, and demolition. The sales of Alfred Nobel's dynamite made him very rich, and he wanted to use that money to honor people who helped humankind in some way. With the money he had earned from selling dynamite, the Nobel Prize was created and funded.

If you win a Nobel Prize, you are called a Nobel Laureate. The youngest person to win a Nobel Prize is Malala Yousafzai—she was only 17 years old when she won the Nobel Peace Prize in 2014.

So maybe someday you will win a Nobel Prize! If you work hard and focus on helping others, you will be in the running for this very important award!

Choose the correct meaning:

YEAR ___ 7 days ___ 365 days

PRESTIGIOUS ___ famous ___ ordinary

AWARD ___ prize ___ punishment

BANQUET ___ quick meal ___ large, formal meal

CONSTRUCTION ___ eating ___ building

CREATED ___ destroyed ___ made

EXPLOSIVE ___ something that blows up when ignited

___ tool that does math

FOCUS ___ pay attention to ___ forget about

FUNDED ___ given time ___ given money

Leonardo da Vinci

What do the Mona Lisa and the parachute have in common? They were created by the same man!

Leonardo da Vinci was a famous Italian artist who was active during the Renaissance, an exciting period of time when there was an explosion of European interest in art and science. Not only was da Vinci a great artist, but he had a knack for designing sophisticated inventions!

Da Vinci was born in the Italian town of Vinci and learned from Andrea del Verrocchio, a renowned painter, and sculptor in Florence. He started becoming famous as he became more and more skilled at painting and drawing.

Today, Leonardo da Vinci is famous not only for his detailed artwork but also for his vast collection of notebooks. Da Vinci kept over 13,000 pages of journal entries, ranging from day-to-day thoughts and records to detailed sketches of wild, imaginative inventions! We have found designs for tanks, flying machines, automated weapons, and even a mechanical knight in his journals!

Since da Vinci painted meticulously accurate portraits of humans, he grew very familiar with how the human body worked. He was able to contribute his findings to the field of anatomy. Leonardo da Vinci was one of the smartest and most talented men ever to live, and he has inspired countless people far beyond his own lifetime.

Find the words in the puzzle and circle.

INVENTIONS   ARTIST   MECHANICAL   ANATOMY   ACCURATE

O	Z	X	V	F	A	N	A	T	O	M	Y	L	H
P	Q	W	M	E	I	O	R	D	K	F	A	S	O
L	A	C	C	U	R	A	T	E	F	L	K	Q	O
Z	M	E	C	H	A	N	I	C	A	L	L	H	B
K	Q	V	F	L	H	B	S	Z	X	V	F	P	Q
W	M	I	N	V	E	N	T	I	O	N	S	E	I

Name:_____

Rome

Rome has been the capital city of Italy since 1870. It is located in central Italy, on the Tiber River. In ancient times Rome was the center of a powerful empire. It is still a great historical and cultural city, visited every year by millions of tourists.

Evidence of Rome's long and fascinating history is found throughout the city. Ancient buildings and modern apartments sit side by side. The people of Rome take great pride in their city's powerful past.

The Colosseum is one of Rome's best-known ancient sites. It is a huge amphitheater, which was built around 80 AD. Wild animals and gladiators would battle in the arena. It was built with amazing architectural features—even including some secret passageways!

The Pantheon is another famous site in Rome. It was built in 27 BC as a place of worship. It has a magnificent dome with an oculus, which is an opening to the sky.

Did you know there is an entire country inside of Rome? Vatican City, the home of the Catholic Church and a separate country, is located within the city of Rome! Saint Peter's Basilica is a huge church there, and it contains many valuable treasures.

There are even more fascinating places and sights to see in Rome. Be sure to read some books or look online to discover them for yourself!

Find the words in the puzzle and circle.

ANCIENT   ARENA   CHURCH   EMPIRE   VALUABLE

E	M	P	I	R	E	S	H	K	X	V	F	L	A
P	Q	W	M	E	I	O	O	D	K	F	A	S	R
L	F	L	K	Q	O	A	N	C	I	E	N	T	E
Z	V	A	L	U	A	B	L	E	Q	O	L	H	N
K	Q	V	F	L	H	B	Q	Z	X	V	F	P	A
W	M	C	H	U	R	C	H	M	E	I	S	E	B

A Visit to Dr. Harrington

"What?" asked John. "I didn't hear you."

"I said that it is time for dinner," said his mom, with a look of concern on her face. This was the third time today that John hadn't been able to hear what she said.

That night John's mom and dad had a conversation about how John seemed to be having a hard time hearing. They decided that it was time to visit an audiologist.

John's mom took him to see Dr. Harrington. The doctor did several tests on John to see how well he could hear. Dr. Harrington then discussed the results with them.

"John, you have a moderate amount of hearing loss in both your left and right ears. We need to figure out why this has happened and how to prevent any further loss. Do you use earbuds?" asked Dr. Harrington.

"Yes," replied John, "I use them to listen to music and at school while on the computer."

"I think we have found the problem," said the doctor. "And it is sadly becoming a common problem among children. The earbuds are damaging your ability to hear."

"Oh no!" exclaimed his mom. "We didn't know they were dangerous."

"They are only dangerous if you use them too loudly or for too long of a time. I will teach you how to use them safely. I also recommend that you use headphones instead of earbuds. They are a safer choice," said Dr. Harrington.

John did what Dr. Harrington suggested, and he shared her information with his classmates. He wanted to spread this important information around to all of his friends!

Read the clues and write the answer in a crossword puzzle:

1. How well you are able to do something

2. With a possibility of causing harm

3. Causing harm

4. Less likely to cause harm

5. Student in the same class

Small but Dangerous!

Can something as small as a tiny pair of earbuds be dangerous to your health? After all, they are so very useful for when you want to listen to music without disturbing the people around you. They are inexpensive, helpful devices, right? Believe it or not, earbuds can be very damaging to your hearing. This may seem untrue since they are so small, but the damage is all due to the volume at which they are often used and the length of time they are used.

This is a problem that is growing among the world's youth, as earbuds have gotten popular. Sadly, the hearing damage being done is permanent—it cannot ever be repaired.

Is there an alternative to earbuds that is not as dangerous? Headphones are a better choice, even though they are more expensive and not as easy to carry around. Since they go over your ears instead of inside of them, they do not cause the same amount of damage to your hearing. But beware: headphones can also cause damage if listened to at a high volume or for too long of a period of time.

So, what can you do to protect your hearing but still enjoy your music? Doctors recommend the 60%/60-minute rule: use your headphones or earbuds at no more than 60% of the maximum volume, and never more than 60 minutes at a time.

It is important to protect your hearing while you are young, so you can continue to listen to your favorite music for many years to come!

Find the words in the puzzle and circle.

DAMAGE   EARBUDS   ALTERNATIVE   DANGEROUS   PERMANENT

E	I	L	H	B	E	Q	O	D	P	Q	W	M	A
V	F	A	L	T	E	R	N	A	T	I	V	E	O
L	F	K	Z	X	P	E	R	M	A	N	E	N	T
E	A	R	B	U	D	S	B	A	Q	O	L	H	M
K	Q	V	F	L	H	B	Q	G	X	V	F	P	Z
W	M	Q	O	D	A	N	G	E	R	O	U	S	L

The Olympics

Do you like sports? Then you probably already know what the Olympics are! The Olympics are the world's biggest sporting event, with more than 200 countries competing in them.

The Olympics include the Summer Games and the Winter Games, each held in a different country once every four years. The very first Olympic Games were in ancient Greece at a site called Olympia—this is where the name Olympics originated.

There is a special Olympic flag that is displayed throughout the games. It has five linked rings on a white background. The rings are red, yellow, black, blue, and green.

The flag represents all of the competing countries' national flags united as one.

The Olympic Games include different sports—there are individual sports, team sports, indoor sports, and outdoor sports. The Summer Games have a wider variety of events than the Winter Games. Some of the Summer Game events are gymnastics, swimming, track and field, baseball, cycling, and volleyball.

All of the Winter Game events are played on snow or ice. Some of the Winter Game events are ice skating, skiing, ice hockey, and bobsled racing. Sometimes new sports are added to the games, such as snowboarding, which was added in 1998.

Watching the Olympics is a fun way to learn about sports different than the ones you may have tried yourself, and a great way to learn a bit about countries other than your own. So be sure to watch the next Olympic Games and cheer on your favorite athletes!

Read the clues and write the answer in a crossword puzzle:

1. Colored fabric that represents some place or thing

2. Sport played with a ball and bat on a field

3. People who play sports

4. Sport that involves bicycles

5. Not the same

Simone Biles

When Simone Biles was a little girl, she had many struggles. Her father had abandoned her family, and her mother was addicted to drugs and alcohol. Simone and her siblings had to be placed in a foster home until her grandparents officially adopted her and her sister. Simone's other two siblings were adopted by an aunt.

Simone also had struggles in school. She suffered from a condition called Attention Deficient Hyperactive Disorder. This disorder caused her to have trouble concentrating in school. Life was very hard for this young girl.

When she was six years old, her day-care group visited a gym where gymnasts trained. Simone couldn't just sit and watch them—she wanted to try their moves! To everyone's surprise, Simone was a natural gymnast! She was so good that one of the coaches at that gym sent a letter home with her, inviting Simone to take gymnastics classes.

Simone loved the classes, and the coaches there could hardly believe their eyes! Very quickly, she was able to perform gymnastics skills that others, who had been training for years, could not. Soon the whole world would get to know this amazing gymnast.

Simone entered gymnastics competitions and performed some of the most difficult moves ever seen in the world of gymnastics. Despite all of her challenges, she worked hard and now has 25 World medals—the most in the history of gymnastics.

Simone has also competed in the Olympics, earning 5 Olympic medals. She will be competing in the Olympics again in the summer of 2021—and the world will be watching her!

Choose the correct meaning:

ALCOHOL   ___ a drink such as beer or wine

                      ___ a drink such as milk or juice

AMAZING   ___ surprisingly bad   ___ surprisingly good

CHALLENGES   ___ advantages   ___ problems

COMPETING   ___ participating in a game   ___ reading a book

DIFFICULT   ___ easy   ___ hard

GRANDPARENTS ___ children of children   ___ parents of parents

HISTORY   ___ events of the future   ___ events of the past

MEDALS   ___ awards given for sports   ___ money given for working

Camels

Camels live in some of the harshest climates on Earth—deserts! In the desert, it is hot and dry during the day and very cold at night. Food and water are very hard to find. Camels have adapted and found ways to survive in the deserts.

Camels have a thick coat of hair. This hair helps to keep them protected from the heat in the day, and it keeps them warm at night. They have long eyelashes to help keep the blowing sand out of their eyes, and their nostrils can open and close, to help keep the sand out of their noses. The most noticeable of their adaptations are their humps! Dromedary camels have one hump, and Bactrian camels have two humps. The humps store fat, which the camel uses for energy when food is scarce. The humps are so helpful to the camels that they can go for several months with no food and one week with no water.

Camels are extremely strong animals. They are often used for people to ride on and to carry heavy loads. Camels are also very fast animals—they can run as fast as a horse! Camels can walk for up to 30 miles (50 km) a day on their long, strong legs! If you'd like to see a camel in its natural habitat, you would need to go on a trip to northern Africa, the Middle East, Australia, or Central Asia. If a trip to one of these countries is not in your future, be sure to visit a zoo to see these amazing animals!

Read the clues and write the answer in a crossword puzzle:

1. Change that makes an animal stronger in its environment

2. Layer of grease and oil found in animals

3. Large yellow animals in the desert

4. Power you can get from eating food

5. Openings in the nose

Billy the Bactrian

Summers were always very hot in Florida, which is where Billy and his sister, Cecilia, were staying while they visited with their grandparents. The temperatures felt like they were getting higher every day!

"I am so hot!" complained Billy. "I wish I had something too cool to drink." Billy and Cecilia were outside helping their grandfather paint his fence.

"Me too!" said Cecilia. "This must be the hottest day ever!"

"Hmm, I suppose we should go in for a little water break," said Grandpa. "After all, you two are not camels!"

"What do you mean, Grandpa? Of course, we are not camels!" said Billy.

"Let's go inside, and I'll tell you what I mean," said Grandpa.

The three of them went inside, and Grandma gave them each a glass of cold ice water.

"Well," said Grandpa, "did you know that camels can survive in climates even hotter than Florida? And they can go up to a week without having a drink of water?"

"Wow! A whole week?" said Cecilia.

"Yes, they store fat in their humps, which gives them energy when they need it. Dromedary camels have one hump, and Bactrian camels have two," explained Grandpa.

"That's awesome!" exclaimed Billy. "I wish I were a Bactrian camel with two humps! Then I could stay outside painting without getting thirsty!" Grandpa laughed. "We could call you Billy the Bactrian!" Billy and Cecilia laughed too, and they all drank their ice water before returning to finish painting the fence.

Choose the correct meaning:

CAMELS   ___ large desert animals   ___ tiny forest animals

DRINK   ___ consume a solid   ___ consume a liquid

FENCE   ___ brick house   ___ wooden or metal barrier

EXPLAINED   ___ made clear for understanding   ___ confused with talking

HOTTEST   ___ warmest   ___ coldest

ICE   ___ liquid water   ___ frozen water

LAUGHED   ___ reacted to something sad   ___ reacted to something funny

OUTSIDE   ___ not in a building   ___ in a building

RETURNING   ___ moving away   ___ coming back

The Great Barrier Reef

The world's largest coral reef system, the Great Barrier Reef, is a source of wonder for people around the world. Located off the coast of Australia, this ecosystem is home to many endangered species and is one of the most popular tourist attractions in Australia.

The Great Barrier Reef is around 2600 kilometers in length—it is so big that astronauts can see it from space! It is the largest living structure on the planet; it is about the same size as Japan!

There are so many animals that live there! Fish, sea turtles, giant clams, stingrays, octopuses, and jellyfish are only some of the different kinds of living things that can be found living in the Great Barrier Reef. There are also thirty species of whales and dolphins living there!

The Great Barrier Reef is made up of around 2900 individual reefs, which are made from over 400 species of coral. The hard coral exoskeletons are what actually forms the reef, slowly building up over time. The Great Barrier Reef has been forming for over 20,000 years! With so many animals depending on the Great Barrier Reef to live, it is very important we all help to care for it. Global warming, pollution, and overfishing are three threats to the health of the Great Barrier Reef. Oil spills and pesticides from farming are additional threats to its health. Be sure to do your part to help protect this amazing part of our Earth!

Choose the correct meaning:

CORAL   ___ to gather and confine

               ___ a hard substance that forms reefs

ECOSYSTEM   ___ community of living things and their environment

               ___ money or pay

GLOBAL   ___ of the world   ___ like a balloon

LARGEST   ___ biggest   ___loudest

LOCATED   ___ where something is   ___ who someone is

OVERFISHING   ___ to deplete the stock of fish   ___to pay too much

PESTICIDES   ___ substance used to kill insects   ___ plants or seeds

POLLUTION   ___ fresh and clean substance   ___ dirty or harmful substance

Down Under

Sandra's family was preparing for a huge adventure—they were traveling to Australia! She and her brother, Danny, were looking online to help plan which sites they wanted to visit once they arrived.

"Wow! Look at this," exclaimed Sandra. "The Sydney Opera House looks like the coolest building I have ever seen! We definitely need to go there!"

"Yes, I agree! I love how it is a building, but it looks like it has huge sails!" said Danny.

"We also definitely need to visit the Great Barrier Reef!" said Sandra. "It says on this website that we could go on a boat to see it up close!"

"That would be awesome!" agreed Danny. "I also want to make sure we see Uluru, also known as Ayers Rock. I have never seen a rock formation like that in the middle of a desert!"

Sandra looked at a picture of Uluru online and she agreed. They would add that to their list.

The siblings had fun finding many more places that they wanted to see while on their trip. They even found one website that taught them vocabulary words commonly used in Australia. They learned that Australia is called "Down Under" since it is in the Southern Hemisphere.

"I just can't wait to travel Down Under!" exclaimed Sandra happily.

desert	sails	Southern	boat
traveling	Ayers	brother	Siblings

Choose a word to complete the sentences.

1. Sandra's family was _ _ _ _ _ _ _ _ _ to Australia.

2. Danny is Sandra's _ _ _ _ _ _ _.

3. Uluru is also known as _ _ _ _ _ Rock.

4. You can take a _ _ _ _ to see the Great Barrier Reef up close.

5. _ _ _ _ _ _ _ _ are brothers and sisters.

6. Australia is in the _ _ _ _ _ _ _ _ Hemisphere.

7. The Sydney Opera House looks like it has _ _ _ _ _.

8. Uluru is in the middle of a _ _ _ _ _ _.

Exploring the Hemispheres

What is the weather like in December? The answer to this question can have very different answers, and it all depends upon which Hemisphere you live in!

A hemisphere is half of the Earth. Geographers, people who study the Earth, have divided our planet into two Hemispheres: Northern and Southern.

How did they divide the Earth? They used an imaginary line! The imaginary line that divides the Northern and Southern Hemispheres is called the Equator. It encircles the Earth's middle. Any place north of the Equator is considered part of the Northern Hemisphere, and any place south of the Equator is considered the Southern Hemisphere.

There are differences in the climates of the Northern and Southern Hemispheres because of the way the Earth is tilted toward and away from the sun. As our planet moves around the sun, the different Hemispheres do not get heated up equally. In the Northern Hemisphere, the warmer months are from June through September, and the colder months are October through May. In the Southern Hemisphere, the warmer months are October through May, and the colder months are June through September!

So, back to our original question: What is the weather like in December? If you live in the Northern Hemisphere, the weather in December is usually getting rather colder, as it is wintertime. If you live in the Southern Hemisphere, the weather in December is warming up, as it is summertime!

heated	Southern	Equator	Sun
Hemisphere	geographers		Northern

Choose a word to complete the sentences.

1. A _ _ _ _ _ _ _ _ _ _ is half of the Earth.

2. People who study the Earth are _ _ _ _ _ _ _ _ _ _ _.

3. Our planet moves around the _ _ _.

4. The _ _ _ _ _ _ _ is an imaginary line.

5. The _ _ _ _ _ _ _ _ Hemisphere is north of the Equator.

6. The Earth does not get _ _ _ _ _ _ up equally.

7. The _ _ _ _ _ _ _ _ Hemisphere is south of the Equator.

Name: _____

Career Day

Frank's class was walking to the auditorium for a special event. The whole school was attending Career Day! They were going to learn all about different jobs that they could have when they were grown up.

When the auditorium was filled with all the students of the school, the principal, Mrs. Carpino, walked onto the stage and introduced the first speaker.

"I'd like you to meet Mr. Roger Delano!" she said.

Mr. Delano was a veterinarian. He spoke to the school about how he tended to many different types of animals. He said he had to go to school for many years to learn how to do his job. Frank thought it would be fun to spend his days taking care of animals!

Next Mrs. Carpino introduced a woman named Ms. Pluth. Her job was an airplane pilot. She said she was able to travel all around the world while working! It was exciting for Frank to imagine flying an airplane up high in the sky!

After Ms. Pluth, they heard from an architect, a florist, and a journalist. Then Mrs. Carpino introduced the final speaker of the day.

"I'd like you to meet Mr. Willis!" she said.

Mr. Willis was a geographer. Frank wasn't sure what a geographer did. Mr. Willis explained that geographers study the Earth. They learn about land formations, the environment, and the people who live in different places. He said that geographers can do many different types of projects to help the Earth function at its best. This career was Frank's favorite—maybe someday he would be a geographer!

Choose the correct meaning:

ENVIRONMENT   ___ surrounding area   ___ happy song

FINAL   ___ the very first   ___ the very last

FORMATIONS   ___ shapes   ___ flavors

FUNCTION   ___ to work in a particular way   ___ to have fun

GEOGRAPHER   ___ one who studies the Earth   ___ one who studies cars

IMAGINE   ___ to remember   ___ to dream or think about

PILOT   ___ one who writes stories   ___ one who flies airplanes

SPEAKER   ___ one who talks to a group   ___ one who dances

STAGE   ___ raised floor or platform   ___ raised ceiling or wall

VETERINARIAN   ___ one who served in the military   ___ animal doctor

The Milky Way

Our Earth is made up of many different countries and many different cultures. Sometimes it seems like we may not have anything in common with people who live in areas different from our own.

But there is something we all have in common with one another—we are all members of the Milky Way galaxy!

The Milky Way galaxy is one of many galaxies in the universe. It is home to our planet and Sun. In fact, it is so huge that in comparison our entire solar system seems tiny!

The Milky Way got its name because in the night sky it can have the appearance of spilled milk! There really is no spilled milk out there, the whitish band is actually billions of stars clustered together out in space.

At the center of the Milky Way is something quite strange—a black hole. Black holes are created when a giant star runs out of energy. The star implodes, causing an explosion called a supernova. Black holes can seem a bit frightening, as they suck up anything that cross their paths because their gravitational force is so strong! Scientists suspect that most galaxies have black holes at their centers.

The shape of the Milky Way is a spiral. Our Earth is situated in a part of the Milky Way most distant from its center—thankfully very far from the black hole!

So, the next time you are outside at night, look up and try to see our Milky Way—and know that together we are all part of this beautiful galaxy!

Choose the correct meaning:

GALAXY   ___ Large group of stars   ___ Large star

GIANT   ___ Tiny   ___ Very big

NAME   ___ What something is called   ___ What something does

NIGHT   ___ Bright part of the day   ___ Dark part of the day

SPILLED   ___ Was put into a container   ___ Fell out of its container

SPIRAL   ___ Circular spinning pattern   ___ Square grid pattern

STAR   ___ Planet we live on   ___ Bright burning lights in the night sky

UNIVERSE   ___ A large city   ___ All of outer space

DISTANT   ___ Far away   ___ Close

EXPLOSION   ___ Gradual fading   ___ Violent destruction

My Very Educated Mother

Every Friday at Rosie's school a guest speaker came to visit. Today the guest speaker was from the city's Lakeview Planetarium! This was exciting to Rosie because she was interested in space. After lunch, Mr. Krumdick, Rosie's teacher, introduced the guest speaker. "Class, I'd like you to meet Ms. Tibble. She is the Assistant Director of the Lakeview Planetarium!" said Mr. Krumdick. Ms. Tibble greeted the class, and took out a huge model of the solar system.

"Does anyone know the names of all the planets in our solar system?" she asked them. Rosie raised her hand. Ms. Tibble asked her to come to the front of the class to demonstrate her knowledge. Suddenly Rosie felt nervous—what if she forgot one of the planet's names in front of the class? Then she would be embarrassed!

Rosie slowly began to name the planets. "Mercury…Venus…Earth…ummm…" Rosie started to blush. She couldn't remember the next planet's name!

"Oh, dear," said Rosie. "I cannot remember the rest!"

"That used to happen to me all the time," said Ms. Tibble kindly, "until I learned about My Very Educated Mother!"

"My Very Educated Mother?" asked Rosie.

"Here is a fun trick to remember the planets' names, just learn this funny sentence: My Very Educated Mother Just Served Us Noodles! Each word represents one of the planets!" explained Ms. Tibble. On the chalkboard she wrote:

My=Mercury Very=Venus Educated=Earth Mother=Mars Just=Jupiter
Served=Saturn Us=Uranus Noodles=Neptune

"Oh!" exclaimed Rosie. "That's a great way to help remember the planets' names!" She felt grateful to Ms. Tibble for teaching them this trick!

knowledge	chalkboard	
remember	planet	planetarium

Choose a word to complete the sentences.

1. I visited the _ _ _ _ _ _ _ _ _ _ _ because I want to learn about stars.

2. My teacher writes on an old _ _ _ _ _ _ _ _ _ _.

3. When you don't forget something, you _ _ _ _ _ _ _ _ it.

4. Venus is a _ _ _ _ _ _.

5. When you learn something, you gain _ _ _ _ _ _ _ _ _.

Gentle Giants of the Sea

Can you imagine seeing the largest animal on the planet? You would be seeing the blue whale, which can be more than 100 feet (30 meters) long and 441,000 pounds (200,000 kilograms)!

The blue whale, scientifically known as Balaenoptera Musculus, is the largest animal ever known to have lived on the Earth. It is even bigger than any known dinosaur—the tongue alone of a blue whale weighs as much as an adult elephant! Blue whales hold another record too. They are the loudest animals on the planet! The call of the blue whale is louder than the sound of a jet engine. They can be heard by others up to 1000 miles (1600 kilometers) away!

Even though the blue whale lives in the water, it is not a fish. All whales are mammals. They breathe air, just like we humans do—except they breathe through a blowhole in the top of their heads!

Blue whales only eat tiny crustaceans called krill. They have never been seen hunting humans or other mammals; therefore, they have gained the nickname of Gentle Giants of the Sea. These giants also can live to be some of the oldest animals on the planet. Blue whales usually live to be 80-90 years old. The oldest one lived to be around 100! Blue whales are an endangered species, as there are not nearly as many blue whales left on the planet as there once were.

Hopefully we humans can help to protect them and we will see their magnificent species flourish once again!

blowhole	Mammals	protect	whale
Endangered	breathe	hunting	

Choose a word to complete the sentences.

1. _ _ _ _ _ _ _ _ _ _ are animals that breathe air and produce milk.

2. _ _ _ _ _ _ _ _ _ _ _ _ animals may die out soon.

3. When you _ _ _ _ _ _ _ something, you keep it from being harmed.

4. A _ _ _ _ _ is a huge aquatic mammal.

5. To survive, humans must _ _ _ _ _ _ _ with their mouths or noses.

6. When you try to kill an animal in the wild, you are _ _ _ _ _ _ _ it.

7. Whales use a _ _ _ _ _ _ _ _ to breathe.

Megan's Big Surprise

The bus pulled up to the entrance of the aquarium, and Megan groaned. She wasn't looking forward to this field trip, and she thought that looking at fish all day would be boring. Mr. Jones, her teacher, announced, "Our field trip includes a viewing of the aquarium's newest addition, so when you enter, please go to the Aquatic Auditorium." "I bet we will just see more fish in there," thought Megan.
She entered the Aquatic Auditorium and was surprised that it wasn't just filled with fish tanks. Instead, there were rows of seats, all surrounding what looked like the biggest swimming pool Megan had ever seen! There was a woman standing at the edge of the pool. "Hello! My name is Diana, and I'd like you to meet a friend of mine," said the woman. Then she blew a whistle. Immediately, an enormous creature came swimming through the water, and stopped right next to Diana! The creature even popped its head up to let Diana pat it! "This is Bailey! Bailey is not a fish but a mammal. Bailey is a beluga whale!" explained Diana.
Megan could not believe what she saw—a whale!
Diana showed the class how intelligent Bailey was, as it was able to do all sorts of tricks. Megan was so captivated; she was disappointed when the show was over. Megan wished she could've stayed there longer! But soon, Mr. Jones was telling the class that it was time to get back onto the bus.
"How did you like the field trip?" Mr. Jones asked.
"I sure was wrong about the aquarium! It wasn't all fish—nor was it boring! Seeing a whale was a big surprise!" replied Megan.

Choose the correct meaning:

AQUARIUM   ___ public place with land animals

                        ___ public place with aquatic animals

BELIEVE   ___ think something is fake   ___ think something is real

BORING   ___ dull ___ interesting

CAPTIVATED   ___ bored ___ interested

CREATURE   ___ an unknown animal ___ a friendly plant

EDGE   ___ outer side ___ very center

ENORMOUS   ___ tiny ___ huge

INTELLIGENT   ___ smart ___ strong

MAMMAL   ___ animal that can breathe and make milk ___ animal that can fly

Name:_____

Rubik's Cubes

While simple in design, the Rubik's Cube has become one of the most popular toys of all time. Over 300 million cubes have been sold!

A standard Rubik's Cube, sometimes called a "3x3x3" cube, is a handheld cube with nine squares on each side. Each square on the cube has a colored sticker on it. There are 6 colors and 9 squares of each color. The goal is to get just one color on each side.

The cube will start with the colors all mixed up, so you will have to twist the rows of squares in a certain order so that the puzzle is solved. Most people will not get it on their first try, but there are certain patterns and strategies you can use to eventually solve the puzzle.

Some people have a passion for solving Rubik's Cubes quickly. These people are called "speedcubers". With practice, world-class speedcubers have been able to solve the puzzle in under five seconds!

To make things more interesting, some speedcubers have added challenges, such as solving the cubes with one hand, blindfolded, or with their feet! There are also competitions for solving larger, more complicated cubes.

If you get the chance, try out a Rubik's Cube yourself and see how long it takes you!

Choose the correct meaning:

COMPLICATED ___ simple ___ complex

CUBES ___ shapes with six trianglular sides

___ shapes with six square sides

EVENTUALLY ___ after a while ___ instantly

HANDHELD ___ able to be worn on your hand ___ able to fit in your hand

INTERESTING ___ fascinating ___ boring

PASSION ___ enthusiasm ___ disgust

PUZZLE ___ a problem to solve ___ a session of physical labor

QUICKLY ___ slowly ___ fast

SOLVING ___ completing a puzzle ___ creating a puzzle

Solving the Cube

It was Thomas's birthday, and he had just one gift left to open. The remaining present was a very small box, small enough to fit in your hand. What could this gift possibly be? Thomas started unwrapping it and soon recognized what it was: a Rubik's Cube! Thomas had read all about Rubik's Cubes and really wanted one. He was very happy with this present!

The next day, he started trying to solve the cube. He twisted the cube over and over again so that the colors would be all jumbled up. Then he began trying to make the colors match up!

The Rubik's Cube concept had seemed easy enough for Thomas, but actually trying to do it proved much more difficult than he'd expected. Getting a single color to match took him over 30 minutes, but he was eventually able to do this. He already had a headache, so he took a break.

After lunch, he went back to it, trying to get a second color to match up. This was even harder since he didn't want to mess up the side he had already completed. It took him almost all afternoon, but he was able to get two sides of the puzzle solved. Throughout the week, Thomas worked on his new puzzle. Some days, he would make lots of progress, and some days he was stumped. But he eventually solved the entire Rubik's Cube!

"Now," he said, "I want to be able to do it faster!"

difficult	solved	twisted	
color	stumped	headache	progress

Choose a word to complete the sentences.

1. I made a lot of _ _ _ _ _ _ _ _ on my homework, answering twelve problems.

2. Dad's confusing riddle had me _ _ _ _ _ _ _!

3. Her favorite _ _ _ _ _ is purple.

4. It is extremely _ _ _ _ _ _ _ _ _ to climb Mt. Everest.

5. Together, my family _ _ _ _ _ _ the jigsaw puzzle.

6. I _ _ _ _ _ _ _ off the cap of the bottle to open it.

7. The math problem gave me a _ _ _ _ _ _ _ _.

Name:_____

Celebrating Holidays

A holiday is a festive day that occurs regularly, usually once a year. Different groups of people celebrate different holidays, and there are holidays celebrated with unique traditions in every country of the world!

Many holidays are religious, and people of the same religion often gather together to observe the special traditions of that day. Religious holidays can help strengthen people's religious faith. For example, Christmas is a holiday that celebrates the birth of Jesus. Most people who are Christians celebrate Christmas with traditions such as gift-giving and a midnight church service. Another popular religious holiday is Vesak, the celebration of the Buddha's birthday. Vesak is celebrated by Buddhists and Hindus and is a time of great joy and happiness.

Other holidays celebrate the seasons or special days of the year, such as New Year's Day. This is a day celebrating the new year and is observed on different days in various countries. Some New Year's traditions include setting off fireworks and gathering with friends and family members to wish each other good fortune for the new year ahead. Certain holidays are unique to one country, as they celebrate a particular historical event that happened there. For example, Independence Day, also known as the Fourth of July, is celebrated in the United States to commemorate the country's independence from England. Chulalongkorn Day is celebrated in Thailand every October 23rd to remember the contributions of King Chulalongkorn. No matter where you live in the world, there are holidays! These special days help to fill the year with joyful celebrations and time spent with family and friends!

Choose the correct meaning:

SPECIAL ___ normal ___ unique

CELEBRATE ___ play a game ___ have a party or ceremony

FESTIVE ___ joyful ___ somber

FIREWORKS ___ explosives used for fun ___ explosives used for warfare

FORTUNE ___ money ___ luck

GATHER ___ assemble ___ break apart

INDEPENDENCE ___ being free from anyone's control

___ being ruled by someone

TRADITIONS ___ personal routines ___ cultural customs

VARIOUS ___ multiple, different ___ exactly one

Name:_____

Gracie's Favorite Holiday

"Grandma and Grandpa are here!" called Gracie happily as she watched them park their car. She had been watching for them to arrive and was so excited that they were finally here! Now they could start the Christmas Eve celebration!

Gracie ran to the door and opened it wide. Soon Grandma and Grandpa were coming up the steps, carrying lots of presents and a dish filled with Grandma's special casserole that she always made for holidays. Gracie helped them carry in their things and then gave them a big hug.

"I'm so glad you are here!" she said. "We are, too," said Grandpa. "It is a very special night—the night before Christmas!" Gracie's mom, dad, brothers, cousins, aunts, and uncles were all at her house too. They were preparing for a meal together, and then they would attend midnight mass at their church. It was an exciting time!

Gracie helped her mom set the table with their fancy dishes. Gracie's brother helped Grandma to place the gifts that they brought around the decorated Christmas tree. Soon the family ate the delicious meal. They now had time to play some games and sing Christmas carols! What fun!

Finally, it was time for mass. The family went to church and prayed together. While there, Gracie started feeling sleepy—she did not usually stay up this late!

As her dad carried her home after mass, Gracie saw the snow starting to fall through her sleepy eyes. She smiled and started to dream about Christmas morning, presents, and how this was her favorite holiday!

presents	church	sleepy	cousins
celebration	decorated	delicious	

Choose a word to complete the sentences.

1. Father John, a priest, works at our _ _ _ _ _ _.

2. Our family has a big _ _ _ _ _ _ _ _ _ _ _ every year for Christmas.

3. You start to feel _ _ _ _ _ _ if you haven't been to bed in a while.

4. Fried chicken is a _ _ _ _ _ _ _ _ _ food.

5. Children receive lots of _ _ _ _ _ _ _ _ on Christmas Day.

6. My aunt and uncle's children are my _ _ _ _ _ _ _.

7. My family and I _ _ _ _ _ _ _ _ _ the house for the holiday.

Flamenco Dancing

Flamenco dancing is a very popular activity for boys and girls in Spain. It is an old tradition that has been preserved by the people there. Seeing a Flamenco dance performed is something you will never forget!

Many Spanish children and adults take lessons to learn how to Flamenco dance. It is not easy! Flamenco dancing requires a lot of practice to get it just right.

Usually, flamenco dancing is done to guitar music, singing, and the clapping of hands. Sometimes the dancer uses castanets while dancing. Castanets are small instruments held in each hand.

They sound like two sticks being tapped together loudly.

It is important for the Flamenco dancer to stomp his or her feet precisely to the beat! The dancers have to wear special shoes to help make the stomping sound even louder! The dancers have to hold their arms in certain positions. One arm is usually held up above the dancer's head.

The dancers also wear special dresses and suits. The dresses are very colorful and have many ruffles. The suits are usually dark-colored and have a matching jacket and pants. Even very young children have these fancy outfits for performing their Flamenco dancing!

Hopefully, you will be able to see Flamenco dancing performed in person. Until then, take a look on the Internet to see samples of this amazing type of dancing!

feathers	glow	auditorium	
travel	months	sounds	microphone

Choose a word to complete the sentences.

INSTRUMENTS ___ things you make food with

___ things you make music with

MATCHING ___ with similar designs ___ with different designs

PRECISELY ___ exactly ___ generally

PRESERVED ___ forgotten ___ kept alive

STOMP ___ hit your hands together ___ hit your foot on the ground

SUITS ___ fancy outfits usually for men ___ fancy outfits only for women

Dancing Around the World

Stephanie was so happy! Today she was going to her older sister's dance recital. Her sister, Janie, had been practicing for months with her dance class, and today was finally the big day! Stephanie and her parents arrived at the auditorium, and found great seats. The lights dimmed, and Stephanie knew that the recital was about to begin!

"Welcome!" said a man on the stage holding a microphone. "We hope you enjoy this very special recital. Our performers have worked hard learning three amazing dances from around the world! Travel to Brazil with our first dance—the Samba!" Suddenly music with a fast beat filled the air, and the light shining on the stage had a yellow glow. The dancers all came out dressed in brightly colored costumes and had feathers in their hair! The Samba was amazing! "Next, travel to Ireland for some traditional Irish Dancing!" said the man. This time the light shined a green glow, and fiddle music was played. The dancers had changed into new costumes and were all wearing curly-haired wigs! The Irish Dancing was great—the dancers' feet moved so quickly, while their upper bodies stayed still! "For our final dance, travel to Spain for some Flamenco Dancing!" announced the man. Guitar music filled the auditorium as the light on stage shined a red glow. The dancers came out wearing dresses with lots of ruffles and wore shoes that made loud sounds when they stomped to the beat. Stephanie felt so proud of Janie and all the dancers. She couldn't wait to sign up for a dance class herself!

feathers	glow	auditorium
travel months	sounds	microphone

Choose a word to complete the sentences.

1. The campfire cast a bright orange _ _ _ _ _ _ on our faces.

2. The school play was held in the _ _ _ _ _ _ _ _ _ _.

3. Clapping is one of the loudest _ _ _ _ _ _ humans can make.

4. There are twelve _ _ _ _ _ _ in a year.

5. You might speak into a _ _ _ _ _ _ _ _ _ _ to make your voice louder.

6. Some people like to _ _ _ _ _ _ in trains.

7. Birds are covered in _ _ _ _ _ _ _ _.

Hiccups

Have you ever been taken by surprise when a loud "HICCUP!" bursts right out of your mouth? How embarrassing! But do not worry, you are not alone. Hiccups happen to everyone. Hiccups happen when the diaphragm—the muscle beneath your lungs—suddenly contracts. And usually, when this happens, it continues to happen for several minutes.

Scientists are not sure why hiccups happen, and they do not seem to serve any purpose. All mammals can get hiccups, even cats, dogs, horses, and mice because they also have diaphragms! Birds, frogs, and snakes cannot hiccup because they do not have diaphragms.

You have probably heard lots of suggestions for how to get rid of hiccups. Maybe you have even tried a few! Holding your breath and counting to ten is one popular way some people can get rid of their hiccups.

Some people say putting sugar under your tongue might help, too. Other people say drinking water from the wrong side of a cup is the best way to get rid of hiccups. And the most popular way is to have someone try to scare you! Boo! Usually, hiccups go away all by themselves after a little while. Very rarely, people have hiccups for days or even years! The longest case of the hiccups lasted from 1922 to 1990! Mr. Charles Osbourne had a case of hiccups that for more than 60 years!

suggestions	Counting	purpose
embarrassing	scare	alone

Choose a word to complete the sentences.

1. My boss gave me _ _ _ _ _ _ _ _ _ _ _ _ on how to work faster.

2. People like to _ _ _ _ _ each other on Halloween.

3. I _ _ _ _ _ _ _ go a day without eating lunch.

4. Shoes serve the _ _ _ _ _ _ _ _ of protecting our feet.

5. _ _ _ _ _ _ _ _ _ from 1 to 100 takes a long time.

6. Losing games can be _ _ _ _ _ _ _ _ _ _ _ _ _.

7. He lives _ _ _ _ _ in a small apartment.

Name:_____

Elliot's Embarrassing Moment

Every kid in the school dreaded the end-of-year presentations. Elliot was no different; he was not looking forward to the speech that he had to give in Mrs. Wilson's class.

"Be prepared to give your speech tomorrow," announced Mrs. Wilson. "It must be at least ten minutes long—and memorized."

Elliot's speech was about Galileo. Elliot practiced his speech many times that evening. He recited it to his mom, dad, sister, and even to his dog! Elliot felt prepared for his presentation, but he still was nervous!

The next morning Elliot woke up early and ate breakfast. He got dressed in his best clothes. He made sure to comb his hair so he would look sharp carefully.

Elliot arrived at school and waited at his desk. Soon Mrs. Wilson started calling students one by one to give their presentations. She called Sarah, who gave a presentation about Leonardo DaVinci. She called Danny, who gave a presentation about the Wright brothers. She called Oliver, who gave a presentation about Diego Rivera.

Then she called Elliot. Elliot nervously walked to the front of the class. His hands were shaking as he stood at the podium. He started his presentation when suddenly a loud "HICCUP!" jumped out of his mouth!

Everyone in the class began to giggle. Elliot blushed and felt very embarrassed.

"Don't worry, Elliot," said Mrs. Wilson kindly. "I get the hiccups all the time. In fact, I know a good trick to help get rid of them." She demonstrated how she drank water, but from the backside of the cup!

Elliot tried the trick, and it worked! Now he was able to successfully give his presentation. He felt so relieved when he was done!

Choose the correct meaning:

ARRIVED   ___ Got somewhere   ___ Left somewhere

BLUSHED   ___ Had a reddened face   ___ Hiccupped

BREAKFAST   ___ Last meal of the day   ___ First meal of the day

DEMONSTRATED   ___ Showed   ___ Learned

EARLY   ___ Before the typical time   ___ After the typical time

EMBARRASSED   ___ Happy and proud   ___ Self-conscious or ashamed

GIGGLE   ___ Laugh loudly   ___ Laugh quietly

NERVOUSLY   ___ Confidently   ___ Anxiously

PRACTICED   ___ Tried repeatedly to get better   ___ Forgot about

RELIEVED   ___ Glad that something's over   ___ Sad that something's over

Name:_____

Domes

There are many incredible buildings around the world that have a similar feature—they all have domes!

While there are many styles of domes, they all are similar in that they are constructed to be a hollow, upper half of a sphere. Architects, people who design buildings, have created some of the most famous domes atop churches, government buildings, and mausoleums.

In the United States, the Capitol Building in Washington DC has the nation's most important dome. There is a statue of a woman on top of the dome called the Statue of Freedom. The statue is 19.5 feet tall!

Another famous dome is in Malaysia. The Putra Mosque has a pink-colored dome, which had been constructed using rose-tinted granite, a very strong type of stone.

The Taj Mahal in India is easily recognizable because of its enormous dome. The dome, made of white marble, looks graceful on top of this huge mausoleum.

Lastly, the Pantheon in Rome is special in many ways. It was built in 120 AD and is still today the world's largest unsupported dome in the world! It has an oculus, a hole in the very top of the dome. This oculus lets in the light; it is called "the eye of the Pantheon" and is quite amazing to see!

There are many more domes in the world—and despite them all sharing certain qualities, each one has a style all its own!

dome	similar	Despite
enormous	constructed	Famous

Choose a word to complete the sentences.

1. The twins had _ _ _ _ _ _ _ features, like their blue eyes and curly hair.

2. The elephant is so _ _ _ _ _ _ _ _; it was the biggest animal in the zoo.

3. The workmen _ _ _ _ _ _ _ _ _ _ _ a bridge over the wide river.

4. _ _ _ _ _ _ celebrities often live in huge mansions.

5. _ _ _ _ _ _ _ their similar looks, the twins' personalities were very different.

6. At the University of Notre Dame, there is a famous

   golden _ _ _ _ atop one of the buildings.

Taj Mahal

India is a huge country with some very remarkable things—soaring mountains, a vast desert, and busy, crowded cities! If you were to travel there, it would be difficult to know what to look at first. Tourists' itineraries vary greatly, as it is the seventh-largest country in the world and there is so much to see!

But there is one place that every traveler to India is certain to visit: the Taj Mahal! The Taj Mahal is a famous mausoleum in Agra, India. It is considered to be one of the most beautiful buildings in the world!

Construction of the Taj Mahal took twenty-two years, beginning in 1631 and finishing in 1653—more than 20,000 people worked its construction. It is built of dazzling white marble, which was transported to the building site from many different countries by over 1000 elephants. The marble seems to change color at various times of day: in the morning, it appears pink, in the midday sun, it looks bright white, and in the moonlight, it appears golden!

The large dome is the central feature of the Taj Mahal. This type of dome is called an "onion dome" because its shape resembles an onion! The large onion dome is surrounded by four smaller onion domes.

So, if you decide to take a trip to India someday, be sure to schedule some time to see the famous Taj Mahal!

desert	Pink	decide	midday
tourists	resembles	mausoleum	

Choose a word to complete the sentences.

1. The _ _ _ _ _ _ is so dry, and the sand there is so hot!

2. A _ _ _ _ _ _ _ _ _ is a building for tombs.

3. _ _ _ _ is the color of my favorite flower.

4. I need to _ _ _ _ _ _ what to eat for lunch, pizza or a sandwich.

5. We eat lunch at _ _ _ _ _ _.

6. The _ _ _ _ _ _ _ _ took photographs while visiting the museum.

7. The little boy closely _ _ _ _ _ _ _ _ _ his father—he looks just like him!

Skyscrapers

A skyscraper is a very tall building with many floors, also known as stories. These huge buildings stretch up into the clouds and soar high above the sidewalks below. Have you ever been up to the top of a skyscraper?

The first skyscraper built was in 1885 in Chicago, Illinois, in the United States. It was called the Home skyscraper, and it was ten stories tall. In those days, people could not believe that a building could be built that high!

Nowadays, there are skyscrapers that reach over 100 stories! The architects that build them use new technology and materials to make that possible. The tallest skyscraper in the world is called Burj Khalifa, and it is located in Dubai, a city in the country of the United Arab Emirates. It has 163 stories!

Some skyscrapers are known for their unusual designs. In the country of Azerbaijan, there are buildings known as the Flame Towers—and they actually look like huge flames rising up 770 feet out of the city! In Sweden, there is a skyscraper called the Turning Torso in which the top is twisted 90 degrees from the orientation of the ground level!

Be sure to check out more interesting skyscrapers, either in person or on the internet. There are many fascinating buildings to admire—and maybe you will be inspired to design a skyscraper of your own someday!

Choose the correct meaning:

ADMIRE ___ to purchase ___ to appreciate

FASCINATING ___ dull or boring ___very interesting

HIGH ___ up in the sky ___ low on the ground

SOAR ___ to feel pain ___ to fly

DEGREES ___ to be dirty or sticky ___ amounts

FLAMES ___ branches of trees ___ tongues of fire

TALLEST ___ the most vertical length ___ the most weight

TURNING ___ to rotate ___ to talk with someone

UNUSUAL ___ same as the rest ___ different from the rest

BUILDING ___ a structure for people to go into ___ an imaginary structure

Uncle Ron's New House

Stanley loved visiting his Uncle Ron's apartment. It was so different than Stanley's house. His Uncle Ron lived in the city, where there was always something exciting going on! Music from street performers seemed to float in through the open windows, as did the delicious smells from the food vendors who were selling all kinds of tasty treats! Stanley never got bored looking out the windows where there were always interesting people walking by. The skyscrapers nearby were amazing to see! Stanley would look way up to try to see the tops of them.

Stanley was sure surprised when his mom told him the news that his Uncle Ron was moving to a new house!

"Why would Uncle Ron move?" asked Stanley. "His apartment is so cool!"

"Uncle Ron wants a bigger home," answered his mom. "He wants a yard to plant a garden in; he wants to move out of the city."

The next Saturday he and his mom went to visit Uncle Ron in his new house. When they arrived, his Uncle Ron was standing in his new yard.

"What do you think of my new house, Stanley?" asked his Uncle Ron.

The neighborhood around the new house was quiet—no exciting music. The air was fresh—no smells from food vendors. There were no people walking by, nor any skyscrapers to look up at. But one thing, the most important thing, was the same. It was his Uncle Ron's home, and Stanley realized that was all that mattered.

"I love it!" said Stanley as he gave his uncle a big hug.

apartment	tasty	realized
vendors	mattered	music

Choose a word to complete the sentences.

1. he _ _ _ _ _ _ _ _ _ had two bedrooms.

2. I love tacos—they are so _ _ _ _ _!

3. The pianist played the most beautiful _ _ _ _ _ I had ever heard.

4. Dad _ _ _ _ _ _ _ _ that he lost his wallet when he couldn't find it in his pocket.

5. The _ _ _ _ _ _ _ sold many types of souvenirs, food, and clothing.

6. My teacher said that our attitudes _ _ _ _ _ _ _ _ more than our grades.

The Moon

Have you ever looked up at night and wondered about our moon? Why does it sometimes appear so big and round, and other times it looks like a thin fingernail with a crescent shape? How can the same object look so different? When the moon is visible in the night sky, it can appear as if it is shining like the sun. But this is not true! The moon does not actually give off any of its own light. It is only reflecting the light coming from the sun.

So, as the moon orbits the Earth, the sun lights up different parts of it, making it seem as if the moon is changing its shape from night to night. The truth is, it is just our view of the moon that is changing!

When the moon appears to be getting bigger, it's "waxing," and when it looks like it is getting smaller, it's "waning." When the moon looks its largest, and it is fully illuminated by the sun, it is called a "Full Moon."

As the moon moves around the Earth, and the portion facing us becomes hidden from the sun until we can hardly see it at all, it is called a "New Moon." It is fun to keep track of the moon's cycle, especially when there are no nighttime clouds to block our view!

wondered	hidden	Until	block
Actually	portion	illuminated	

Choose a word to complete the sentences.

1. Sally _ _ _ _ _ _ _ _ where her lost book was.

2. A _ _ _ _ _ _ _ of my homework is done, but not all of it.

3. To _ _ _ _ _ to the bright sun, she closed the curtains.

4. _ _ _ _ _ you eat your vegetables; you cannot have dessert.

5. _ _ _ _ _ _ _ _, I prefer to eat vegetables more than dessert!

6. The lamp _ _ _ _ _ _ _ _ _ _ _ the family room in the evening.

7. The moon was _ _ _ _ _ _ behind some clouds last night.

Name:_____

Gordon and the Night Sky

The window in Gordon's bedroom was even better than the television. From it, he could see trees, a bird's nest, and even his neighbor Mrs. Mishkoff's garden. In the mornings, the sun would shine through the sheer curtains to wake Gordon up.

But Gordon's favorite part about having a bedroom window was the view he had at night. Every time he went to bed, Gordon looked out and could see the moon. Gordon loved looking out and seeing the moon shining in the dark sky. Sometimes there were clouds covering his view of the moon, but Gordon didn't mind. He knew the moon was there behind them.

At school, Gordon learned about the lunar cycle, and he kept track of which phase the moon was going through every night. He loved the way the full moon seemed to fill the sky with such bright light, and he loved the way the crescent moon looked like his fingernail!

He wondered what it would be like to fly to the moon someday in a rocket ship. Gordon thought that maybe he would study to become an astronaut when he grew up so he could.

On Gordon's birthday, he was surprised by a special gift from his parents. They bought him a telescope. Together they set the telescope up in Gordon's bedroom. With the telescope, Gordon could see the features of the moon even more clearly. Gordon was so grateful to have the telescope, his window, and his amazing nightly view!

| clouds | bright | moon | track |
| astronaut | telescope | window | |

Choose a word to complete the sentences.

1. The gray _ _ _ _ _ _ in the sky meant that it was going to rain.

2. I saw a cat in our yard when I looked out the _ _ _ _ _ _.

3. The _ _ _ _ orbits around the Earth.

4. To become an _ _ _ _ _ _ _ _ _ you need to go to college.

5. Looking through a _ _ _ _ _ _ _ _ _ you can see stars more clearly.

6. The new lamp was so _ _ _ _ _ _ because it used two lightbulbs.

7. I kept _ _ _ _ _ of how many days until vacation.

Petra

The world is filled with some amazing, magical places! One of those amazing places is called Petra!

What is so amazing about Petra? It is an ancient city, one of the oldest cities in the world. It was established in 312 BC! But what makes Petra so amazing is not just its age; it is also amazing because the city was built by being carved into enormous, rocky cliffs!

To see Petra for yourself, you would need to travel to the country of Jordan, which is located in Western Asia. It is located in the desert, which makes it even more interesting—how did the original inhabitants, so many years ago, get water and other resources needed to survive? How did they construct such an amazing city in the desert?

The people who built Petra were a tribe called the Nabataeans. The Nabataeans were excellent carvers, plumbers, and stonemasons—and ingenious water collectors! Not only did they build an elaborate city, but they somehow managed to grow lush gardens in the desert!

The city they built became a thriving and wealthy trading center. When it was at its peak, Petra was home to about 30,000 people. Sadly, in 363 AD, Petra was mostly destroyed by a gigantic earthquake. Many of the people had to leave the area, and the city was abandoned.

An explorer from Switzerland named Johann Ludwig Burckhardt discovered the remains of Petra in 1812. It is now protected as an important historical site, and many people visit it every year! Hopefully, you will get to see it for yourself someday!

Choose the correct meaning:

ANCIENT   ___ extremely wealthy   ___ extremely old

BUILT   ___ created   ___ destroyed with fire

ENORMOUS   ___ very large   ___ very angry

ESTABLISHED   ___ began   ___ ended

INGENIOUS   ___ clever   ___ false

CLIFFS   ___ a towering tree   ___ a steep rock face

DESTROYED   ___ made unusable   ___ made colorful

ELABORATE   ___ with no detail   ___ with lots of detail

DESERT   ___ dry, arid environment   ___ a tasty sweet treat

EARTHQUAKE   ___ a natural disaster   ___ a dessert with ice cream

Kelly Protects the World

One day in school, Kelly was learning about World Heritage sites. Her teacher, Mrs. Swanson, explained how a particular place could be chosen to be designated as a World Heritage site.

"World Heritage sites are special places that are being protected," she told the class. "These sites are cultural treasures and important natural habitats."

Kelly raised her hand as she had a question.

"Yes, Kelly?" said Mrs. Swanson.

"Where are all the World Heritage sites? And how many are there?" Kelly asked.

"World Heritage sites are all over the world! They are located in more than 160 different countries! Right now, there are over 1000 sites,

and the list continues to grow!"

Kelly raised her hand again. "Yes, Kelly?" asked Mrs. Swanson.

"Why do these places need to be protected?" Kelly asked.

"There are various reasons these sites need protection. Sometimes important landmarks have gotten destroyed in wars; other times, natural disasters like floods have destroyed places. If a site has the World Heritage designation, great efforts will be made to help protect it or rebuild it, if necessary," explained Mrs. Swanson.

Kelly liked the idea of protecting special places on the Earth. After school, she looked online to view images of World Heritage sites. She saw amazing photos of faraway places: the Taj Mahal, the Great Barrier Reef, Petra, and Venice. She was surprised by how many beautiful places there were in the world. She dreamed of visiting them all someday!

Kelly was pleased that they would be protected by the World Heritage organization, and she promised to do her part to protect them too!

floods	faraway	destroyed
protection	organization	

Choose a word to complete the sentences.

1. When the _ _ _ _ _ _ came many people's homes filled with water.

2. It was sad to see that the fire _ _ _ _ _ _ _ _ _ the building.

3. Sometimes valuable things need extra _ _ _ _ _ _ _ _ _ _ _ from harm.

4. I dreamed of going to a magical castle in a _ _ _ _ _ _ _ land.

5. An _ _ _ _ _ _ _ _ _ _ _ _ _ is a group of people working towards

a common goal.

Name:_____

The Armadillo

The word "armadillo" means "little armored one," and if you take a look at one, you can see why! Armadillos are small mammals that have tough armor made of bony plates that protects them from enemies and other dangers.

No other type of animal has armor like this. The bony plates cover their backs, their legs, their heads, and their tails. The way the plates overlap one another adds even more protection.

The four legs of the armadillo are very strong, and they have big claws on their toes. The claws on their front toes are huge, and they are useful for digging. They live in holes in the ground, which they dig for themselves.

Insects, plants, and some fruits make up the diet of the armadillo. Sometimes they will eat small birds found on the ground. They have very poor eyesight, so they rely upon their strong sense of smell to find their food. They can smell things that are even 20 centimeters below the ground!

Armadillos live in the hot regions of Central and South America, and one species of them live in the southern United States. They do not have very much body fat to keep them warm, so they do not like cold weather!

The armadillo is a really interesting animal. They do not make good pets, as they prefer to live in the wild—and because they are nocturnal! They would keep you awake all night!

Choose the correct meaning:

AWAKE ___ sleeping ___ not sleeping

SOMETIMES ___ every moment ___ not always

RELY ___ depend upon ___ to catch a ball

SPECIES ___ a special song ___ a special type

BELOW ___ underneath ___ on top of something

TOUGH ___ very soft and delicate ___ hard and strong

CLAWS ___ sharp nails on fingers or toes ___ a sharp stick

POOR ___ extremely strong ___ very weak or insufficient

FRONT ___ where something begins ___ where something ends

NOCTURNAL ___ awake during the day ___ awake during the night

Name:_____

Unique Animal Week

On Monday, Rebecca's teacher announced that each student was to spend the week learning about a unique animal. The students would each have read about the animal, watch videos about the animal, write a report about the animal, and then give an oral presentation about the animal to the class on Friday.

At lunchtime, all the students were talking about the big assignment.

"What animal are you going to learn about?" asked Sarah, a girl in Rebecca's class.

"I don't know yet," answered Rebecca. "Do you?"

"I'm going to learn about the Mangalitsa pig! I saw a picture of one online, and I think they are cute!" said Sarah.

"I am going to learn about the armadillo," said Robert, a boy who was also in Rebecca's class. "I think they look amazing, like little four-legged knights!"

Rebecca started feeling worried, as she had no idea which unique animal she should learn about!

At home after school, her little sister Maggie was playing with her toys.

"Why do you look so sad, Rebecca?" asked Maggie.

"I can't think of what animal to learn about for my big school assignment," replied Rebecca.

"You can learn about unicorns," said Maggie as she handed Rebecca her toy unicorn doll. Unicorns were Maggie's favorite thing.

"No, I need to learn about a real animal. Unicorns are pretended," said Rebecca.

"I know," said Maggie,

"but narwhals are real! They are called the unicorns of the sea!"

Rebecca smiled and said, "You are right! I would love to learn more about narwhals! Maggie, you are so smart!"

favorite	Monday	Narwhals
unique	sea	smart	knights

Choose a word to complete the sentences.

1. _ _ _ _ _ _ is the first day of the school week.

2. _ _ _ _ _ _ _ _ are very unusual animals!

3. Every snowflake is _ _ _ _ _ _; no two are alike!

4. Strawberry ice cream is good, but chocolate is my _ _ _ _ _ _ _ _!

5. Many kinds of fish live in the _ _ _.

6. The student was so _ _ _ _ _ that he won a special award.

7. The kingdom was protected by _ _ _ _ _ _ _ many years ago.

Ants

You might not like ants when they are crawling in your kitchen, or on your picnic blanket, or on your peanut butter sandwich, but they are quite interesting insects! Ants live in colonies. That means they live in a large group together. Each ant in the colony has a special job to do. The colony is very organized; the ants all know what to do to help the colony grow.

There is one queen ant, and she lays the eggs. The other ants are worker ants. They build the anthill and find food. They also act like soldier ants. Soldier ants protect the colony and sometimes attack other colonies.

Ants range in size from 2 to 25 millimeters, and they can be yellow, brown, red, or black depending on which species they belong to—and there are more than 10,000 different species!

The body of an ant is divided into three sections: the head, the thorax, and the abdomen. Two antennae are located on top of the ant's head, which are used for smelling or communicating with each other.

Ants are tiny animals but extremely strong! They can carry 20 times their own body weight as they deliver food and other items to different parts of the colony. That would be like you lifting a car and carrying it around the neighborhood!

colony	divided	communicating
soldier	queen	hill lifting

Choose a word to complete the sentences.

1. Dad found a _ _ _ _ _ _ of ants living in our backyard.

2. I _ _ _ _ _ _ _ the cake into eight pieces.

3. The telephone is a great way for _ _ _ _ _ _ _ _ _ _ _ _ _ with one another.

4. She joined the army because she wanted to become a _ _ _ _ _ _ _.

5. The _ _ _ _ _ ruled the kingdom with kindness.

6. Do you know that a _ _ _ _ is like a very small mountain?

7. My arm was sore after _ _ _ _ _ _ _ the heavy piece of wood.

Picnic Pests

It was a beautiful sunny day, and Amelia's whole family was going on a picnic in the park. Amelia helped her mother to pack up the picnic basket with all kinds of delicious foods. "I love fried chicken!
I cannot wait to take a bite!" said Amelia as she put the fried chicken into the basket.
"It all sure smells good," said her dad as he walked into the kitchen.
"Are you ready to go?" "I think so," said her mom. "Is Billy ready?"
Billy was Amelia's younger brother.
Billy came running into the kitchen carrying a bag of candy. "Can I bring this old candy with me on the picnic?" he asked. "It is leftover from Halloween."
"Sure," said his mom. The family loaded up the car and drove to the park. Once they arrived, they spread a colorful blanket down on the ground. They took the picnic basket out and began enjoying the food.
Amelia noticed something small and black crawling on her piece of chicken.
"Oh no!" said Amelia. "An ant!"
Her dad said, "If there is one ant, there are probably more because ants live in colonies. These pests are rarely alone!"
Sure enough, her dad was right. Soon the whole blanket seemed to be covered with little black ants! "These ants are looking for something sweet to eat," said her mom. "Too bad they are eating our chicken."
"I have an idea," said Billy. Billy ran to the car and came back with his bag of candy. "The ants can eat this old candy!" he said. He spread the old candy out nearby the blanket. Sure enough, the ants preferred the old candy, and left the family alone to eat their delicious picnic!

fried	park	probably	Candy
picnic	pests	Nearby	blanket

Choose a word to complete the sentences.

1. _ _ _ _ _ is usually very sweet.

2. Having a _ _ _ _ _ _ is a fun way to spend the day.

3. My grandfather enjoyed eating _ _ _ _ _ chicken on Sundays.

4. The swings and slide at the _ _ _ _ were being used by children.

5. I _ _ _ _ _ _ _ _ will go to the movies tonight, but I'm not sure yet.

6. The mosquitos were being _ _ _ _ _ to the fishermen.

7. _ _ _ _ _ _ _ the school is the public library.

8. On cold winter nights I love to snuggle up with a _ _ _ _ _ _ _ _.

Niagara Falls

Did you know that there is an amazing natural wonder that can be viewed from two different countries? The Niagara Falls, a trio of three huge waterfalls, is located on the border of Canada and the United States. You can view it from whichever country you happen to be in!

Each of the trios of waterfalls has its own name: the American Falls, the Bridal Veil Falls, and the Horseshoe Falls. The three waterfalls together create the highest flow rate of any waterfall on Earth.

The waterfalls were created by glacier activity around 10,000 years ago. It is quite a remarkable sight, totally designed by nature! Scientists believe that Niagara Falls will be gone within 50,000 years due to erosion.

Many tourists visit the Niagara Falls every year, about 13 million! There are special boat rides that take you around the basin of the falls. If you decide to ride in one of them, prepare to get wet! The spray of the falling water gets everyone soaked! Some people have tried to go over the falls, even though it is illegal to do so. The very first person was a teacher named Annie Edson Taylor. In 1901 she traveled down the falls in a barrel! Luckily, she survived. Many who have tried to follow her example have not. So, if you are ever in Canada or the United States and you want to see an amazing sight be sure to put the Niagara Falls on your itinerary!

barrel	soaked	prepare	illegal
created	countries	itinerary	

Choose a word to complete the sentences.

1. My friend _ _ _ _ _ _ _ a beautiful picture using colored pencils.

2. There are many _ _ _ _ _ _ _ _ _ in the world.

3. To _ _ _ _ _ _ _ for the math test I studied a lot.

4. We prepared an _ _ _ _ _ _ _ _ _ for our vacation.

5. The big old _ _ _ _ _ _ was full of dirty water.

6. The rain came down so fast that we got _ _ _ _ _ _.

7. The police arrested the man who had the _ _ _ _ _ _ _ weapon.

The Best Vacation Ever

Linda and Geraldine walked home from school while talking excitedly about the vacation their family was planning. It was only two days away!

"I cannot wait to see the hotel!" said Linda. "Mom told me that it has a swimming pool!"

"I can't wait to ride on the boat! I read online that it takes you so close to the falls!" exclaimed Geraldine.

When the sisters arrived home, their third sister, Carol, was already there. She had stayed home from school because she was feeling a bit sick in the morning.

"Hi Carol," they both said to her. "How are you feeling?"

"Worse," Carol said sadly. "Mom said that I have a fever. If I don't get better, we will have to cancel the vacation!"

All three sisters felt worried that their vacation would be canceled.

"How can we help Carol to feel better?" asked Linda.

"Let's make her some chicken soup," said Geraldine. "That should help."

They made a pot of soup and brought it to Carol. She drank it and then went to sleep.

In the morning, Linda and Geraldine rushed in to see Carol.

"How are you?" they asked. "Mom said I still have a fever!" Carol replied.

"Oh no! The vacation is only one day away!" said Linda.

"Let's make her some more soup," said Geraldine. They made more soup. Carol drank it and rested for the rest of the day. The next morning, Linda and Geraldine rushed in again to see Carol. But she wasn't in her bed! She was packing her suitcase!

"Mom said my fever is gone! We can go on vacation!" said Carol happily.

"This is going to be the best vacation ever!" they all said.

worried	vacation	talking	
suitcase	hotel	soup	fever

Choose a word to complete the sentences.

1. The bowl of _ _ _ _ was very hot.

2. The _ _ _ _ _ was near Niagara Falls.

3. Grandma _ _ _ _ _ _ _ about her lost kitten.

4. My neighbor likes _ _ _ _ _ _ _ with my parents.

5. A _ _ _ _ _ _ _ _ can be a special time for a family.

6. My _ _ _ _ _ _ _ _ was filled with clothes for the trip.

7. Your temperature goes up if you have a _ _ _ _ _.

Human Bones

How many bones are in the human body? Well, did you know that the answer to this question is not the same for babies as it is for adults?

At birth, the human skeleton is made up of around 300 bones. But by adulthood, some of those bones will have fused together, leaving you with 206 bones.

The size and shape of these bones are very different from one another, and so is their function. Some bones serve to protect delicate parts of the body, like the brain and heart. Other functions of bones are to support your body, to help with movement, and to produce blood cells.

The longest bone in your body is the femur bone, which is in the upper part of your leg, called the thigh. The smallest bone in your body is the stirrup bone, which is located in the ear—it is only 2.8 millimeters long!

The area of your body with the most bones is your hand, fingers, and wrist. There are 54 different bones there—all ready to help you write your name, pick up a sandwich, or throw a ball!

It is important to take good care of your bones by getting plenty of calcium in your diet. So, drink your milk and eat your cheese to keep your bones strong and healthy!

strong	Babies	bone	blood
protect	longest	skeleton	

Choose a word to complete the sentences.

1. _ _ _ _ _ _ are so tiny when they are born!

2. I wear a helmet to _ _ _ _ _ _ _ my head while riding a bike.

3. My science teacher has a model _ _ _ _ _ _ _ _ in the classroom.

4. That girl has the _ _ _ _ _ _ _ hair that I've ever seen!

5. I will be _ _ _ _ _ _ after exercising every day.

6. My brother broke a _ _ _ _ when he fell off the swing.

7. When I cut my finger a little bit of _ _ _ _ _ came out.

The Halloween Parade

October 31 was Michael's favorite day of the year. It was Halloween! Halloween was a fun holiday that he celebrated with his friends and family. All the kids dressed up in costumes and went around the neighborhood to get candy!

This year his school, Glenwood Elementary School, was joining in the fun with a Halloween parade to take place at the end of the school day! All of the students were to bring their costumes in a bag, and then they would be allowed to put them on for the parade.

"Mom, I know what I want to dress up as this year," said Michael.

"I want to be a skeleton!"

"Oh my!" said his mom. "Are you sure that won't be too scary?"

Michael laughed and said, "It won't be!"

The next day he worked at making his costume. Michael gathered an old black shirt and some old black pants. He used white paint to create bones on the clothing. Then he found a black hat to put on his head. Now he was all ready for the big day!

October 31 arrived. Michael put his costume in a bag and brought it with him to school. As the day progressed, Michael watched the clock tick slowly—but finally, it was time for the parade!

Everyone loved Michael's skeleton costume, and he had such fun at the parade! Afterward, he and his brothers went around the neighborhood saying, "trick-or-treat!" They received a lot of candy as they wished his neighbors a "Happy Halloween!"

holiday	costume	wished	parade
neighborhood	received	laughed	

Choose a word to complete the sentences.

1. Which _ _ _ _ _ _ _ do you prefer to celebrate most?

2. The princess _ _ _ _ _ _ _ _ looked so cute on the little girl.

3. Dad _ _ _ _ _ _ _ at all of my jokes.

4. The street was full of people as the _ _ _ _ _ _ went by.

5. Grandma _ _ _ _ _ _ _ _ the letter I sent to her.

6. There are 35 houses in our _ _ _ _ _ _ _ _ _ _ _ _ _.

7. I _ _ _ _ _ _ _ my mom a happy birthday and gave her a gift.

Braille

Two hundred years ago, a French boy named Louis Braille became blind as a result of an accident he had. This means he could not see anymore. Being blind made many activities hard. Instead of giving up on these activities, Louis looked for ways to make them possible for blind people.

When he was only fifteen years old, he invented a way of writing for blind people. His invention, which is called Braille, has been used by many blind people all around the world.

Braille is a tactile alphabet. Tactile means using your sense of touch. Instead of ordinary letters, Braille uses dots that are raised on the page. Every letter of the alphabet has a special arrangement of dots to represent it. Using the tips of their fingers to feel the dots, a person can learn this alphabet just as they would one written in ink!

Entire books written in Braille have been created to assist blind people in reading. Additionally, many public signs include words in Braille, in order to help blind people be more independent when out of their homes. Special Braille typewriters have been created, allowing blind people to write on their own.

Louis Braille is honored every year on his birthday, January 4th.

This day is celebrated as "World Braille Day." This day spreads awareness about Braille and the importance of independence for people who are blind.

typewriters	assist	alphabet
independence	accident	blind

Choose a word to complete the sentences.

1. The car was in an _ _ _ _ _ _ _ _ and its window was broken.

2. The _ _ _ _ _ man walked down the busy street using a cane and a trained dog to help him.

3. In English there are 26 letters in the _ _ _ _ _ _ _ _.

4. The writers used _ _ _ _ _ _ _ _ _ _ _ to compose their stories.

5. I can _ _ _ _ _ _ my grandma by helping her clean her house.

6. Many people take pride in their _ _ _ _ _ _ _ _ _ _ _ _; they like to do things for themselves.

Scott's Special Cousin

Scott was nervous. He and his mom were going to visit with his aunt and cousin David, who lived many hours away.
He and David were the same age,
but that was where the similarities ended. David was blind.
Scott was nervous because he'd never spent time with a blind person before.
"Don't be nervous, Scott," said his mom. "You and David will have fun together!"
Scott didn't think that would be possible. What could David even do? How could they play together if he couldn't see?
When they arrived, David was waiting by the door.
"Hi, Scott," David said. "What do you want to do?"
"Umm, I don't know," said Scott. He didn't think David would be able to do anything!
"We could play games, listen to music, or get something to eat!" said David.
"I'd like something to eat," said Scott shyly.
"Me too!" said David. Using a cane to guide his steps, David showed Scott the way to the kitchen. He knew exactly where the cookies were kept.
"These are my favorite cookies!" exclaimed Scott, who was no longer feeling so shy.
"Mine too!" said David, munching on one. "Do you like Harry Potter?"
"I love those books and have read them all!
Did your mom read them to you?" asked Scott.
"No, I read them myself," said David. "I have Braille editions of Harry Potter." David showed Scott the books. Scott was interested in how the little dots felt and couldn't believe David knew how to read them!
When it was time to go, the boys made plans to visit again soon. Scott was so happy to discover that he had such a special cousin!

exactly	aunt	myself	boys
visit	waiting	munching	

Choose a word to complete the sentences.

1. My _ _ _ _ is my mom's sister.

2. Sometimes I like to go for walks by _ _ _ _ _ _.

3. Do you ever _ _ _ _ _ the Science Museum?

4. The bunny rabbit was _ _ _ _ _ _ _ _ a bright orange carrot.

5. My dad was _ _ _ _ _ _ _ for my mom to finish getting ready.

6. The _ _ _ _ were playing video games all afternoon.

7. The identical twin brothers looked _ _ _ _ _ _ _ alike!

Name:_____

Queen of the Adriatic

How would you like to live in a city where there are no cars, only boats? Where some of the streets are so narrow that two people are unable to walk side by side? Where most of the buildings are over 500 years old? If you would, you may like to live in Venice, Italy!

Venice is known to be one of the most beautiful, unusual cities in the world. It is actually a city built upon 118 islands separated by canals. These canals are connected by hundreds of bridges—over 400 of them!

This magnificent city is situated in a body of water called a lagoon, at the edge of the Adriatic Sea. Because it is completely built on the lagoon, roads for cars do not exist. Special boats called gondolas are used for getting from place to place through the canals, as well as other types of boats.

Venice is known to have a uniquely charming atmosphere and a very rich history. Some of the most famous places in Venice include the Rialto Bridge, the Doge's Palace, the Bridge of Sighs, and St. Mark's Basilica. Many tourists visit Venice every year to see these landmarks.

Venice has many nicknames: City of Bridges, City of Canals, Queen of the Adriatic, The Floating City, and City of Masks are just a few of them! Despite not being able to agree on a nickname, one thing most everyone can agree on—Venice is an extraordinary city!

atmosphere	landmarks	narrow
bridge	Canals	gondolas	Islands

Choose a word to complete the sentences.

1. The trail was so _ _ _ _ _ _ that we had to hike in a single file line.

2. I love to walk over the river on the _ _ _ _ _ _.

3. _ _ _ _ _ _ are a type of waterway for boats to travel on.

4. While on vacation, we visited many historic _ _ _ _ _ _ _ _ _.

5. _ _ _ _ _ _ _ are completely surrounded by water.

6. Riding in _ _ _ _ _ _ _ _ would be an exciting way to travel!

7. The _ _ _ _ _ _ _ _ _ _ at the surprise party was filled with excitement.

The Violinist of Venice

Little Antonio loved living near the water. He was born in Venice, Italy, which was surrounded by water. He loved the canals, the bridges, and the gondolas throughout the city.

But there was something he loved even more. He loved music!

Antonio's father played the violin, and he taught Antonio how to play too. The two of them would perform together for the people of Venice.

As Antonio grew up, he realized that he also loved his Catholic religion so much that he wanted to become a priest. So, he did! The people of Venice would recognize him and call him the "Red Priest" because he had bright red hair!

While Antonio was a priest, he still was able to continue playing his violin. He even taught music to children, particularly to girls who lived in an orphanage near his church.

Antonio became quite popular for also writing music. People would come from miles around to hear the beautiful music that he had written. He wrote over 500 pieces of music for not only violins, but for full orchestras!

Antonio lived from 1678-1741, but he is still very famous today for the beautiful music that he wrote. People still love to hear it and perform it—especially the people of Venice. Antonio Vivaldi is the much-loved violinist (and composer!) of Venice!

Orchestras	orphanage	perform
church	religion	written	taught

Choose a word to complete the sentences.

1. The actor liked to _ _ _ _ _ _ _ on the theater stage.

2. An _ _ _ _ _ _ _ _ _ _ is a special home for children who have no parents.

3. My grandfather _ _ _ _ _ _ me how to read.

4. People of the same _ _ _ _ _ _ _ _ often pray together.

5. Many books were _ _ _ _ _ _ _ by J.K. Rowling.

6. _ _ _ _ _ _ _ _ _ _ are made up of different instruments.

7. A _ _ _ _ _ _ is often a very large building.

The Roller Coaster

Adam and his family woke up very early. They were going to an amusement park today! They had to drive three hours to get there, so they wanted to get an early start. "You can sleep in the car, Adam," said his mom, "if you are still sleepy."

"I am too excited to be sleepy!" exclaimed Adam.

When they arrived at the amusement park, Adam was surprised by all the rides! It was like nothing he had ever seen before in his life! Adam felt as if he were on another planet! There was a carousel with colorful figures of horses that people could ride on! There was a Ferris Wheel that took riders way up high where they could see the whole park from above!

There was a ride where people rode in little boats and got splashed with water! But the ride that Adam was most excited to see was the roller coaster. The roller coaster was the tallest and fastest of all the rides. Adam watched as people rode the roller coaster, and he heard them as they shouted with excitement.

The roller coaster looked thrilling, but it also looked really scary.

Adam was not sure he wanted to go on it.

"Adam, which ride do you want to go on first?" asked his dad.

"Let's try the carousel," Adam said. They rode on the carousel.

"Which should we ride on next?" asked his mom.

"Let's go on the boat ride," Adam said. They rode on the boat ride.

"Well," said Adam's dad, "are you ready for the roller coaster?"

Adam looked up at the roller coaster.

He felt so nervous! But he also felt very excited! "Okay!" he said. "Let's do it!"

They got in line for the roller coaster. It was finally their turn. Adam held onto the safety bar of the roller coaster car very tightly!

The ride began and started out slowly; the car moved up, up, up into the air. Then suddenly the car stopped moving up, and— whoosh! —the car raced downward and all around the roller coaster track! Adam yelled out in delight!

He loved riding on this roller coaster! What a thrill!

1. How long did it take to get to the amusement park?
   It took three hours to get to the amusement park. ✓

2. Which ride had colorful figures of horses to ride?
   The carousel had colorful figures of horses to ride. ✓

3. Which ride did Adam go on second?
   a. the roller coaster
   b. the carousel
   c. the Ferris Wheel
   d. the boat ride ✓

4. How did Adam feel about the roller coaster at the end of the story?
   Adam loved the roller coaster at the end of the story. ✓

Peter's Lucky Pebble

Peter and his older brother, Christopher, liked to run. They would run around in their backyard, and they would run at the park. They would run whenever they could! They were always racing to see who was faster, Peter or Christopher. Christopher, who had longer legs, usually won.

One day while the brothers were at the beach, they decided to have a race to the top of the biggest sand dune.

"This will be a hard race," said Peter. "It is a big sand dune!"

"Yes," said Christopher, "but we can do it!"

The sand was very hot, so they put on their shoes. They did not want to burn their feet while running!

The race began, and Christopher was in the lead. Peter was trying his best but was still falling further behind. Just when he thought he was going to lose again, he felt something in the shoe on his left foot. There was something in his shoe rubbing against his toes. It did not feel good!

"Should I stop?" thought Peter. "There must be a pebble in my shoe. Should I quit the race to shake the pebble out of my shoe?"

Peter kept going. In fact, he started running faster. He wanted to finish the race so he could take his shoe off! Peter ran faster than he ever ran before. He passed Christopher! He won the race to the top of the dune!

"Wow!" exclaimed Christopher. "How did you do that? How did you run so fast?"

Peter sat down and took his left shoe off. He shook the shoe, and out came a little brown pebble. He held the pebble up for Christopher to see.

"This little pebble helped me to win!" said Peter, laughing.

Christopher laughed too. "That is your lucky pebble. Are you going to always race with it in your shoe?"

"I will always race with it," said Peter, "but I think I will keep it in my pocket instead of my shoe!" The brothers ran back down the sand dune with Peter's lucky pebble!

1. Which brother was older?
   Christopher was the older brother. ✓

2. What helped Christopher to usually win the races?
   a. He had shorter hair.
   b. He had longer arms.
   c. He had longer legs. ✓
   d. He had stronger muscles.

3. Why did they put their shoes on for the race at the beach?
   Peter and Christopher put their shoes on because the sand was very hot and they did not want to burn their feet while running. ✓

4. How did the pebble help Peter to win the race?
   Peter wanted to finish the race so he could shake the pebble out of his shoe, so he ran faster than ever before. ✓

The Most Amazing Tree

Evelyn felt very happy because she was going to her grandparents' house. Their house was located deep in the woods. It was a special, very peaceful place to visit. There were all kinds of interesting things to see inside of their house. Evelyn loved to look at all of the old photographs and to read the old books that they had. She loved the cookies that her grandmother baked for her!

But what Evelyn loved the most were the woods outside of her grandparents' house—she thought those woods were magical!

"Grandfather, please, let's go for a walk in the woods!" Evelyn said.

Her grandfather smiled and put on his hiking boots. Evelyn put on her boots too.

"Today, I will show you the most amazing tree in the woods! It is the oldest tree, even older than me!" said her grandfather.

Together they walked on the trail. Evelyn saw little flowers growing beneath the branches of big trees. She saw birds making nests and squirrels chasing one another through the leaves. She even saw a mouse hiding under a pile of sticks. "Where is the most amazing tree, Grandfather?" Evelyn asked. "We are almost there," her grandfather answered.

"You will soon see." They walked a little further, and then Evelyn's grandfather stopped in front of the tallest, widest, oldest tree Evelyn had ever seen. "This is the tree! Isn't it amazing?" said her grandfather.

Evelyn looked way up high into the branches of the old tree. She walked all around the trunk of the tree. She touched the bark of the tree. She picked up a leaf that had fallen off of the tree.

"Yes, Grandfather, this is the most amazing tree I have ever seen. I think it is the grandfather of these woods!" said Evelyn. "Thank you for showing it to me."

Evelyn gave her grandfather a big hug.

Evelyn and her grandfather walked back to the house. There, her grandmother had just finished baking cookies. While they ate the cookies, Evelyn told her grandmother all about the tree. Evelyn had a wonderful time seeing the amazing tree and seeing her amazing grandparents!

1. Where was Evelyn's grandparents' house?
   The house was located deep in the woods. ✓

2. Name four things that Evelyn saw while walking in the woods.
   Evelyn saw flowers, birds, squirrels, and a mouse while walking in the woods. ✓

3. Why did Evelyn call the tree the "grandfather of these woods?"
   Evelyn called the tree the "grandfather of these woods" because it was the oldest (or biggest) tree. Or ...because it was amazing, like her grandfather. (answers may vary) ✓

4. What did Evelyn's grandmother bake?
   a. cookies ✓
   b. cakes
   c. pies
   d. spaghetti

Carly's New Friend

"Come on, Carly!" called her mom. "We are going to be late!"

It was Thursday afternoon, and every Thursday afternoon Carly and her mom volunteered at the animal shelter. The animal shelter was filled with dogs and cats that did not have a home.

Carly did not feel like going to volunteer today. Helping at the animal shelter was a lot of work—and it usually smelled bad there! She had to clean out cages, feed the animals, and fill their water bowls. Carly wanted to stay home and watch TV today. But she knew her mom would never allow that! "I'm coming, Mom!" Carly said, and she hurried to the car.

When Carly and her mom arrived at the animal shelter, the director asked her to do a new job. Carly was asked to walk the dogs on leashes around the yard outside. She was to help them to get some exercise.

The first dog Carly walked was a big shaggy black dog named Max. It was very strong and pulled Carly along as they walked around the yard.

The second dog was a small white dog named Rizzo, who barked the whole time. He barked at everything he saw!

The third dog was a medium-sized brown dog who had no name, as he was new to the animal shelter. This dog was very shy and did not want to come out of his cage. Carly had to encourage him to come out by petting him and speaking to him in a calming voice.

When this dog finally came out, he would not leave Carly's side. Carly did not mind. In fact, she really liked this dog! The director said, "Wow! This dog really likes you! I think you made a new friend! Maybe you can help to think of a name for him?"

Carly said, "I know the perfect name for this dog—Buddy!"

"Then his name will be Buddy!" said the director.

The next Thursday, Carly couldn't wait to get to the animal shelter to volunteer. She couldn't wait to see Buddy again. Carly's mom asked if she would want to adopt Buddy and bring him home to live with them. Carly was so happy to have her new friend become a part of their family!

1. Which day of the week did Carly volunteer at the animal shelter?
   Carly volunteered at the animal shelter every Thursday. ✓

2. With whom did Carly go to the animal shelter?
   a. her brother
   b. her best friend
   c. her aunt
   d. her mom ✓

3. How did Carly encourage the shy dog out of his cage?
   Carly encouraged the shy dog out of his cage by petting him and speaking to him in a calming voice. ✓

4. Who was Carly's new friend?
   Carly's new friend was Buddy the dog. ✓

Ronnie and the Chess Tournament

When Ronnie was only five years old, his father taught him to play the game of chess. Ronnie learned very quickly how to move the different pieces, and he learned how to capture the pieces of his opponent.

Over the next four years, Ronnie got even better at the game. He loved playing chess with his family and friends. They all knew that he would usually win, even though he was so young.

One day, when Ronnie was nine years old, his father saw a sign at the library advertising for a chess tournament. The sign said that all ages were welcome to play in the tournament.

"Ronnie, would you like to play in a chess tournament?" asked his father. "You would get to play chess with lots of other people who love to play the game."

"Yes!" exclaimed Ronnie. "I want to play in the tournament!"

Ronnie's father signed him up for the tournament. It was going to take place on Saturday at the library.

Saturday morning, Ronnie woke up early. He and his father walked to the library. There were a lot of tables and chess boards set up. The man in charge told Ronnie where to go.

Ronnie sat down, and so did a man who looked very old. He even looked older than Ronnie's father! The man was surprised he was going to play chess with a little boy. They started their chess match, and Ronnie thought very carefully about each move. He won the game!

"Congratulations," said the man. "You played a great game of chess!" The man shook hands with Ronnie.

The tournament continued, and Ronnie played six more games, and he won every one of them! He was declared the champion of the tournament!

Ronnie walked home with his father after the tournament, proudly carrying a giant golden trophy.

"Thank you," Ronnie said to his father. "Thank you for teaching me how to play chess!"

1. How old was Ronnie when he learned how to play chess?
   Ronnie was five years old when he learned to play chess. ✓

2. Where was the chess tournament?
   a. at the school
   b. at the park
   c. at the book store
   d. at the library ✓

3. Why was the man surprised that he was going to play chess with Ronnie?
   The man was surprised because Ronnie was very young. ✓

4. What did Ronnie receive after winning the tournament?
   Ronnie received a giant golden trophy. ✓

Washing Dishes with Grandma

Helen was on vacation from school. She had an entire week to do anything she wanted—and she wanted to go to her grandma's house!

Helen and her grandma loved to do many things together. They would sometimes go shopping together. They would sometimes go to the movies together. They would sometimes play card games together.

But Helen's favorite thing to do with her grandma was to help her wash the dishes! At Helen's house, there was a dishwasher to do this chore, but not at her grandma's house! So, this was a special job that she only got to do while at her grandma's house.

Whenever there were dirty dishes in the sink, Helen and her grandma would have a fun time washing them together. "Today, let's sing songs while we wash the dishes," said Helen one day. "Lovely idea!" her grandma responded. Together they sang their favorite songs while washing all the dishes. The next day Helen said, "Today, let's tell each other jokes while we wash the dishes!"

"Fabulous idea!" her grandma responded. Together they giggled at the funny jokes they told to each other while washing all the dishes. Every day they found something fun to do while washing dishes—they told scary ghost stories, they made up silly rhymes, they even quizzed each other on math problems!

On the last day of Helen's vacation, she was feeling sad that she would have to leave her grandma's house.

"I have an idea," said her grandma. "Today, let's be grateful for all the fun things that we did together this week!"

"Wonderful idea!" Helen responded. Together they remembered all the activities that they did during Helen's vacation and planned new ones for the next time they would be together.

"Let's not forget the activity I am most grateful for..." Helen said, "...washing dishes with you!" Helen's grandma gave her a big, soapy hug!

1. Where did Helen want to go on vacation?
   Helen wanted to go to her grandma's house. ✓

2. Why didn't Helen wash dishes at her own house?
   Helen didn't wash dishes at her own house because they had a dishwasher. ✓

3. How was Helen feeling on the last day of her vacation?
   Helen was feeling sad on her last day of vacation. ✓

4. What was one thing Helen and her grandma did not do while washing the dishes?
   a. tell jokes
   b. read books ✓
   c. sing songs
   d. tell ghost stories

The Baby

Johnny was feeling very nervous. His mom and dad were coming home today from the hospital. His mom had a baby! The baby was coming home too.

Johnny was not sure what it would be like to have a new baby in the family.

"Johnny, you will love your new baby brother," said his grandmother. "You will help to take care of him."

But Johnny was not sure about that. He did not know how to take care of a baby! How could he help?

When his parents came home, they gave him a big hug and introduced him to the baby, who was sleeping. The baby's name was Timmy. Johnny was not sure what to think about this new baby.

"Johnny, would you like to hold the baby?" asked his mother. "Come and sit on the couch next to me. I will show you how to safely hold the baby."

"I don't think I can," said Johnny. "I am afraid I won't do it right."

"Let's try," said his mom. "I think you can do it!"

Johnny went to the couch with his mom. She showed him how to hold Timmy. Johnny could not believe that he was actually holding a baby!

He could not believe this little baby was his new brother!

Timmy opened his eyes. He started to cry a little bit. Johnny started to get worried again. "Mom, please take the baby from me. He is crying!"

"Don't worry, Johnny. Timmy is just hungry. Would you like to help feed him?" asked his mom.

"I don't think I can," said Johnny. "I am afraid I won't do it right."

"Let's try," said his mom. "I think you can do it!"

Johnny's mom brought him a bottle filled with special milk for the baby. She showed him how to hold the bottle so Timmy could take a drink from it.

Timmy stopped crying and started drinking the milk. Johnny could not believe he was feeding the baby!

"You are a wonderful big brother, Johnny," said his mom. Johnny smiled. He loved being able to help, and he loved his baby brother!

1. Where did Johnny's mom go to have the baby?
   a. to the library
   b. to the police station
   c. to the hospital ✓
   d. to the restaurant

2. What was the baby's name?
   The baby was named Timmy. ✓

3. How did Johnny feel at the beginning of the story?
   At the beginning of the story Johnny felt nervous (or worried). ✓

4. Johnny's mom showed him how to hold the baby. What else did she show him?
   Johnny's mom showed him how to feed the baby. ✓

Cloud Stories

Sarah was so excited! She was spending the day with her cousin Beth and her Aunt Linda. Together they were going on a picnic.

Aunt Linda drove them to a park with lots of green grass, where they spread out a big blanket. Beth brought a basket filled with sandwiches, carrot sticks, fruits, and cookies. Sarah brought bottles of cold lemonade.

"This is the best picnic ever!" Sarah said. They had eaten all of the delicious food and were now sipping on the lemonade.

"Yes," agreed Beth, "even the fluffy clouds look happy up in the beautiful blue sky."

"Today is the perfect day to tell cloud stories!" exclaimed Aunt Linda.

"What is a cloud story?" asked Sarah.

"A cloud story is when you look up at the clouds and find images within the shapes they make. Then you use your imagination to create a story about those images!" answered Aunt Linda.

"Oh! Let me try!" said Beth. "Let's see...that cloud looks like a polar bear! I think the polar bear is making an ice cream sundae...with a cherry on top!" They all giggled at Beth's polar bear cloud story!

Next, Aunt Linda thought of a cloud story. She pointed up towards a cloud and said, "That cloud looks like a horse! I think that horse was running in a race and just won first place!"

"It is your turn, Sarah!" said Beth. "What do you see? Tell us a cloud story!" Sarah looked up at the clouds and tried to see an image. She was having trouble finding an image to tell a story about. But then a breeze shifted the clouds in the sky, and suddenly one of them seemed to look just like a bunny rabbit!

While pointing up at the cloud, Sarah said, "That bunny rabbit over there just finished munching on a carrot stick that he took from our picnic basket!" They all laughed! What a perfect day for cloud stories!

1. How was Beth related to Sarah?
   Beth is Sarah's cousin. ✓

2. What was in Beth's basket?
   There are sandwiches, carrot sticks, fruits, and cookies in Beth's basket. ✓

3. Who told a cloud story about a horse?
   a. Aunt Linda ✓
   b. Beth
   c. Sarah
   d. Uncle Frank

4. What was Sarah's cloud story about?
   Sarah's cloud story was about a bunny rabbit who just finished munching on a carrot stick that he took from their basket. ✓

Lauren's Loose Tooth

Everyone else in Lauren's class at school had already lost at least one baby tooth. Richard had already lost two baby teeth. Lauren's best friend Grace had already lost four baby teeth! Lauren still had not lost even one baby tooth. She was feeling very frustrated!
"Don't worry," her mother told her,
"your baby teeth will fall out when they are ready."
"But I'm ready now!" Lauren complained. She didn't want to wait any longer! She wasn't a baby anymore; why'd she still have her baby teeth?
"Are any of your teeth wiggly?" asked her older brother, Matthew.
Lauren tried wiggling each tooth in her mouth. One of them was wiggly!
"Try eating something crunchy," advised Matthew. "That will help get the tooth looser."
Lauren went to the kitchen for some crunchy food. First, she tried a big red apple. She chomped on the apple, but the tooth still didn't come out.
Next, Lauren tried a bright orange carrot. She bit down on the crunchy carrot, but her tooth still did not come out.
Then, Lauren tried some little brown peanuts. She chewed the crunchy peanuts, but her tooth still did not come out.
"Don't worry," her mother said, "perhaps tomorrow your tooth will be ready to come out."
Lauren went to school feeling a bit sad the next day. She could feel the wiggly tooth moving back and forth in her mouth, but why wouldn't it fall out? Would she have her baby teeth forever?
At lunchtime, Lauren sat next to her friend, Grace. While she was eating her sandwich, something felt funny in her mouth…her tooth fell out!
"Your tooth!" exclaimed Grace. "Let's go to see the school nurse."
She will help you." The nurse helped Lauren to rinse her mouth with water and then gave her a special little bag in which she put the tooth.
Lauren felt very proud to have lost her first baby tooth! She smiled widely for everyone to see!

1. Who had already lost four baby teeth?
   - a. Lauren
   - b. Richard
   - c. Bernie
   - d. Grace ✓
2. How did Matthew advise Lauren?
   Matthew told Lauren to eat something crunchy. ✓
3. Which three crunchy foods did Lauren eat to try to loosen her tooth?
   Lauren ate an apple, a carrot, and some peanuts. ✓
4. Who gave Lauren a special little bag for her tooth?
   The school nurse gave Lauren a special little bag for her tooth. ✓

Teddy's New Bicycle

"Today is the day!" declared Teddy's father.
"Today, we are going to try out your new bicycle!"
Teddy looked up from his cereal bowl with a worried look on his face. His new bicycle was really big. It only had two wheels instead of three, like his old tricycle. Teddy wasn't sure that he'd be able to ride his new bicycle.
"I like my tricycle," he said. "I can save my new bicycle for next summer."
"I think you will like your new bicycle better," his father said.
"You are taller now, so a bigger bicycle is what you need. Come on, let's take it to the park to try it out."
The park by their house had many trails where people liked to go for walks, to go for jogs, and to ride bicycles. Teddy and his father brought the new bicycle to one of the trails.
His father held onto the back of the bicycle as Teddy tried to sit and balance on it. He had to stretch his legs out in order to reach the pedals with his feet. Teddy felt very nervous.
"You can do it!" his father exclaimed. They started moving on the trail.
Teddy held on tightly to the handlebars and moved the pedals with his feet. His father ran along behind him, still holding onto the bicycle.
"Don't let go!" Teddy shouted. "I don't want to fall!"
"You are doing a great job! You can do this all by yourself. If you fall, we can try again," encouraged Teddy's father.
Teddy kept pedaling and steering with the handlebars. He was starting to enjoy his new bicycle! As he was moving along, his father let go.
Soon Teddy lost his balance, and the bicycle fell over.
Teddy looked at his scraped knees and dirty hands. He looked at the bicycle, which was on the ground next to him. He didn't like falling, but it really didn't hurt too much. "I can do this!" he thought.
Teddy's father ran up to him and helped him to his feet.
"Are you okay?" he asked. Teddy nodded.
"Let's try again!" Teddy said with a smile. "Today is the day!"

1. How many wheels did the new bicycle have?
   The new bicycle had two wheels. ✓
2. What didn't people do on the trails at the park?
   - a. go for a walk
   - b. go for a swim ✓
   - c. ride bicycles
   - d. go for a jog
3. How did Teddy's father help to get him started on the bicycle?
   Teddy's father held onto the back of the bicycle and ran along with it. ✓
4. Teddy felt more confident at the end of the story. How do you know?
   Teddy demonstrated his confidence by wanting to try again after he fell off of the bicycle. ✓

Playing in the Band

Andrea felt very excited. She was going to the high school, where her older sister Chloe was a student. Chloe was a clarinet player in the band at the high school, and they were having a concert!
"Mom, can I wear my new blue dress to the concert?" Andrea asked.
"Sure, that dress will be perfect for tonight's concert!" said her mom. Chloe had a special band uniform that she was wearing. After Andrea put the dress on, her mom braided her hair. Her mom braided Chloe's hair too. Andrea and her family were finally all ready to go to the concert.
When they arrived at the high school, Chloe went to warm-up with the other musicians.
"Good luck, Chloe!" Andrea said. She gave her sister a hug before she went.
Andrea and her parents found seats in the school auditorium. The auditorium was such a big place! On the stage there were many seats set up for the band.
Soon the band members started to come onto the stage and sit in their seats. Andrea saw Chloe carrying her clarinet! She also saw many other students with flutes, trumpets, oboes, trombones, and saxophones. There were some students standing in the very back with percussion instruments.
Then a man carrying a short stick in his hand came out and stood in front of the band.
"Who is that? Why is he holding a stick?" Andrea whispered quietly to her dad.
"He is the conductor of the band. That stick is called a baton and he uses it to direct the band," her dad answered.
The band started playing and Andrea heard the most beautiful music she had ever heard in all her life. She thought the band was wonderful! When it was over, she clapped her hands and felt so proud that her sister was one of the musicians.
"I cannot wait until I am in high school!" Andrea exclaimed. "I also want to be in the band!" That night when Andrea went to sleep, she dreamed that she had a clarinet of her own and was playing in the band!

1. Did Andrea enjoy the band concert?
   Yes, Andrea enjoyed the band concert. ✓
2. What is a baton?
   a short stick that the conductor uses to direct the band. ✓
3. What color was Andrea's new dress? dress was blue. ✓
4. Which instrument does Chloe play?
   - a. flute
   - b. clarinet ✓
   - c. tuba
   - d. oboe

The Time Machine

A big brown box had arrived at Ellie's house. Inside the box was the new washing machine that her parents had ordered. Ellie was not interested in the new washing machine, but she was interested in the big brown box!
It was big enough for her to sit inside—big enough for her and a friend!
"Can I please have this box?" Ellie asked her mom.
"Sure," said Ellie's mom. "Why do you want this big empty box?"
"You'll see!" replied Ellie. Ellie took the big box outside to the yard. Her best friend, Oscar, came over from his house next door.
"Wow! Cool box!" said Oscar. "What should we do with it?"
"Let's make a Time Machine!" exclaimed Ellie.
Ellie and Oscar used markers, paint, crayons, colored paper, and glue to decorate the inside and outside of the box. They made dials, switches, buttons, and colorful designs. Now it looked like a Time Machine!
The two friends sat inside the Time Machine. They were ready to go!
"Where in time should we travel?" asked Oscar.
"Hmmm…" thought Ellie. "I have an idea!" She ran inside the house and returned with a book about dinosaurs.
"Let's go back in time to see the dinosaurs!" said Ellie.
"That will be awesome!" said Oscar. They pushed their buttons, turned their dials, and counted to ten, and, using their imaginations, traveled to the time of the dinosaurs!
Ellie and Oscar imagined being surrounded by huge dinosaurs. They looked in the book to learn the names of the dinosaurs that they imagined were walking all around their Time Machine. It was amazing!
"Where should we go next?" Ellie asked. "I have an idea," said Oscar. He ran home and returned with a book about knights and castles. "Let's go!" exclaimed Ellie. They said goodbye to the dinosaurs and set the dials for the Middle Ages!

1. Why had a big brown box arrived at Ellie's house?
   The big brown box had the new washing machine inside of it. ✓
2. What did the friends use to decorate the box?
   markers, paint, crayons, colored paper, and glue to decorate the box. ✓
3. What kind of book did Ellie get from her house? About dinosaurs ✓
4. Where did Oscar live?
   - a. next door to Ellie ✓
   - b. on a boat
   - c. in a different city
   - d. deep in the woods

Julia and the Bird's Nest

Spring had finally arrived! Julia was happy to be able to open the windows of the house and let in the fresh air. It had felt like a long winter. Now that the cold, snowy days were over, Julia was excited to see signs of spring popping up all over the place!

"Look, Mom!" exclaimed Julia. "I see a yellow flower in the yard!"

"That is a daffodil. Daffodils are one of the first flowers of springtime!" said Julia's mom.

"Look, Dad!" exclaimed Julia. "The leaves are growing on the trees!"

"The leaves come back in the springtime!" said Julia's dad. Julia noticed new signs of spring every day. One day while playing outside, she heard a chirping sound coming from a nearby tree. Julia walked over to the tree and saw a bird sitting in a nest! She quickly went and got her parents. She wanted to show them!

"That is a mother robin," said her dad. "You know it is springtime when the robins return!" The mother robin flew from the nest. Julia saw that there were three small blue eggs in the nest! "Eggs!" exclaimed Julia happily. "Three eggs!"

"There will be baby robins in this nest soon," said Julia's mom.

Over the next several weeks, Julia kept a close watch on the mother robin and the eggs. Most days the mother robin sat on the nest all day long.

"The mother robin is sitting on the eggs to keep the eggs warm," explained Julia's dad. One morning Julia went outside to see the mother robin. But the mother robin was not there. She peeked into the nest, and to her surprise, the eggs were not there either! Instead, there were three baby birds! Julia's mom and dad came out to see the baby birds too. They watched as the mother robin returned. She had a little worm in her beak that she was bringing to the baby birds to eat. "This bird's nest was the best sign of spring!" exclaimed Julia.

1. Which season has cold, snowy days?
   a. spring
   b. summer
   c. autumn
   d. winter ☑

2. What color are daffodils? ☑
   Daffodils are yellow.

3. Why did the mother robin sit on the eggs?
   The mother robin sat on the eggs to keep them warm. ☑

4. Who brought the baby birds a worm to eat?
   The mother robin brought a worm for the baby birds to eat. ☑

Nina's Secret

Nina loved school. She especially loved math! But lately, that had changed. She was getting math problems wrong because she couldn't see the board clearly.

"Nina, could you please come up to my desk?" her teacher asked.

Nina walked slowly up to the teacher's desk. She knew why the teacher had called her up there—she had gotten all of her math problems wrong.

"Nina, you are a very good math student," said her teacher.

"But you copied the math problems down incorrectly from the board. I think you may need to visit the eye doctor."

The next week, Nina's mom brought her to the eye doctor. There she was fitted with eyeglasses to help her see things that were far away. Nina was amazed at how clear everything suddenly looked!

But now Nina had a new problem: she felt embarrassed about wearing her glasses. She wasn't sure what the other kids at school would say about them. She decided to keep her glasses a secret.

At school the next day, Nina carefully hid her eyeglasses in her backpack.

"No one will ever know about my eyeglasses," thought Nina.

The teacher announced to the class that they were going to have a math contest! The students were divided into two teams, and whichever team got the most problems correct would get a prize—a candy bar!

The teams had to copy down math problems from the board and take turns answering them. It was very exciting! The score was tied, and it was the final problem. Nina felt very nervous. It was her turn, and she couldn't see the problem on the board! She did not want to let her team down.

"Wait a moment, please!" Nina said. She hurried to her backpack and took out her new eyeglasses. The students were all surprised to see Nina wearing them. Nina could now see the board clearly. She completed the math problem, and her team won the contest!

"Hooray for Nina!" the other students shouted! Nina felt very proud. She was so happy to have her new eyeglasses!

1. Why was Nina getting her math problems wrong?
   Because she couldn't see the board clearly. ☑

2. Who took Nina to the eye doctor?
   a. her teacher
   b. her dad
   c. her classmate
   d. her mom ☑

3. Why did Nina want to keep her glasses a secret?
   Nina wanted to keep her glasses a secret because she felt embarrassed about wearing them. Or; Nina wasn't sure what the other kids at school would say about them. ☑

4. What was the math contest prize?
   The math contest prize was a candy bar. ☑

Ruthie and the Swim Class

Summer was coming soon. This summer was going to be the best ever—her family was getting a swimming pool!

"Our swimming pool will be so awesome!" Ruthie said. "I cannot wait to jump into the cool water on a hot day!"

"Yes, having a swimming pool will be awesome," said her dad, "but you will not be jumping into it until you learn how to swim!"

"That is why we signed you up for a swim class," said Ruthie's mom, "so you will know how to be safe in our new pool. You start swim class tomorrow after school."

The next day Ruthie arrived at the swim class. Her mom sat on a bench to watch while Ruthie got into the pool with the instructor. The instructor showed Ruthie how to float. They practiced putting their heads under the water. They also practiced kicking their legs while holding onto the side of the pool. "Am I swimming yet?" asked Ruthie.

"Not yet," said the instructor. "You are first learning skills that will help you swim. Every week you will learn more skills to make you a strong swimmer."

Ruthie felt impatient! She wanted to learn how to swim now!

Each week Ruthie went to class and did exactly what the instructor taught her. She was motivated to become a very strong swimmer so she would be allowed to jump into her family's new pool!

After many classes with the swim instructor, Ruthie could swim on her back and her front. She enjoyed learning how to swim!

"You are becoming a very good swimmer," the instructor said, "but remember that no matter how well you swim, an adult must always be watching while you are in the pool." "I will always remember that rule," said Ruthie.

When summer came, the new pool at Ruthie's house was installed. Ruthie's parents went over all the rules with her about using the pool safely. Then finally, Ruthie got to jump into the pool with a big splash!

1. When was Ruthie's family's getting swimming pool?
   Ruthie's family was getting a swimming pool in the summer. ☑

2. What does Ruthie want to do on a hot day?
   Ruthie wants to jump into the cool water of the pool on a hot day. ☑

3. Name one of the skills that the instructor taught Ruthie.
   Answers may vary: The instructor taught Ruthie how to float
   OR how to put her head under water OR how to kick her legs. ☑

4. An important rule the instructor told Ruthie was:
   a. Always swim alone.
   b. Always swim with your shoes on.
   c. An adult must always be watching while you are in the pool. ☑
   d. Only swim on your back.

The Haircut

Deena had very long hair. It was so long that it hung all the way down her back! Her mother often braided her hair into two beautiful thick braids.

Deena's cousin Kara had long hair too. Whenever they visited one another, they would take turns brushing each other's long hair and pretend that they worked in a hair salon! It was such fun!

Today Kara was coming to Deena's house for a visit, and Deena was so excited to see her. Kara had told her that she had a big surprise to show her. Deena wondered what the surprise could be!

"Kara is here!" Deena's mom said. Deena came running to the front door to greet her cousin. When Deena saw Kara, she could not believe her eyes! Kara had gotten a haircut! Kara's hair was now very short!

"What do you think of my surprise?" asked Kara. "Don't I look grown-up?"

Deena thought that Kara did look very grown-up with her new haircut. Deena suddenly felt like a baby with her own long hair in braids.

"We can still play hair salon," said Kara. Deena didn't think playing hair salon would be much fun with Kara's short hair—but then she got an idea.

"I want to look grown-up too," said Deena. "Do you think you can give me a haircut in our hair salon? A haircut like yours?"

"Sure!" said Kara. "I will cut your hair just like mine!"

Deena found scissors in her mom's sewing kit and quietly snuck them into her bedroom. She wanted her new haircut to be a surprise for her mom!

"Okay," said Kara, "you sit in this chair and I will be the hair stylist." Kara had the scissors and was about to cut off one of Deena's long braids when Deena's mom came into the room.

"Girls!" exclaimed Deena's mom. "What are you doing?"

"I'm getting a haircut," said Deena. "I want to look grown-up too!"

Deena's mom took the scissors. She told Deena that if she wanted a haircut, they could go to a real salon. Deena decided that she still liked her long hair. Maybe she would get her hair cut some day—but not today!

1. What did Deena and Kara like to pretend?
   a. that they were famous singers
   b. that they worked in a restaurant
   c. that they were movie stars
   d. that they worked in a hair salon ☑

2. What was Kara's big surprise?
   Kara's big surprise was that she got a haircut. ☑

3. Why did Deena feel like a baby?
   Deena felt like a baby because she still had her long hair in braids. ☑

4. What did Kara plan to do with the scissors?
   Kara planned to give Deena a haircut with the scissors. ☑

Fireworks!

It was the day of the annual Summer Fun Festival, and Danny felt very excited. The festival helped to raise money for the local school. His family went to the festival every year and always had a wonderful time!

"Is it time to go yet?" Danny asked his mother. The festival was in a park which was a short drive from Danny's home.

"Almost," she said, "I just have to finish icing this cake."

Danny's mother liked to help with the Cake Walk at the festival. She would bake cakes, cookies, and pies to donate to the Cake Walk. Many people would try to win his mother's delicious desserts!

"I'm ready to go! I've been practicing my aim!" said Danny's brother.

Danny's brother liked to play the Ring Toss game. It was his favorite because one year, he won a bouncy red ball while playing it. He was going to try to win another ball this year! "And I am hungry!" said Danny's father with a wink.

Danny's father liked to sample all of the food vendors' dishes. He liked the burgers, tacos, hot dogs, and pizzas that were sold at the festival. Yum!

But Danny's favorite part of the festival was at the very end of the day after the sun went down and the sky grew dark. That was when the fireworks display began!

Danny's family arrived at the festival and enjoyed a wonderful day. All of his mother's desserts were won, his brother played the Ring Toss game three times, and his father tried every food available!

Finally, the sun started to set, and the sky grew dim. Danny and his family made their way to the grassy area of the park and laid down a blanket to sit on while they relaxed and watched the display. The fireworks were amazing! Bright colors decorated the sky and seemed to rain down from high above. Loud booms, exciting pops, and surprising whistles filled the air. Danny loved watching the fireworks with his family! "This is my favorite part of the Summer Fun Festival!" Danny exclaimed happily. "I really love fireworks!"

1. For what did the Summer Fun Festival raise money?
   The Summer Fun Festival raised money for the local school. ✓

2. How did Danny's mother help with the festival?
   Danny's mother helped by baking desserts for the Cake Walk. ✓

3. What game did Danny's brother like to play at the festival?
   a. the Cake Walk
   b. the Ring Toss ✓
   c. the Cake Toss
   d. basketball

4. Which part of the festival did Danny like the best?
   Danny liked the fireworks display the best. ✓

Logan's Hiccups

It was Logan's turn to read aloud during class. He had been practicing at home, so he felt confident about all of the new vocabulary words in the story. Just as he started reading, a hiccup jumped out of his mouth! Logan felt embarrassed. The other boys and girls laughed.

"Excuse me," he said. He started again. Another hiccup jumped out!

"Oh dear," said Ms. Zayner, his teacher. "Why don't you go get a drink of water to help your hiccups go away."

Logan quickly went to the drinking fountain in the hallway. He took a long sip of water and then returned to the classroom.

"Let's try again," said Ms. Zayner. Logan started to read, but then all of a sudden—"Hiccup!" Another hiccup jumped out of his mouth!

"Hmmm…why don't we give Anna a turn reading until your hiccups go away," said Ms. Zayner.

Soon it was lunchtime, and all the students went to the cafeteria. Logan still had the hiccups! His best friend, Zachary, tried to help him.

"Boo!" shouted Zachary as he snuck up behind Logan in the lunch line.

"Hey!" said Logan, startled. "Why did you do that? I almost dropped my lunch tray!" The other kids around him all giggled.

"Haven't you heard? Scaring someone is the best way to get rid of the hiccups!" said Zachary. "I'm just trying to help!"

"Hiccup! Well, it doesn't seem to have helped," said Logan sadly.

Logan's hiccups continued all afternoon. When he arrived home, his mother asked, "Why do you look so sad?"

"I have had the hiccups all day!" replied Logan. "I didn't get to have my turn reading in class, and the other kids laughed at me."

"Oh, I'm sorry," said his mother. "Let's see…I remember my grandmother had a cure for the hiccups…try this spoonful of honey mixed in water."

Logan slowly sipped on the spoonful of honey in water. His great-grandmother was right! His hiccups went away! Finally!

1. Who is Ms. Zayner?
   Ms. Zayner is Logan's teacher. ✓

2. What happened to Logan when he started to read aloud?
   When Logan started to read aloud, a hiccup jumped out of his mouth.
   Or: When Logan started to read aloud, he got the hiccups. ✓

3. How did Zachary try to help Logan?
   Zachary tried to help Logan by scaring him. ✓

4. What was Logan's great grandmother's cure for hiccups?
   a. sipping on a spoonful of honey mixed in water ✓
   b. eating an egg
   c. scaring the hiccups away
   d. reading a scary story

Stanley Builds a Treehouse

Stanley enjoyed being outside. He would much rather be out in the fresh air than inside the house. He didn't mind the cold weather or even the rainy weather! He just always preferred to be outside!

"Stanley," called his mom, "it is time for you to come in. You must do your homework!"

"I can do it out here!" said Stanley. He ran in to get his backpack and brought it back outside with him. He sat in the sunshine and worked on his homework.

The next several days, Stanley continued to do his homework outside. He did math outside, he read his science book outside, and he wrote his history report outside. He was so pleased that he could stay outside!

But then the weather changed. The sunshine that had filled the sky disappeared behind heavy clouds. The rain started falling, and his books started to get wet.

"Uh-oh," thought Stanley, "I don't mind the rain, but my books do! I need to go in." Stanley stared gloomily out the window. He always felt so much better when he was surrounded by fresh air, but he could not let his books and papers get wet. Then he had an idea—he would build a treehouse!

Stanley told his mom and dad about his idea and asked if they would allow him to build a treehouse. They decided to help him build a treehouse! On Saturday, they went to the hardware store to buy the supplies. Stanley and his parents found a good spot in a tree in their backyard for the treehouse.

"This is going to be the best treehouse ever!" Stanley said. They worked for two days building the treehouse together. It had a strong floor to sit on and a roof to keep Stanley dry. It was perfect!

"Thank you!" said Stanley to his parents. They were all very proud of the treehouse that they had built together. The next day, Stanley could not wait to bring his homework outside and work on it in his new treehouse!

1. What does Stanley like about being outside?
   a. Stanley likes to watch TV outside.
   b. Stanley likes only warm weather outside.
   c. Stanley likes the fresh air outside. ✓
   d. Stanley likes bringing his radio outside.

2. What problem did Stanley have while doing his homework outside?
   Stanley's books got wet when it rained. ✓

3. Who helped Stanley to build the treehouse?
   Stanley's parents helped him to build the treehouse. ✓

4. Where is Stanley's treehouse located?
   Stanley's treehouse is located in his backyard. ✓

Renee's First Sleepover

Friday night was coming soon, and Renee felt worried. She had been invited to a sleepover at her friend Henrietta's house. Renee was worried because she had never slept at someone else's house before.

"You will have a fun time," her mother reassured her. "You have played at Henrietta's house before."

"But I have never slept there," replied Renee. "What if I get scared in the dark? What if I have a bad dream? What if I want to come home?"

"I have an idea," said her mother. "Let's get your things ready. We will pack useful items. You will be prepared for anything!"

Renee and her mother started to gather items she would need for the sleepover. They put pajamas, slippers, a toothbrush, and clothes for the next day in her backpack. They rolled up her sleeping bag and a pillow.

"Now," said Renee's mother, "you are worried about the dark?"

"Yes," said Renee. "I have a nightlight at home. What if Henrietta does not have a nightlight? What if her room is very dark?"

"Why don't you pack this small flashlight in your backpack. If Henrietta doesn't have a nightlight, and it gets too dark, you can use this flashlight!"

"Oh, that's a good idea!" said Renee smiling. She packed the flashlight.

"Next, you're worried about having a bad dream?" said Renee's mother.

"Yes," said Renee. "What if I dream about monsters or snakes?"

"Well," said Renee's mother, "your teddy bear usually helps you to sleep soundly here at home. Why don't you bring him with you?"

"I can bring him with me?" asked Renee excitedly.

"Of course!" her mother answered. "And if you still want to come home, call me, and I will come to pick you up, even if it is late."

Friday night arrived, and Renee went to the sleepover. The girls had so much fun! They watched movies and played games. They ate pizza and popcorn. Renee forgot all about being worried! She had a wonderful time and never had to call her mother to pick her up!

1. Who invited Renee to a sleepover?
   Henrietta invited Renee to a sleepover. ✓

2. What items does Renee pack?
   a. pajamas and roller skates
   b. a sleeping bag and a tent
   c. pajamas and a toothbrush ✓
   d. a pillow and a book

3. What helpful item does Renee's mother suggest she pack in case it is too dark?
   Renee's mother suggests that she pack a small flashlight in case it is too dark. ✓

4. What did the girls eat at the sleepover?
   The girls ate pizza and popcorn at the sleepover. ✓

Harry's Newspaper

The houses in Harry's neighborhood all looked pretty similar. They were built from stucco and were painted white. Harry was interested in learning more about the people who lived inside of these similar-looking houses.

He saw many of his neighbors coming and going, but they all felt like strangers who didn't say hello or wave to one another.

"I'd like to know the people who live in our neighborhood," Harry said.

"I bet they would like to know you too!" said his mom.

Harry thought for a while and then came up with a plan. "I'm going to start a neighborhood newspaper!" Harry used his computer to type up an article all about himself and his family. He wrote another one about his pet bird, another about his favorite sports teams, and another about what music he liked. He also requested to interview anyone who'd be willing to be featured in a future edition of his newspaper.

Harry printed out his newspaper and made enough copies for every house in his neighborhood. The next morning, he woke up very early and delivered a copy of his newspaper to each house in his neighborhood.

By the next day, Harry had received many calls from people who were willing to be interviewed! Harry took a notebook and a pen and headed out to start his interviews. The first person he interviewed was an older adult who lived three houses from Harry's. The man, Mr. Kubin, was a fascinating person. He had worked his whole life in a paper factory. He also had been in the army. Mr. Kubin was now retired and had a small pet dog. Harry wrote it all down.

Next, he interviewed the Ayala family that had moved to the neighborhood from Mexico. They knew how to speak Spanish and taught Harry a few words, like "hola" and "amigo." Harry wrote it all down.

Harry felt so good learning about the people in his neighborhood. He would spend lots more time interviewing the rest of the neighbors and printing out many more newspapers! In time, the neighbors did not feel like strangers to one another. The neighbors all loved reading Harry's newspaper and loved getting to know one another!

1. What did the houses in Harry's neighborhood look like?

   The houses in Harry's neighborhood were built from stucco and painted white.

2. Harry has a pet _____ . ✓
   - a. cat
   - b. bird ✓
   - c. dog
   - d. turtle

3. Where had Mr. Kubin worked?

   Mr. Kubin had worked in a paper factory. ✓

4. How did Harry help his neighbors get to know one another?

   Harry helped his neighbors get to know one another
   by starting a neighborhood newspaper. ✓

Oliver the Artist

The morning school bell rang, and Miss Anderson gathered the excited students onto the bus. Today they would not be sitting at their desks to study. Today they were going on a field trip to the Art Museum! Oliver and his friends, Joshua and Connor, were excited about having a field trip but not very happy that it was to the Art Museum. They did not like art. They thought art was boring and wanted to go on a field trip to somewhere more exciting, like to the Space Museum.

"I don't want to go look at old paintings all day!" complained Oliver.

"At least at the Space Museum, we could see cool stuff," said Joshua.

"Yeah, I will probably fall asleep during the boring tour," laughed Connor.

When they arrived at the Art Museum, Miss Anderson introduced the class to their guide, a young man named Justin. He said he had just graduated from college. Oliver was surprised that Justin would want to work at the boring Art Museum. He seemed like a cool guy; why would he work here?

Justin walked them all around the museum, where they saw artwork from painters, sculptors, and even artists who created figures out of glass! Some of the artwork was very old, some of it more modern, but none of it was boring.

Oliver started to think that he was wrong about this field trip!

"So, do you kids want to check out my favorite room of the museum?" asked Justin. "Follow me!" Justin took them to a room filled with paints of every color and lots of paintbrushes. There were lots of easels around the room with blank paper hanging on them. "This is where you get to become an artist! Have fun making your own masterpiece!" Oliver and his classmates each got to paint a picture. Then their artwork was displayed on a huge bulletin board in the museum.

"Now when other people visit the museum, they will admire your work too! You are all artists!" said Justin. Oliver felt very proud of his painting.

On the bus ride back to school, Oliver, Joshua, and Connor agreed that the Art Museum was much cooler than what they expected. Oliver wondered how many people would see his painting when they visited the museum. He liked being Oliver the Artist!

1. Where did Oliver's class go on their field trip?

   Oliver's class went to the Art Museum. ✓

2. At first, what did Oliver and his friends think about the Art Museum?

   At first, Oliver and his friends thought the Art Museum would be boring. ✓

3. Who was the guide at the Art Museum?
   - a. Joshua
   - b. Connor
   - c. Oliver
   - d. Justin ✓

4. Where was Oliver's artwork displayed?

   Oliver's artwork was displayed on a huge bulletin board in the museum. ✓

Kyle Plays Tennis

Kyle's school had many sports teams. There was a football team, a soccer team, a basketball team, a track team, and a volleyball team. There was even a golf team and a swim team. But Kyle could not find a sports team that he wanted to join.

One day there was an announcement that a new sports team was forming.

The school was going to have its first-ever tennis team. Kyle had never played tennis before, but he was interested in finding out about it. He signed up to go to the informational meeting being held after school.

At the meeting, there were lots of other boys and girls.

The teacher in charge was Mr. Heintz. "Welcome to the tennis team informational meeting!" said Mr. Heintz. "I think we are going to have a great school tennis team!" He explained when the practice sessions would be and when they would have tennis matches against other schools. Kyle hurried home with all the information on paper. He excitedly showed it to his dad and mom. "Can I join?" asked Kyle.

"Mr. Heintz said that the school would provide all of the equipment!"

"Of course!" said his parents. "Tennis is a really fun sport!"

At the first practice, Kyle felt nervous. Would he be any good at playing tennis? He wasn't even sure how the game was played.

Mr. Heintz explained to the students the rules of tennis and the complicated scoring system. He gave each student a racket and a bright yellow tennis ball.

They all walked onto the tennis courts and were assigned a partner. They were to practice hitting the ball back and forth.

Kyle served the ball, and it went right over the net! He was so pleased!

He and his partner continued to practice hitting the ball to one another. Kyle was having so much fun! Mr. Heintz came over to watch them.

"Kyle, you are very good at playing tennis!

I cannot believe this is your first time!" said Mr. Heintz. Kyle felt very proud of himself!

Kyle continued to attend all of the tennis team practices. He did very well in the tennis matches. Kyle became the school's star tennis player!

1. What sports teams did Kyle's school have? Name at least three.

   Kyle's school had football, soccer, basketball, track, volleyball, golf, swim,
   and tennis teams. (Only 3 needed. Answers may vary.) ✓

2. Who was the teacher in charge of the tennis team?

   Mr. Heintz was the teacher in charge of the tennis team. ✓

3. What did Mr. Heintz give to the students at the first practice?
   - a. a racket and a uniform
   - b. a book about tennis and a bright yellow ball
   - c. a racket and a shoe
   - d. a racket and a bright yellow ball ✓

4. How did Kyle feel at the end of the story?

   Kyle felt proud of himself (or happy) at the end of the story. ✓

The Haunted Attic

Gabriel and Claudia always enjoyed visiting their grandma and grandpa's house. It was a big old house with lots of rooms to explore. The rooms were filled with all kinds of interesting items like old books, games, and antiques. They would spend hours looking at all the cool old stuff.

One day while playing at their grandparents' house, Gabriel said, "There is one place in this house that we have never explored—the attic!"

"The attic!" exclaimed Claudia. "I don't think we should go up there!"

"Why not?" asked Gabriel. "Grandma said we could go anywhere."

"Hmm," said Claudia thoughtfully, "I suppose we could go take a peek."

Gabriel and Claudia found the staircase to the attic and slowly walked up the creaky old stairs. It was quite dark, as there were very few lights in the attic. Gabriel brought a flashlight, and he turned it on.

"Oh wow! Look at all this stuff!" Gabriel exclaimed. There were old chairs, boxes of fancy old clothes, a broken mirror, a dusty trumpet, an antique dollhouse, a large clock...so much stuff! Suddenly they heard a strange squeaky sound coming from the corner. Both Gabriel and Claudia got so startled that they screamed in fright and ran down the stairs. They were sure there was a ghost in the attic!

"Grandma! Grandpa!" they yelled. "The attic is haunted!"

"Haunted?" asked Grandma calmly. "Hmmm...there are many things in that attic, but I don't think a ghost is one of them!"

"Why don't we all go up together and see if we can figure out what really scared you, kids," said Grandpa.

Together they all went back up into the attic. Gabriel pointed to the corner where the strange sound came from. Grandpa bravely walked to the corner with a flashlight. He lifted up an old sheet that was on the floor, and underneath, they saw a family of mice living there! They all started laughing! Gabriel and Claudia felt relieved.

"I guess this attic isn't haunted," said Gabriel, "just home to a family of spooky, squeaky mice!"

1. Which place in the house had the children not yet explored?

   They had not yet explored the attic. ✓

2. Why did they need a flashlight to look around in the attic?

   They needed a flashlight because there were very few lights in the attic
   (so it was quite dark). ✓

3. Why did the children think the attic was haunted?

   The children thought the attic was haunted because they heard
   a strange squeaky sound. ✓

4. What was living in the attic? ✓
   - a. a ghost
   - b. a monster
   - c. a family of mice ✓
   - d. a family of birds

Maizy Moves Away

Maizy and Rachel had been neighbors since they were tiny babies. They spent time together almost every day. They went to the same school and played on the same soccer team. They were best friends.

One day Maizy's mom had some news to share. "Maizy's dad got a new job. It is in a different state, and our family will be moving there."

Maizy and Rachel both felt very sad about this news. Together they cried.

Maizy and Rachel both felt very sad about this news. Together they cried.

"This is awful news," said Rachel. "I will miss you so much. Who will I play soccer with? Who will I walk to school with? I don't want you to go!"

"I think it is awful too," said Maizy. "I don't want to go to a new school. I don't want a new house. I wish my dad didn't have a new job!"

The girls spent many hours feeling sad and worried. They cried many tears.

Rachel's mom said, "Let's find on a map where Maizy's new house will be." She got out a big map and together they found the new state. They saw that Maizy's new house would be only two hours away.

Maizy's mom said, "We would love for Rachel to come to visit—we can have a sleepover! And there is a beach near our new house—we could all go spend time together at the beach! Won't that be fun?"

Maizy and Rachel agreed that a sleepover and the beach did sound like fun. They stopped crying and started to make plans.

Over the next several weeks, Rachel helped Maizy to pack up her things. They sometimes cried a little more, but they also shared lots of laughs!

"The moving truck is all ready," Maizy said sadly to Rachel on the day of the move. They looked out to the street and saw a gigantic truck waiting to go.

They gave each other a big hug and didn't want to let go.

"Girls, I have a present for each of you!" said Rachel's mom. She handed them small boxes wrapped with matching pink satin bows. Inside the boxes were pretty stationery, matching envelopes, and new pens.

"We can write letters to each other," said Rachel. "And send pictures!"

"I may be moving away, but we will always be best friends!" said Maizy.

1. How long have Maizy and Rachel known one another?
   - a. since yesterday
   - b. since they were tiny babies ✓
   - c. since last year
   - d. since they were grown ups
2. What sport do the girls like to play?
   The girls like to play soccer. ✓
3. Why is Maizy moving?
   Maizy is moving because her dad got a new job in a different state. ✓
4. What can the girls do with their new stationery?
   The girls can write letters to one another with their new stationery. ✓

Nora's Nickname

Nora wanted a nickname. She thought it would make her feel special if people called her by a special name. But the name "Nora" didn't seem to have a nickname to go along with it.

"How about we call you 'Nory?'" her little sister Becky suggested.

"No," said Nora, "that doesn't sound quite right. It is not special."

"Maybe we can call you Nor-Nor," said her brother Jimmy.

"No," said Nora, "that sounds silly, not special."

"Why don't we call you Ra-Ra?" asked her cousin Lizzie.

"No," said Nora, "that isn't special either."

Nora felt jealous. Her name wasn't special without a nickname. Becky was a nickname for Rebecca, Jimmy was a nickname for James, and Lizzie was a nickname for Elizabeth. She was the only one without a special name. Nora went out to sit by herself in her favorite place, the garden.

Nora's mother went outside to pick vegetables from the garden and noticed Nora sitting there looking sad. "What's wrong, Nora?" she asked.

"My name isn't special! Why didn't I get a special name?" Nora said.

"Nora, do you like this garden of ours?" asked her mother.

"Of course, I do! You know that it's my favorite place. We have the loveliest vegetables, fruits, and flowers growing here," said Nora.

"Well, this garden was started many years ago, by your great-grandmother. She also loved to work in this garden, and she grew many of these same kinds of vegetables, fruits, and flowers. Your great-grandmother taught me how to take care of a garden," she said. "Her name was Nora."

Nora's eyes grew wide.

"You were named after your great-grandmother. I wanted to honor the woman who was most special in my life," explained her mother.

Nora hugged her mother tightly and said,

"Thank you for giving me the most special name of all!"

1. Why didn't Nora think her name was special?
   Because she didn't have a nickname. ✓
2. What did Becky suggest they call Nora?
   - a. Nory ✓
   - b. Nor-Nor
   - c. Ra-Ra
   - d. Aron
3. Where was Nora's favorite place?
   Nora's favorite place was the garden. ✓
4. What was special about Nora's name?
   Nora's name was special because she was named
   after her great-grandmother. (Answers may vary) ✓

Victor's Robot

Victor had so many chores to do. His mom had made a list of chores he had to do every day. Victor was not allowed to play with his friends until his chores were done. He did not like this rule!

"Victor, want to come to play video games?" asked his friend Leland.

"I wish I could," said Victor, "but I need to do my chores." Victor felt sad that he couldn't go play with Leland. He wished someone else would do his chores for him. He wished he had a robot!

"Yes, a robot would be awesome," thought Victor. "I would never have to make my bed, take out the trash, mow the lawn, feed the cat, fold the laundry...I would be able to play video games all day!"

Victor lay on his unmade bed and thought about how cool a robot would be to have in his house. He wondered if he would be able to build one.

Then he heard a noise outside of his bedroom. He got up and opened the door—and there stood a robot! It was very tall and made of silver metal and had bright blue lights for eyes. It had wheels instead of feet and an antenna on top of its head. It was looked amazing!

"Hello, Victor. I am Marvin. I am your robot. I will do anything you tell me to do," said the robot in a funny-sounding voice. "Shall I make your bed? Take out the trash? Feed the cat?"

Victor couldn't believe his eyes! This was great! Now he could go play video games with Leland while the robot did all of his chores for him!

The robot started to make his bed, but instead of straightening out the blanket, he ripped it to shreds! The robot then took the trash out—by throwing it out the window! Then he headed to the cat...

"No!" shouted Victor, "Wait! Stop, Marvin! I'll take care of the cat!" Victor was terrified at what the robot might do to his cat!

Suddenly Victor felt someone shaking him.

"Wake up, Victor! You are having a bad dream! Who is Marvin?" said his mom.

Victor opened his eyes. He must have fallen asleep!

This was all a dream! He laughed and told his mom about Marvin the robot. She laughed too, and together they made his bed.

1. What did Leland want to play with Victor?
   - a. soccer
   - b. chess
   - c. tennis
   - d. video games ✓
2. Why couldn't Victor play with Leland?
   Victor could not play with Leland because his chores were not done yet. ✓
3. How did Marvin take out the trash?
   Marvin took out the trash by throwing it out the window. ✓
4. Was Marvin the robot real?
   No, Marvin the robot was not real. Victor was having a dream. ✓

The Cat Who Liked to Read

Summertime in Dolton, Missouri, was very hot. Miss Gish, the librarian at the Dolton Public Library, was very grateful that the library had air conditioning to help keep it cool. Many people would come into the library to read, relax, and escape from the outdoor summer heat.

One summer day, Miss Gish heard a meowing sound coming from behind a bookshelf. She peeked behind it and was surprised to see a gray striped cat sitting there! The thin cat appeared to be very hungry and thirsty.

"Oh my!" said Miss Gish. "Where did you come from, little kitty?" The cat did not have a collar or any sort of identification tags on her.

Miss Gish got a small bowl and put some water into it and set it in front of the cat. The cat quickly started to lap up the water. She purred happily.

After the cat finished the water, Miss Gish said, "Okay, kitty, I think your owner may be looking for you. You are such a pretty little kitty!" Miss Gish put the cat back outside to find her way home.

The next day Miss Gish was putting some books away onto the library shelves when she felt something furry rub up against her leg. "Oh my!" said Miss Gish in surprise. "How did you get back in here?"

The cat went and sat on a pile of books. Several people in the library came over to see what was going on. They all smiled, seeing a cat sitting atop the books!

"That cat must like to read!" said Mr. Norris, a man who often came to the library. Mr. Norris looked closely at the cat. "I recognize this cat! This cat is a stray who wanders around the streets. She has no home."

"The poor kitty must have been so hot outside in this heat," said Miss Gish.

"I think this cat snuck into the library when the door was open. I think this cat wanted to cool down in your air conditioning!" said Mr. Norris.

Miss Gish gave the cat some more water. She decided that this stray cat needed a home, and she decided that the library needed a cat!

Miss Gish adopted the cat and named her Paige. Everyone who visited the library loved to see Paige, the cat who liked to read!

1. Where did Miss Gish work?
   - a. Dolton Public Zoo
   - b. Dolton Public Animal Shelter
   - c. Dolton Public Library ✓
   - d. Dolton Public Park
2. How was the weather in Dolton, Missouri, in the summertime?
   The weather in Dolton, Missouri, was very hot in the summertime. ✓
3. Why did Mr. Norris say that the cat must like to read?
   Mr. Norris said the cat liked to read because she was sitting atop a pile of books.
   Or: ...because she snuck into a library. ✓
4. What name did Miss Gish give to the cat?
   Miss Gish named the cat Paige. ✓

Uncle Arthur's Camera

Jane and her brother, Brian, were traveling from Pennsylvania to California to visit their Uncle Arthur. She and Brian were excited to go! They had never been to California before!

"Welcome to California!" exclaimed Uncle Arthur when they arrived.

"Are you ready to do some sightseeing?"

"Yes!" both Jane and Brian shouted. "Where are we going first?"

"Sequoia National Park!" said Uncle Arthur. They got into Uncle Arthur's car, and he drove them to Sequoia National Park. It was amazing there—Jane and Brian saw trees so big and tall that they felt like little ants standing next to them.

"Smile!" said Uncle Arthur as he took a picture of them with his camera in front of the huge trees. Jane and Brian smiled widely at the picture.

The next day they went to see the Golden Gate Bridge. It was so cool to see! Jane and Brian could not believe their eyes.

There were no bridges like this in Pennsylvania!

"Smile!" said Uncle Arthur as he took a picture of them by the bridge.

The following days they visited many more interesting places, such as Santa Monica Pier, Hollywood, and even Alcatraz Island! Uncle Arthur brought his camera to each place and took lots of pictures.

"Goodbye," Jane said as she gave her Uncle Arthur a big hug. "We will miss you—and we will miss California!"

"We loved sightseeing with you!" said Brian. "We will miss you and your camera!"

Two weeks after Jane and Brian had returned home, a package arrived.

"What could this be?" wondered Brian. They quickly opened up the box.

Inside was a beautiful photo album. It was filled with pictures that Uncle Arthur had taken of them while they were in California! They were able to remember all the fun places they had visited by looking at the pictures!

Jane and Brian were very grateful to Uncle Arthur for the photo album and for his wonderful camera!

1. **Where do Jane and Brian live?**
   Jane and Brian live in Pennsylvania. ✓

2. **Why are Jane and Brian going to California?**
   Jane and Brian are going to California to visit their Uncle Arthur. ✓

3. **Which was the first place they went sightseeing?**
   a. Alcatraz Island
   b. Hollywood
   c. Golden Gate Bridge
   d. Sequoia National Park ✓

4. **What helped Jane and Brian to remember all of the places they had visited in California?**
   The photo album sent by their Uncle Arthur helped them
   to remember all the places they had visited. ✓

Cousin Camp

Jackson had a big family—he had five sisters! He loved his sisters all very much, but he was the only boy in the family, and sometimes he wished he had a brother. Especially when his sisters all left to go to Girl Scout Camp in the summer, and he was left home without them.

One day his mom came into his room and said, "Jackson, how would you like to go to visit your cousins this summer?" Jackson had three older cousins: Tristan, Gavin, and Adrian. They lived in a town about an hour away.

They were so much fun! They knew how to do so many things!

"Yes!" exclaimed Jackson. "I would love to visit them!"

So, when Jackson's sisters were all going to Girl Scout Camp, Jackson went to stay with his cousins for a week. They called it Cousin Camp!

Jackson was so excited to be surrounded by other boys all week! He went for nature hikes with them, he rode bicycles with them, he watched movies with them, and he played video games with them!

One day Tristan said, "Jackson, would you like to learn a magic trick?"

"Sure!" replied Jackson. Tristan taught Jackson a magic trick using a coin.

Another day Gavin taught Jackson how to play chess.

"You are really good at chess!" Gavin said. Jackson felt so proud!

"Do you know how to play ping pong, Jackson?" asked Adrian.

Jackson had never played ping pong before, so Adrian taught him.

When the week of Cousin Camp was over, Jackson's mom came to pick him up. He showed her the magic trick and challenged her to games of chess and ping pong!

"Wow, Jackson! You have learned a lot this week!" said his mom.

"Cousin Camp was the best! Can I come again next summer?" asked Jackson.

"I think so," said his mom, "as long as your cousins would like that."

Tristan, Gavin, and Adrian all agreed that Cousin Camp should be an annual event. Jackson was so happy to have these boy cousins!

1. **How many sisters did Jackson have?**
   Jackson had five sisters. ✓

2. **Where did his sisters go in the summer?**
   His sisters went to Girl Scout Camp in the summer. ✓

3. **Who taught Jackson how to do a magic trick?** ✓
   a. Tristan ✓
   b. Gavin
   c. Adrian
   d. His mom

4. **What two games did Jackson learn from his cousins?** ✓
   The two games that Jackson learned how to play were chess and ping pong.

Clouds

Have you ever looked up into the sky and admired the beautiful white puffs floating up there? Or have you ever looked outside to a darkened sky, knowing that it was going to rain soon? You are seeing clouds!

Clouds are actually large groups of very tiny water droplets that are visible in the air. Some clouds look white because they reflect light from the sun, others; look gray because they are filled with so many water droplets that they no longer reflect the sun's light.

Scientists have identified three main types of clouds: stratus, cumulus, and cirrus. These three types of clouds have different characteristics, and they help scientists to know what kind of weather is happening. You can learn to tell the different types of clouds apart.

Stratus clouds hang low in the sky and are gray in color.

They mean snow or rain is coming!

Cumulus clouds are the largely white, fluffy clouds seen on days when the sky is clear and blue. They often appear on warm, sunny days.

Cirrus clouds are found high in the sky. They are small and wispy. A cirrus cloud often means there will be a change in the weather.

The next time you are outside, take a look up in the sky.

What kind of clouds do you see?

Find the words in the puzzle and circle.

CLOUD   CUMULUS   DROPLET   REFLECT   WEATHER

S	H	Z	C	I	O	O	P	A	V	K	Q	V	L
P	E	O	L	F	K	Z	C	U	M	U	L	U	S
L	B	M	O	R	E	F	L	E	C	T	D	V	E
W	A	K	U	E	Q	X	O	E	K	I	S	F	L
Z	H	X	E	Q	K	Q	U	A	H	M	E	S	D
W	E	A	T	H	E	R	D	R	O	P	L	E	T

The Water Cycle

Water is necessary for all living things. Plants, trees, animals, and people all need water to survive. On our Earth, water is found in three states of matter: solid, liquid, and gas. Solid water, called ice, is found in glaciers and snow. It is most commonly found in places where it is very cold, such as the North Pole and the South Pole.

Liquid water is found in oceans, lakes, and rivers. It can even be found in soil and underground. Water vapor, a gas, is found in the atmosphere around the Earth.

Water can change from one state of matter to another by following the path of the water cycle. Solid water and ice can change into a liquid when it gets warm. This process is called melting. Melting ice flows in the Earth's oceans, lakes, and rivers.

The heat from the sun causes water to evaporate from oceans, lakes, and rivers. When liquid water evaporates, it turns into water vapor. The water vapor enters the atmosphere and can form clouds.

As the water vapor in the clouds cools down, it becomes liquid again. This process is called condensation. Condensation is the opposite of evaporation.

When a cloud becomes full of liquid water, it falls from the sky like rain or snow. This is called precipitation. The rain and snow fill the oceans, lakes, and rivers, and the water cycle starts all over again.

It is important for us to learn about the water cycle and to keep our water clean!

Find the words in the puzzle and circle.

ATMOSPHERE   CONDENSATION   EVAPORATION   OCEANS   HEAT

C	O	N	D	E	N	S	A	T	I	O	N	P	E
F	L	K	E	O	K	P	E	O	L	C	M	O	H
P	A	T	M	O	S	P	H	E	R	E	O	E	E
C	O	N	F	L	V	L	B	M	O	A	C	A	A
E	V	A	P	O	R	A	T	I	O	N	E	C	T
P	A	A	H	M	E	S	D	V	B	S	S	H	Z

The Cloud Race

Martin liked to look out the windows of the car while his father drove him to school in the mornings. He would often notice things in the sky, such as birds, airplanes, and clouds.

Clouds were his favorite thing to see. If they were the large, fluffy white clouds he could look for shapes in them! Sometimes he could see clouds shaped like dragons with giant wings. Other times he saw turtles crawling slowly along. Once he even saw a huge whale swimming through the sky!

"Dad, today is a perfect day to see cloud shapes!" Martin said one morning. The sky was blue and the white clouds were high overhead.

"Tell me if you see any cool shapes!" His dad said as he started the car.

Martin pressed his face against the window and looked up towards the sky. He looked and looked for a shape, but couldn't see anything special. They were almost to his school when he noticed a cloud shaped exactly like a horse!

"Dad! There is a beautiful horse! And he is going to win a race!" said Martin. His dad parked the car at the school. They got out, and Martin pointed up to where he saw the horse shape in the sky.

"That does look like a fast horse, but I think you are faster! Let's get on the grass and see if you can beat him in the race!" said his dad.

Martin hurried over to the grass and started running along, imagining that he was racing the horse! It was a great day to see cloud shapes!

Read the clues and write the answer in a crossword puzzle:

1. Tiny water droplets gathered together in the air

2. A lawn, usually kept trimmed and free of weeds

3. Time of day when you first wake up

4. Push up against

5. Formation

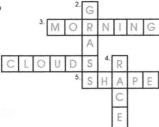

```
                    2.
                    G
              3.
              M  O  R  N  I  N  G
                    A
         1.                  4.
         C  L  O  U  D  S     R
                   5.
                   S  H  A  P  E
                            C
                            E
```

The Wright Brothers

Have you ever flown in an airplane? If so, you have the Wright brothers to thank! Orville and Wilbur Wright invented the first airplane. They spent years experimenting with the design and technology and finally made the first flight on December 17, 1903.

Wilbur was older than Orville by four years. They also had five other siblings! They were American and grew up in the states of Indiana and Ohio, as their family moved to different houses a few times.

The brothers loved to invent things and became interested in flying when their dad gave them a toy helicopter. When they were young, they loved to build kites and fly them for fun. They also were very interested in how bicycles worked, and when they were young men, they opened a bicycle shop.

They decided to try out their first plane in Kitty Hawk, North Carolina. They chose Kitty Hawk because it had strong breezes to help the plane and soft sand below in case it crashed. The first flight only lasted 12 seconds!

Orville and Wilbur Wright were very courageous to attempt such an invention and very smart to figure out how to make it work! They are known as the Fathers of Modern Aviation, and you can see their original airplane on display at the Smithsonian Air and Space Museum in Washington D.C.

Find the words in the puzzle and circle.

AVIATION   EXPERIMENT   INVENT   HELICOPTER   TECHNOLOGY

```
H  E  L  (E  X  P  E  R  I  M  E  N  T) L
S  H  Z  A (T  E  C  H  N  O  L  O  G  Y)
F  L  V  L  B  M  O  A  V  I  C  O  N  F
(H  E  L  I  C  O  P  T  E  R) K  E  M  E
T  E  C  P  A  E  M  E  N  T  P  E  O  A
E  X  P  E (A  V  I  A  T  I  O  N) C  C
```

Nicholas and his Brother

Nicholas loved doing things with his younger brother. Today they were playing on the swings in the park. Nicholas was very good at swinging—he could go so high that he felt like he was flying!

"I'm flying!" Nicholas shouted happily as his mother gently pushed his younger brother on the baby swing nearby.

"Are you flying like a bird?" asked his mother with a smile.

"No," said Nicholas, "I'm flying like an airplane! I love airplanes!"

Before they returned home, they stopped by the library. There Nicholas and his mother found a book about airplanes. They checked the book out and brought it home. While his brother was taking a nap, Nicholas and his mother read the book. It had lots of colorful photographs of airplanes and lots of interesting information about how they were invented.

"Wow! I didn't know that two brothers invented the airplane!" exclaimed Nicholas. He looked closely at the photograph in the book that showed Orville and Wilbur Wright. "Yes," said his mother. "The Wright brothers worked hard to figure out how to design and build a new type of machine."

Nicholas looked over at his brother, who was still napping in his crib.

"Maybe we will invent something together someday, brother," he whispered quietly. "Just like the Wright brothers!"

Read the clues and write the answer in a crossword puzzle:

1. Knowledge that you could get from a picture or a book

2. A mechanical tool made to do something

3. The Wright Brothers' invention

4. A place to find great books

5. A short sleep

```
                              4.
              5.        2.    L
         1.
         I  N  F  O  R  M  A  T  I  O  N
              A           A     B
              P           C     R
                          H     A
                          I     R
                       3.        Y
                       A  I  R  P  L  A  N  E
                          E
```

Penguins

Everyone seems to agree that the penguin is a cute animal! The way they waddle around in their black and white tuxedos is truly adorable! But did you know that the penguin is not only cute but one of the unique birds in the world? What makes it so unique?

The penguin is a flightless bird. This means it does not fly in the air. The penguin swims in the water instead! A penguin can spend at least half of its time swimming in the water. Their bodies are shaped in a streamlined way to help them to be able to dive deep into the water, and their sleek shape helps them to be very fast swimmers! Penguins can swim comfortably in very cold water because they have a thick layer of blubber under their skin. Blubber is a special type of fat that helps to insulate their bodies and keep them warm.

And while their black and white feathers are fun to look at, they also serve an important purpose—they help to camouflage the penguins from predators while swimming. The black feathers on their backs are hard to see from above, and the white feathers on their fronts look like the sun reflecting off the surface of the water when seen from below! These special adaptations help to make the penguin quite a unique, remarkable bird—and cute too!

Find the words in the puzzle and circle.

ADORABLE   CAMOUFLAGE   FEATHERS   INSULATE   UNIQUE

```
U  (C  A  M  O  U  F  L  A  G  E) P  E  R
N  A  D  O  R  N  E  X  P  E  I  N  O  N
I  H  E  L  I  (I  N  S  U  L  A  T  E) A
F  E  A  T  E  Q  T  I  O  N  C  M  E  N
I  N  A  V  I  U  (A  D  O  R  A  B  L  E)
C  A  M  N  (F  E  A  T  H  E  R  S) G  Y
```

Penelope Goes to the Zoo

Penelope had an exciting day planned—she was going to see lions, monkeys, and gorillas. She was going to see zebras, giraffes, and elephants. She was going to the zoo! Penelope's dad made sure they brought their sunhats and sunblock, as it was a hot, sunny day. Penelope's mom prepared a bag with water bottles and snacks. Penelope had her camera to take pictures.

When they arrived, Penelope got a zoo map showing where the different animals were located. They decided to see the giraffes first. At the giraffe habitat, it was hard to see the giraffes because they were standing far from the visitors in the shade of a tree.

"It is so hot outside. The giraffes are not feeling friendly," said Penelope's dad. Penelope felt a bit disappointed.

They went next to see the lions. They were just lying in the grass, swatting flies with their tails. Penelope could not see them well enough to get a picture. She felt even more disappointed.

"I have an idea," said her mom. "Let's go to one of the indoor exhibits, where it will not be so hot. Perhaps those animals will be easier to see."

They went to a building that had various birds in it. There Penelope saw a type of bird she had never seen before—a penguin! The penguins were happily swimming around in their cool watery habitat, and Penelope got lots of cute photographs.

"These penguins are my favorites!" exclaimed Penelope. "I love the zoo!"

Read the clues and write the answer in a crossword puzzle:

1. Feeling unhappy about the results of something
2. People who come for a short amount of time
3. Place where specific animals live best
4. Paper that shows where things are
5. Within a building

Crossword answers shown:
- 4. M (MAP - down, "HABITAT" vertical with letters H A B I T A T)
- 1. DISAPPOINTED (across)
- 5. INDOOR (down)
- 2. VISITOR (across)

The Pyramids

Randy and Mary are students at Grandacre Elementary School. One morning, Mary sees Randy reading a large book called About the Egyptians.

"That looks like a very interesting book, Randy!" says Mary. "Can you tell me about it?"

"Sure," says Randy, turning to a different page. "Here's an interesting part of the book. It's all about the Egyptian pyramids! Listen to this: the first pyramid was built in 2680 BC! This pyramid does not look like the famous pyramids. It is called a step pyramid since it was built by stacking smaller and smaller layers on top of each other. The sides of this pyramid look like a staircase."

"Wow!" said Mary. "I thought all the pyramids looked the same. Who built this strange pyramid?"

Randy shows Mary the page. "A man named Imhotep built the pyramid for Djoser, an Egyptian pharaoh," he replies. "Pharaohs were rulers of ancient Egypt. Imhotep was Djoser's architect." Randy turns a few more pages and shows Mary another picture. "Here is the Great Pyramid of Giza. This pyramid had smooth sides. It is the largest Egyptian pyramid, over 450 feet tall! It was built as a tomb for a ruler named Khufu. In ancient Egyptian culture, it was important for powerful people to have great tombs constructed for them. It probably took over 20 years to build."

"That's amazing, Randy. I learned so much about the pyramids!" says Mary.

"Thank you for sharing."

Find the words in the puzzle and circle.

ANCIENT   ARCHITECT   CONSTRUCT   PYRAMIDS   TOMB

C	O	N	F	L	K	O	A	N	C	I	E	N	T
P	A	R	C	H	I	T	E	C	T	S	H	Z	C
E	X	P	E	M	L	O	A	R	C	T	I	O	N
Q	S	P	Y	R	A	M	I	D	S	W	A	K	U
O	P	A	O	E	I	B	L	B	M	O	K	F	O
C	O	N	S	T	R	U	C	T	P	Y	R	A	E

Sir Isaac Newton

Sir Isaac Newton, born in England in 1643, is considered one of the most important scientists in history. Some people think he was the smartest person who ever lived! He made many scientific discoveries throughout his life, and he developed important inventions that are still used today.

One of Newton's most famous discoveries was the theory of gravity. This theory helped to explain the movements of the planets around the sun. It also explains how we stay on the earth instead of floating out into space!

Newton also invented a whole new type of mathematics which he called "fluxions." Today we call this type of math "calculus." It is an important type of math used in engineering and science.

The reflecting telescope, which uses mirrors to reflect light and form an image, was invented by Newton. Astronomers today still use telescopes based on Newton's original design. Newton wrote a book that is considered one of the most important science books ever written. It is called Philosophiae Naturalis Principia Mathematica, which means Mathematical Principals of Natural Philosophy.

We all have something in common with Sir Isaac Newton—he lived during a pandemic, just as we have done! Some of his greatest discoveries were made while he was staying at home during the Great Plague of 1665-1667. Later in his life, Newton was made an honorary knight by the Queen of England in 1705. That is why he has the word "Sir" in front of his name!

Find the words in the puzzle and circle.

DISCOVERIES   GRAVITY   INVENTIONS   PLAGUE   THEORY

G	R	A	V	I	N	V	E	N	T	I	O	N	S
T	D	I	S	E	X	P	E	M	H	C	O	N	F
H	O	P	A	P	L	A	G	U	E	H	X	E	Q
E	A	R	C	T	I	O	N	B	O	S	H	Z	C
O	P	D	I	S	C	O	V	E	R	I	E	S	U
F	K	Z	G	R	A	V	I	T	Y	P	Y	R	A

Ashley Sees the Stars

The car ride to Uncle Edgar's house was very long. He lived out in the rural countryside where there was nothing to look at but farm fields. Ashley was worried that she would be bored while visiting him.

"Cheer up, Ashley," said her mother. "We will have a great time visiting—my brother Edgar always has some interesting things to look at!" Ashley doubted that she would think anything out here in the countryside would be interesting to her.

When they finally arrived, Uncle Edgar was waiting for them on the porch. There he stood beside a strange piece of equipment. Ashley had no idea what it was, and she didn't really care. She figured it was probably something boring.

She carried her suitcase inside the house and stayed there while everyone else visited outside. Soon it became evening, and it was time for dinner.

"Ashley, come on out. We are going to eat outside at Uncle Edgar's picnic table," said her mother. While eating dinner, Ashley couldn't help but look up into the night sky. There she saw millions of twinkling stars! It was amazing how much she could see without the bright lights of the city interfering! Uncle Edgar noticed her looking at them.

"Ashley, would you like to take a closer look at those stars?" asked Uncle Edgar.

"A closer look? How?" asked Ashley.

Uncle Edgar showed her the strange piece of equipment that he had on the porch—a telescope! Through it, Ashley saw the most amazing stars!

Read the clues and write the answer in a crossword puzzle:

1. An instrument used for viewing far away objects
2. Luminous celestial bodies visible in the night sky
3. A tool used to do something
4. An outdoor part of a house
5. An area far from any city

Crossword answers shown:
- 2. STAR (across)
- 1. TELESCOPE (down)
- 5. RURAL (down)
- 3. EQUIPMENT (across)
- 4. PORCH (across)

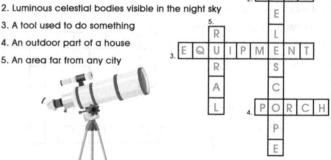

Galileo

Galileo Galilei was an Italian astronomer born in 1564. He is famous for performing revolutionary experiments and challenging old ideas about science.

For example, Galileo once disproved old beliefs about gravity. In those days, people believed that heavier objects always fell faster than lighter objects. To test this, Galileo climbed to the top of the Leaning Tower of Pisa and dropped two balls of different weights at the same time. They fell and hit the ground together!

About ten years later, news of the telescope had reached Italy. Most of the people interested in this invention thought it would be a great tool in battle, but Galileo had other plans. Galileo modified the telescope so that it could be used to look up at the stars.

Galileo went on to discover many things with the telescope. First, he looked at Earth's moon up close, finding that its surface was rough and full of craters. Then he saw four odd spots traveling around Jupiter. At first, he thought they were stars, but then he realized that they were moons of Jupiter!

In those times, most people believed that the Earth was the center of the universe. However, Galileo learned about old ideas that the Earth and other planets actually revolved around the Sun. He supported these ideas and wrote about them. His books and ideas were widely rejected during his lifetime, but they are now famous!

Find the words in the puzzle and circle.

REVOLVED   TELESCOPE   UNIVERSE   PLANETS   DISCOVERY

A	S	D	K	E	F	R	E	V	O	L	V	E	D
V	F	U	N	I	V	E	R	S	E	Z	O	D	O
T	E	L	E	S	C	O	P	E	W	M	Q	S	O
L	H	B	E	Q	X	B	P	L	A	N	E	T	S
K	Q	V	F	L	H	B	Q	A	X	V	F	P	Z
F	L	K	O	K	D	I	S	C	O	V	E	R	Y

The Jigsaw Puzzle

Are you looking for an entertaining, inexpensive way to have fun with your family and friends? Consider doing a jigsaw puzzle! While attempting to solve a jigsaw puzzle, you will try to correctly arrange oddly shaped, interlocking pieces. Each piece has a portion of a picture printed onto it. When all pieces are arranged correctly, they create a complete, unified picture.

Does that sound easy? Well, some jigsaw puzzles are easy—if they only have a few pieces to arrange—but some jigsaw puzzles have thousands of pieces! Those are quite difficult! The first jigsaw puzzles were made in the 1760s by a mapmaker named John Spilsbury. He drew maps onto pieces of wood and then cut them into small pieces. He gave the puzzles to a local school to help the children there learn their geography lessons. These puzzles were a big success!

These days, you can find jigsaw puzzles with many different pictures on them, not just maps! Animals and nature images, cartoon characters, city skylines, and abstract colorful designs can all be found on jigsaw puzzles. You can even have a photograph of your own family made into a personalized jigsaw puzzle!

Scientists have even discovered that by regularly working on jigsaw puzzles, you can help your brain to stay healthy! Jigsaw puzzles make good gifts for your grandparents and friends, and they usually do not cost very much money.

So, turn off the television set and try out a jigsaw puzzle! Your family, friends, and even your brain will thank you!

Find the words in the puzzle and circle.

HEALTHY   JIGSAW   ABSTRACT   ARRANGE   BRAIN

Q	O	L	H	M	E	A	B	S	T	R	A	C	T
L	F	V	Z	O	A	R	R	A	N	G	E	M	A
E	I	S	L	F	K	Z	A	P	W	M	Q	S	O
B	H	X	V	F	L	J	I	G	S	A	W	D	O
K	Q	V	F	L	H	B	N	A	X	V	F	P	Z
H	E	A	L	T	H	Y	A	S	D	K	E	Q	W

Mike's Puzzling Day

Mike didn't know what to do today. It was Saturday, so he didn't have school. He had finished his homework and chores.

"What are we going to do today?" he asked his dad.

"I'm sorry, Mike," said his dad. "I'm busy fixing the car today."

"Okay," said Mike, "I'll ask Mom what we're doing."

Mike found his mom in the kitchen. She was baking cookies. "I'm sorry, but I'm busy today baking cookies for the church bake sale."

Mike went to play with his sister, but she was still working on her homework. Mike felt upset that everyone else in his house was busy. He did not know what to do all by himself. Mike looked around his bedroom and found a box under his bed. It was a gift that he had gotten last year for his birthday. Mike had forgotten all about this gift—it was a jigsaw puzzle! Mike opened up the puzzle and spread the pieces out. The goal of the puzzle was to make a picture of a hot air balloon. Mike started working on it.

Soon his sister walked into the room. She had finished her homework and asked if she could help with the puzzle.

"Sure!" said Mike. Next his dad finished fixing the car. He asked if he could help too.

"Sure!" said Mike. Then his mom came into the room with a plate of cookies. "Would you like some of these extra cookies?" asked his mom.

"Sure!" they all said.

Together they all worked on the jigsaw puzzle and ate cookies!

Read the clues and write the answer in a crossword puzzle:

1. A special kind of puzzle with interlocking pieces

2. The date on which someone was born

3. Having many things to do

4. An activity that you try to solve

5. Small, sweet treats, usually circular

5. C O O K I E S
2. B I R T H D A Y
4. P U Z Z L E

Hot Air Balloons

Have you ever looked up in the sky and seen a giant, colorful balloon floating by? Then you are really lucky, as it is not often that hot air balloons are out traveling around!

A hot air balloon is a type of flying machine. But it doesn't have an engine or use batteries…it uses fire to heat the air inside the huge balloon! The warmed-up air is lighter than the cool, unheated air outside of the balloon. The balloon, therefore, rises up once there is enough warm air inside of it! Attached to the bottom of the balloon is a large basket that holds the mechanism from which the fire is controlled. This basket is also big enough to carry passengers for a ride!

Did you know that the very first hot air balloon passengers were a sheep, a duck, and a chicken? This ride took place in France in 1783. Soon after, people started taking rides in them—this makes it the oldest form of flying technology used by humans!

Hot air balloons can only be used on days when there is no rain. This is because the raindrops would get boiling hot when in contact with the inflated balloon and destroy the balloon's fabric.

So, on a dry, sunny day, be on the lookout for a hot air balloon! Perhaps you will get to go for a ride in one someday!

Find the words in the puzzle and circle.

BALLOONS   PASSENGERS   GIANT   BOILING   MACHINE

Z	G	K	Q	V	S	H	K	Q	O	L	H	M	E
L	I	B	A	S	D	K	M	A	C	H	I	N	E
P	A	S	S	E	N	G	E	R	S	E	Q	W	A
V	N	B	H	X	V	F	L	D	O	M	Q	S	O
F	T	B	O	I	L	I	N	G	F	L	H	P	Z
A	X	V	F	F	K	B	A	L	L	O	O	N	S

Computers

If you've ever read an email, played a video game, or searched for something online, you've used some kind of computer. Computers play many important roles in our lives today, but they weren't always so powerful.

The first computers were built in the 1930s. These computers were much different than the ones we use today; they were really just big calculators. These early computers couldn't do much more than mathematical calculations, and they were so big that they took up whole rooms!

The first computers were made for government workers. However, in the 1970s, the first PCs (personal computers) were released. These allowed typical people to have and use household computers.

An even greater invention came in the 1980s: the internet! With the internet, computers are able to communicate with one another. This is how you can send and receive emails, play online games, or visit websites.

At the same time, laptop computers were being popularized. Laptops are very convenient computers that can be carried around and used anywhere. They fold up when not in use and are usually very portable.

However, they aren't as portable as smartphones!

The smartphone was invented in the 1990s. Smartphones feature "touchscreen" displays, meaning you control them by touching their screens with your finger. These computers are very small compared to the early ones; they can fit right into your pocket!

Find the words in the puzzle and circle.

CALCULATOR   INFORMATION   SMARTPHONES   CONVENIENT   ONLINE

S	H	Z	S	M	A	R	T	P	H	O	N	E	S
E	Q	X	B	E	O	M	Q	S	O	N	L	W	A
K	Q	O	L	H	M	E	S	D	K	L	Z	O	M
L	B	A	V	C	O	N	V	E	N	I	E	N	T
I	N	F	O	R	M	A	T	I	O	N	H	P	Z
C	A	L	C	U	L	A	T	O	R	E	V	F	K

Grandma and the Computer

It was summer vacation and Rachel was visiting her grandma's house. Rachel was excited to be out of school for the summer, and she was happy to get to spend time with her grandma.

"How did you do in school this year?" asked her grandma.

"Oh, it was a great year!" replied Rachel. "I really liked my teacher, and I did well on my final report card. Would you like to see it?"

"Sure! Did you bring it with you?" asked her grandma.

"No, my report card is not printed on paper, it is on the computer! It is posted onto the school's website," Rachel explained.

"I do not really understand what that means," said her grandma. "I still do not know how to use the computer that your parents bought for me. It just sits on the desk—I do not even know how to turn it on!"

"Oh, Grandma! I can teach you! You will love it." Together Rachel and her grandma went into the room with the computer.

Rachel showed her how to turn the computer on, how to get onto the internet, and how to look up different websites. She showed her grandma her report card!

"How wonderful—both your report card and this computer!" exclaimed her grandma. "The computer is like a whole new world for me. Thank you, Rachel, for teaching me!"

"Today's lesson is just the beginning. Tomorrow I will teach you even more!" Rachel was so happy that her grandma could finally use the computer!

Read the clues and write the answer in a crossword puzzle:

1. The online community that computers connect to
2. A machine made for searching the internet
3. Last and most recent
4. The day after today
5. The day it is now

Crossword answers:
- 4 across: TOMORROW
- 2 down: COMPUTER
- 5 down: TODAY
- 3 down: FINAL
- 1 across: INTERNET

Polar Bears

Do you want to impress your family and friends with an amazing fun fact? Tell them that polar bears are not really white! This is true because their fur is actually made up of clear, hollow tubes that reflect the light, causing the bears to appear white. The skin beneath polar bears' fur is black!

The polar bear is the world's largest land predator; they hunt for and eat seals. Polar bears live in the countries that ring the Arctic Circle: Norway, Greenland, Canada, Russia, and the United States (Alaska). They live on sea ice, which is frozen ocean water. That is why you will not find a polar bear in warmer climates. But do not worry about the polar bears getting too cold while out in the snow and ice! They are insulated with two layers of fur and under the fur, a thick layer of fat. In fact, they have more problems with overheating than they do with getting too cold!

Polar bears are excellent swimmers. They can swim for long distances to get from one piece of sea ice to another. Their large paws are specially adapted for swimming, and they use them to paddle through the icy water.

As the world is going through a period of global warming, polar bears are at risk. Their sea ice is melting, and so they are losing their natural habitat. It is important to learn more about how to help protect polar bears and to save this unique species!

Find the words in the puzzle and circle.

FROZEN   POLAR   PREDATOR   SPECIES   ADAPTED

S	H	Z	O	M	Q	S	O	L	W	A	K	P	F
H	M	E	S	D	E	P	R	E	D	A	T	O	R
A	D	A	P	T	E	D	E	I	S	F	L	L	O
L	B	A	V	K	Q	V	L	E	Q	X	B	A	Z
P	Z	H	X	S	P	E	C	I	E	S	R	R	E
F	K	Z	O	M	E	Q	V	F	L	D	V	B	N

Brock Saves the Polar Bears

One day Brock was watching television and saw a show about global warming. The show explained how the Earth's temperature is rising and why that is a major problem—especially for the polar bears.

Polar bears thrive in areas where it is very cold. They live around the icy, frozen ocean waters of the Arctic Circle called sea ice. Brock learned that those icy areas are beginning to melt because the Earth's temperature is too warm to freeze the water. The polar bears' entire ecosystem is at risk because the sea ice is disappearing.

"This is terrible," said Brock. "I wish I could do something to help."

"Well, Brock," said his mom, "we could try to help. We can raise awareness about this problem. We can give people ideas of how changes in their daily behavior could reduce global warming."

"Yes! I want to help! I want to help save the polar bears!" exclaimed Brock.

Together they researched information about ways to help, such as planting trees, using the car less often, and using less electricity. Brock and his mom decided to form a club to spread this useful information. Brock named the club the Save the Polar Bears Club!

At the first meeting, Brock explained to the group what global warming is and the simple ways we could help. Then the club members all planted new trees in a nearby park. Brock felt proud that he was helping to save the polar bears!

Read the clues and write the answer in a crossword puzzle:

1. The way that someone acts
2. How hot or cold something is
3. Energy that powers machines
4. Huge, furry animals with large teeth
5. Natural environment in which plants and animals live

Crossword answers:
- 3 down: ELECTRICITY
- 4 down: BEAR
- 2 across: TEMPERATURE
- 1 across: BEHAVIOR
- 5 across: ECOSYSTEM

Antarctica

"I'm so excited!" said Noah, Timothy's best friend. "My dad is coming into class today!" The bell rang, and Timothy was excited. Noah's father walked in through the door.
"Class, we have a guest today, so please give him your full attention," said Mrs. Kranz, the teacher.
"Hello, everyone, my name is Mr. Casal. Today, I'm going to tell you about my job as a glaciologist. A glaciologist is someone who studies glaciers! And I have just returned from an amazing trip to a very interesting place: Antarctica."
The whole class gasped. Some kids started whispering.
Mr. Casal continued. "I learned so much about Antarctica during my trip. Did you know that it's actually a desert?" This confused Timothy. What did he mean? Antarctica is full of ice, not sand!
"It's true that Antarctica is cold and covered in ice," said Mr. Casal, "but it is considered a desert because it has very little rain or snow. In fact, Antarctica is the driest continent on the planet!"
"Did you see any penguins?" asked Suzie, one of Timothy's classmates.
"Well, I was quite busy, but I did see a few! They were beautiful in their natural habitat."
"How cold was it?" asked Josh, another student.
"On most days, it was far colder than the inside of your freezer! However, it was not as cold on the coast."
"Could I ever go there?" asked Timothy.
Mr. Casal smiled. "If you study hard!"

Read the clues and write the answer in a crossword puzzle:

1. Flightless birds that can live in Antarctica
2. Quickly inhaled in surprise
3. Huge chunks of ice
4. Least wet or moist
5. Frozen water

Crossword answers:
- 3. GLACIERS
- 4. DRIEST
- 2. GASPED
- 5. ICE
- 1. PENGUINS

Rainforests

Did you know that approximately 25% of all medicines come from the rainforest? Rainforests are full of unique plant species that have been proven to provide various health benefits.
Not all plants in the rainforest are used for medicine, though! Sugar, pineapples, and cinnamon originate from the rainforest, along with cocoa beans, which are used to make chocolate!
The rainforest is also home to many unique animals, including sloths, orangutans, poison dart frogs, and macaws. In fact, about 50% of the world's plant and animal species can be found somewhere in the rainforest!
Unfortunately, the world's rainforests are in trouble. A big problem called deforestation poses a threat to these amazing places. Deforestation is the gradual loss of forest area due mostly to people cutting down trees for lumber to create room for farms or buildings.
Over half of the world's rainforests have vanished since 1950 due to deforestation. At its current rate, at least 150 acres of rainforest are lost to deforestation every minute!
If we don't stop or dramatically slow down deforestation, millions of irreplaceable plant and animal species could be lost forever. It's very important that we make good decisions that positively affect the environment.

Find the words in the puzzle and circle.

MEDICINES   PLANT   RAINFORESTS   THREAT   UNIQUE

S	H	Z	P	I	O	O	D	A	V	K	Q	V	L
P	E	O	L	F	K	Z	O	M	E	Q	K	Q	O
L	B	R	A	I	N	F	O	R	E	S	T	S	E
W	A	K	N	E	Q	X	B	U	N	I	Q	U	E
Z	H	X	T	H	R	E	A	T	H	M	E	S	D
M	E	D	I	C	I	N	E	S	E	I	S	F	L

The Unexpected Artwork

Julia was excited to be starting her new job.
She was going to be the babysitter for a four-year-old boy named Tyler. Julia gathered some supplies to bring with her: a box of crayons and paper to color on and a few books that she thought Tyler might like to read with her. She was all ready for her new job!
She arrived and showed Tyler her supplies.
"Would you like to read a book?" asked Julia.
"Yes! I love books!" said Tyler. Together they took out the books that Julia had brought. Tyler picked up the book titled Diego. It was about the mural artist Diego Rivera. They read it, and Tyler loved the book!
"Let's make some artwork too!" said Julia. She took out the crayons and paper. As she was clearing off a table for them to work upon, Tyler quietly went into the other room. When Julia turned around, she realized Tyler had gone—with the crayons!
"Tyler! Where are you?" she called.
"In here!" Tyler said happily. "I'm making my own mural! Just like Diego!"
Julia ran to the other room and saw Tyler coloring on the wall!
"Oh no!" she cried. "We are supposed to color on paper, not the wall!"
"But I want to be like Diego!" said Tyler.
"How about I help me clean up your mural, and we can color on paper and then hang it on the wall?" suggested Julia.
Tyler agreed. Luckily, the crayon marks came off the wall with soapy water! Then they got to work coloring new artwork—on paper this time!

Choose the correct meaning:

AGREED	_X_ Accepted a suggestion	___ Rejected a suggestion
COLORING	___ Making art with paint	_X_ Making art with crayons
CRAYONS	_X_ Colored sticks of wax	___ Pieces of paper
EXCITED	_X_ Enthusiastic and eager	___ Bored and tired
LOVED	___ Really hated	_X_ Really liked
MURAL	_X_ Painting on a wall	___ Drawing on paper
SOAPY	___ Containing dirt and grime	_X_ Containing soap
SUPPLIES	_X_ Useful materials	___ Useless items
WALL	___ Horizontal structure you walk on	
	_X_ Flat, vertical structure	

Diego Rivera

Diego Rivera was born on December 8, 1886, in Guanajuanto, Mexico. People from all over the world have heard of him. Why? Because he helped to change the meaning of art.
Instead of making paintings to hang in museums and galleries, Diego Rivera painted murals in public spaces for everyone to see. For Diego, the public wall was the perfect place to express his deep respect both for the common people of Mexico and for the working-class people around the world.
Diego Rivera loved his Mexican heritage so much that he wanted to create an art form that was entirely Mexican. This is why he was asked to paint murals all over the country of Mexico. He painted murals in schools, palaces, and government buildings.
Diego's reputation of being a talented artist stretched beyond his own country. He was also asked to paint murals in various states of the United States, such as California, Michigan, and New York.
People everywhere love seeing his colorful artwork! Other artists have been inspired by his murals and have painted murals of their own. This style of artwork brings cheer to a community and is often appreciated by visitors as well!
It has been estimated that in his lifetime Diego Rivera painted more than two and a half miles of murals! Those public walls are now so much more than simple brick and mortar!

Read the clues and write the answer in a crossword puzzle:

1. Liked and recognized
2. Set of cultural traditions
3. Admiration of someone
4. Distances of 5280 feet
5. Roughly guessed

Crossword answers:
- 2. HERITAGE
- 3. RESPECT
- 1. APPRECIATED
- 4. MILES
- 5. ESTIMATED

Easter Island

In the Pacific Ocean, thousands of miles away from the nearest civilization lies Easter Island. It is a strange and mysterious place famous for what happened there many years before and the unique kind of evidence that has been left behind.

The island, called Rapa Nui in the local language, got its English-language name from Holland's Capitan Jacob Roggeveen, who landed there on Easter Sunday in 1722. Roggeveen found a strange culture on the island and even stranger statues called Moai.

The Moai are giant rocks, about 13-feet-tall and weighing more than 14-tons, shaped into faces. Scientists determined that they were made between 1400 and 1600 AD. They are found all along the coastlines as if guarding the island's people from intruders. To this day, no one knows who made them or how they did it.

In all, 887 Moai have been found, many still in stone quarries on the island. But how exactly did the islanders move the 14-ton moai? In those days, the powerful machinery that we have today did not exist. Historians believe the islanders may have used wooden logs as rollers, and ropes and ramps to help set them upright.

As for the people of Easter Island, they mostly died out, leaving their numbers only in the hundreds. Historians believe at the height of their civilization as many as 10,000 Rapa Nui people lived on the island. It is believed that the decline of their culture was caused by the deforestation of almost all the island's trees.

Today, the descendants of the Rapa Nui people work hard to preserve the island's culture and traditions—and to preserve the Moai!

Read the clues and write the answer in a crossword puzzle:

1. Unlike others, unexpected
2. Unknown, puzzling
3. Gradual worsening
4. Two thousand pounds
5. Unlike any other

Crossword:
- 1 down: STRANGE
- 2 across: MYSTERIOUS
- 4 down: TONNAGE
- 5 down: UNIQUE
- 3 across: DECLINE

Sophia's Tree

Sophia's family visited their cousins who live in Brazil near the Amazon rainforest. They had traveled all the way from the United States, so it was a very far trip!

"Wow! What a beautiful place this is!" Sophia exclaimed.

"I have never seen so many trees!"

"I wish you could have seen this area ten years ago," said her Uncle Rogelio. "There were many more trees then."

"Why are there fewer trees now?" asked Sophia.

"There are fewer trees because people are cutting them down. They want to use the land for other purposes, so they are taking the trees down. It is called deforestation."

"That makes me feel so sad. What happens to all of the animals who live in those trees? Where will they go?" asked Sophia.

"They usually have trouble finding new homes, and they may die. Also, fewer trees means more carbon dioxide in the atmosphere, which is contributing to global warming," replied Uncle Rogelio.

"Is there anything we could do to help? How can we stop deforestation?" asked Sophia.

"Reforestation is a great way to fight back. That means we should plant more trees and encourage other people to do the same. We should also write letters to our government officials to encourage them to make laws to protect the rainforests," said Uncle Rogelio.

When Sophia returned home, she and her family planted a tree in their yard. The tree always reminded Sophia of what she learned while in Brazil.

Read the clues and write the answer in a crossword puzzle:

1. Dense group of trees with lots of rainfall
2. Support someone by talking to them
3. Place, region
4. Traveling vacation
5. Reasons for using or doing something

Crossword:
- 5 down: PURPOSES
- 4 down: TRIP
- 1 across: RAINFOREST
- 2 across: ENCOURAGE
- 3 down: AREA

Nelson Mandela

Our world is made up of people who have skin colors different from one another. Sadly, sometimes people are treated differently because of their skin color; this is called discrimination.

Nelson Mandela is someone you should know about because he helped to move us towards a world where everyone is treated fairly and equally. Even though there is still a lot of discrimination in the world today, Nelson Mandela's work made a positive difference in many people's lives.

Nelson Mandela, born in 1918, lived in the country of South Africa, where there are many different cultures and races of people. When he was growing up, there was a huge racial divide in the country.

White people ran the country, and they had all the good jobs, and the white children went to good schools. Most black people did not have access to good jobs or schools. They were not even allowed to vote in the elections.

Nelson Mandela felt that everyone deserved to be treated the same, no matter what their skin color was. He worked hard to change the laws of South Africa, so this could be a reality. He was even put into prison for trying to make this change. Eventually, Nelson Mandela's hard work gained support from people around the entire world. He even became South Africa's first black president! For his work towards equal rights in South Africa, Nelson Mandela won the Nobel Peace Prize in 1993.

Read the clues and write the answer in a crossword puzzle:

1. Events in which leaders are chosen by the people
2. Reward for your actions
3. Leader of a country
4. Make a choice in an election
5. Time without fighting or conflict

Crossword:
- 4 down: VOTE
- 2 down: PRIZE
- 3 across: PRESIDENT
- 5 down: PEACE
- 1 across: ELECTIONS

The Nobel Prize

The Nobel Prize is one of the most prestigious awards that you can receive. There are six given out every year, in six different subject areas. The areas are physics, chemistry, medicine, literature, economics, and peace. The Nobel Prize honors people from around the world who have done outstanding work in one of these areas.

The Nobel Prize winners receive a gold medal, a diploma, and some money. The prizes are given out at a very fancy banquet in Stockholm, Sweden, every year on December 10th, which is the birthday of Alfred Nobel.

Alfred Nobel was a Swedish scientist who invented an explosive called dynamite. Dynamite was used for mining, construction, and demolition. The sales of Alfred Nobel's dynamite made him very rich, and he wanted to use that money to honor people who helped humankind in some way. With the money he had earned from selling dynamite, the Nobel Prize was created and funded.

If you win a Nobel Prize, you are called a Nobel Laureate. The youngest person to win a Nobel Prize is Malala Yousafzai—she was only 17 years old when she won the Nobel Peace Prize in 2014.

So maybe someday you will win a Nobel Prize! If you work hard and focus on helping others, you will be in the running for this very important award!

Choose the correct meaning:

YEAR	_X_ 7 days	___ 365 days
PRESTIGIOUS	_X_ famous	___ ordinary
AWARD	_X_ prize	___ punishment
BANQUET	___ quick meal	_X_ large, formal meal
CONSTRUCTION	___ eating	_X_ building
CREATED	___ destroyed	_X_ made
EXPLOSIVE	_X_ something that blows up when ignited	
	___ tool that does math	
FOCUS	_X_ pay attention to	___ forget about
FUNDED	___ given time	_X_ given money

Leonardo da Vinci

What do the Mona Lisa and the parachute have in common? They were created by the same man!

Leonardo da Vinci was a famous Italian artist who was active during the Renaissance, an exciting period of time when there was an explosion of European interest in art and science. Not only was da Vinci a great artist, but he had a knack for designing sophisticated inventions!

Da Vinci was born in the Italian town of Vinci and learned from Andrea del Verrocchio, a renowned painter, and sculptor in Florence. He started becoming famous as he became more and more skilled at painting and drawing.

Today, Leonardo da Vinci is famous not only for his detailed artwork but also for his vast collection of notebooks. Da Vinci kept over 13,000 pages of journal entries, ranging from day-to-day thoughts and records to detailed sketches of wild, imaginative inventions! We have found designs for tanks, flying machines, automated weapons, and even a mechanical knight in his journals!

Since da Vinci painted meticulously accurate portraits of humans, he grew very familiar with how the human body worked. He was able to contribute his findings to the field of anatomy. Leonardo da Vinci was one of the smartest and most talented men ever to live, and he has inspired countless people far beyond his own lifetime.

Find the words in the puzzle and circle.

INVENTIONS   ARTIST   MECHANICAL   ANATOMY   ACCURATE

O	Z	X	V	F	A	N	A	T	O	M	Y	L	H
P	Q	W	M	E	I	O	R	D	K	F	A	S	O
L	A	C	C	U	R	A	T	E	F	L	K	Q	O
Z	M	E	C	H	A	N	I	C	A	L	L	H	B
K	Q	V	F	L	H	B	S	Z	X	V	F	P	Q
W	M	I	N	V	E	N	T	I	O	N	S	E	I

Rome

Rome has been the capital city of Italy since 1870. It is located in central Italy, on the Tiber River. In ancient times Rome was the center of a powerful empire. It is still a great historical and cultural city, visited every year by millions of tourists.

Evidence of Rome's long and fascinating history is found throughout the city. Ancient buildings and modern apartments sit side by side. The people of Rome take great pride in their city's powerful past.

The Colosseum is one of Rome's best-known ancient sites. It is a huge amphitheater, which was built around 80 AD. Wild animals and gladiators would battle in the arena. It was built with amazing architectural features—even including some secret passageways!

The Pantheon is another famous site in Rome. It was built in 27 BC as a place of worship. It has a magnificent dome with an oculus, which is an opening to the sky. Did you know there is an entire country inside of Rome? Vatican City, the home of the Catholic Church and a separate country, is located within the city of Rome! Saint Peter's Basilica is a huge church there, and it contains many valuable treasures.

There are even more fascinating places and sights to see in Rome. Be sure to read some books or look online to discover them for yourself!

Find the words in the puzzle and circle.

ANCIENT   ARENA   CHURCH   EMPIRE   VALUABLE

E	M	P	I	R	E	S	H	K	X	V	F	L	A
P	Q	W	M	E	I	O	O	D	K	F	A	S	R
L	F	L	K	Q	O	A	N	C	I	E	N	T	E
Z	V	A	L	U	A	B	L	E	Q	O	L	H	N
K	Q	V	F	L	H	B	Q	Z	X	V	F	P	A
W	M	C	H	U	R	C	H	M	E	I	S	E	B

A Visit to Dr. Harrington

"What?" asked John. "I didn't hear you."

"I said that it is time for dinner," said his mom, with a look of concern on her face. This was the third time today that John hadn't been able to hear what she said.

That night John's mom and dad had a conversation about how John seemed to be having a hard time hearing. They decided that it was time to visit an audiologist.

John's mom took him to see Dr. Harrington. The doctor did several tests on John to see how well he could hear. Dr. Harrington then discussed the results with them.

"John, you have a moderate amount of hearing loss in both your left and right ears. We need to figure out why this has happened and how to prevent any further loss. Do you use earbuds?" asked Dr. Harrington.

"Yes," replied John, "I use them to listen to music and at school while on the computer."

"I think we have found the problem," said the doctor. "And it is sadly becoming a common problem among children. The earbuds are damaging your ability to hear."

"Oh no!" exclaimed his mom. "We didn't know they were dangerous."

"They are only dangerous if you use them too loudly or for too long of a time. I will teach you how to use them safely. I also recommend that you use headphones instead of earbuds. They are a safer choice," said Dr. Harrington.

John did what Dr. Harrington suggested, and he shared her information with his classmates. He wanted to spread this important information around to all of his friends!

Read the clues and write the answer in a crossword puzzle:

1. How well you are able to do something
2. With a possibility of causing harm
3. Causing harm
4. Less likely to cause harm
5. Student in the same class

Crossword answers:
- 2 down: DAMAGING
- 1 across: ABILITY
- 5 down: CLASSMATE
- 3 across: DANGEROUS
- 4 across: SAFER

Small but Dangerous!

Can something as small as a tiny pair of earbuds be dangerous to your health? After all, they are so very useful for when you want to listen to music without disturbing the people around you. They are inexpensive, helpful devices, right? Believe it or not, earbuds can be very damaging to your hearing. This may seem untrue since they are so small, but the damage is all due to the volume at which they are often used and the length of time they are used.

This is a problem that is growing among the world's youth, as earbuds have gotten popular. Sadly, the hearing damage being done is permanent—it cannot ever be repaired.

Is there an alternative to earbuds that is not as dangerous? Headphones are a better choice, even though they are more expensive and not as easy to carry around. Since they go over your ears instead of inside of them, they do not cause the same amount of damage to your hearing. But beware: headphones can also cause damage if listened to at a high volume or for too long of a period of time.

So, what can you do to protect your hearing but still enjoy your music? Doctors recommend the 60%/60-minute rule: use your headphones or earbuds at no more than 60% of the maximum volume, and never more than 60 minutes at a time.

It is important to protect your hearing while you are young, so you can continue to listen to your favorite music for many years to come!

Find the words in the puzzle and circle.

DAMAGE   EARBUDS   ALTERNATIVE   DANGEROUS   PERMANENT

E	I	L	H	B	E	Q	O	D	P	Q	W	M	A
V	F	A	L	T	E	R	N	A	T	I	V	E	O
L	F	K	Z	X	P	E	R	M	A	N	E	N	T
E	A	R	B	U	D	S	B	A	Q	O	L	H	M
K	Q	V	F	L	H	B	Q	G	X	V	F	P	Z
W	M	Q	O	D	A	N	G	E	R	O	U	S	L

The Olympics

Do you like sports? Then you probably already know what the Olympics are! The Olympics are the world's biggest sporting event, with more than 200 countries competing in them. The Olympics include the Summer Games and the Winter Games, each held in a different country once every four years. The very first Olympic Games were in ancient Greece at a site called Olympia—this is where the name Olympics originated.

There is a special Olympic flag that is displayed throughout the games. It has five linked rings on a white background. The rings are red, yellow, black, blue, and green.

The flag represents all of the competing countries' national flags united as one.

The Olympic Games include different sports—there are individual sports, team sports, indoor sports, and outdoor sports. The Summer Games have a wider variety of events than the Winter Games. Some of the Summer Game events are gymnastics, swimming, track and field, baseball, cycling, and volleyball.

All of the Winter Game events are played on snow or ice. Some of the Winter Game events are ice skating, skiing, ice hockey, and bobsled racing. Sometimes new sports are added to the games, such as snowboarding, which was added in 1998.

Watching the Olympics is a fun way to learn about sports different than the ones you may have tried yourself, and a great way to learn a bit about countries other than your own. So be sure to watch the next Olympic Games and cheer on your favorite athletes!

Read the clues and write the answer in a crossword puzzle:

1. Colored fabric that represents some place or thing
2. Sport played with a ball and bat on a field
3. People who play sports
4. Sport that involves bicycles
5. Not the same

Crossword answers: 3. ATHLETES 4. CYCLING (5 down) DIFFERENT (1 down) FLAG (2 down) BASEBALL

Simone Biles

When Simone Biles was a little girl, she had many struggles. Her father had abandoned her family, and her mother was addicted to drugs and alcohol. Simone and her siblings had to be placed in a foster home until her grandparents officially adopted her and her sister. Simone's other two siblings were adopted by an aunt.

Simone also had struggles in school. She suffered from a condition called Attention Deficient Hyperactive Disorder. This disorder caused her to have trouble concentrating in school. Life was very hard for this young girl.

When she was six years old, her day-care group visited a gym where gymnasts trained. Simone couldn't just sit and watch them—she wanted to try their moves! To everyone's surprise, Simone was a natural gymnast! She was so good that one of the coaches at that gym sent a letter home with her, inviting Simone to take gymnastics classes.

Simone loved the classes, and the coaches there could hardly believe their eyes! Very quickly, she was able to perform gymnastics skills that others, who had been training for years, could not. Soon the whole world would get to know this amazing gymnast. Simone entered gymnastics competitions and performed some of the most difficult moves ever seen in the world of gymnastics. Despite all of her challenges, she worked hard and now has 25 World medals—the most in the history of gymnastics.

Simone has also competed in the Olympics, earning 5 Olympic medals. She will be competing in the Olympics again in the summer of 2021—and the world will be watching her!

Choose the correct meaning:

ALCOHOL	_X_ a drink such as beer or wine
	___ a drink such as milk or juice
AMAZING	___ surprisingly bad _X_ surprisingly good
CHALLENGES	___ advantages _X_ problems
COMPETING	_X_ participating in a game ___ reading a book
DIFFICULT	___ easy _X_ hard
GRANDPARENTS	___ children of children _X_ parents of parents
HISTORY	___ events of the future _X_ events of the past
MEDALS	_X_ awards given for sports ___ money given for working

---

Camels

Camels live in some of the harshest climates on Earth—deserts! In the desert, it is hot and dry during the day and very cold at night. Food and water are very hard to find. Camels have adapted and found ways to survive in the deserts.

Camels have a thick coat of hair. This hair helps to keep them protected from the heat in the day, and it keeps them warm at night. They have long eyelashes to help keep the blowing sand out of their eyes, and their nostrils can open and close, to help keep the sand out of their noses. The most noticeable of their adaptations are their humps! Dromedary camels have one hump, and Bactrian camels have two humps. The humps store fat, which the camel uses for energy when food is scarce. The humps are so helpful to the camels that they can go for several months with no food and one week with no water.

Camels are extremely strong animals. They are often used for people to ride on and to carry heavy loads. Camels are also very fast animals—they can run as fast as a horse! Camels can walk for up to 30 miles (50 km) a day on their long, strong legs! If you'd like to see a camel in its natural habitat, you would need to go on a trip to northern Africa, the Middle East, Australia, or Central Asia. If a trip to one of these countries is not in your future, be sure to visit a zoo to see these amazing animals!

Read the clues and write the answer in a crossword puzzle:

1. Change that makes an animal stronger in its environment
2. Layer of grease and oil found in animals
3. Large yellow animals in the desert
4. Power you can get from eating food
5. Openings in the nose

Crossword answers: 1. ADAPTATION 4. ENERGY (3 down) CAMELS (2 down) FAT (5 down) NOSTRILS

Billy the Bactrian

Summers were always very hot in Florida, which is where Billy and his sister, Cecilia, were staying while they visited with their grandparents. The temperatures felt like they were getting higher every day!

"I am so hot!" complained Billy. "I wish I had something too cool to drink." Billy and Cecilia were outside helping their grandfather paint his fence.

"Me too!" said Cecilia. "This must be the hottest day ever!"

"Hmm, I suppose we should go in for a little water break," said Grandpa. "After all, you two are not camels!"

"What do you mean, Grandpa? Of course, we are not camels!" said Billy.

"Let's go inside, and I'll tell you what I mean," said Grandpa.

The three of them went inside, and Grandma gave them each a glass of cold ice water.

"Well," said Grandpa, "did you know that camels can survive in climates even hotter than Florida? And they can go up to a week without having a drink of water?"

"Wow! A whole week?" said Cecilia.

"Yes, they store fat in their humps, which gives them energy when they need it. Dromedary camels have one hump, and Bactrian camels have two," explained Grandpa.

"That's awesome!" exclaimed Billy. "I wish I were a Bactrian camel with two humps! Then I could stay outside painting without getting thirsty!" Grandpa laughed. "We could call you Billy the Bactrian!" Billy and Cecilia laughed too, and they all drank their ice water before returning to finish painting the fence.

Choose the correct meaning:

CAMELS	_X_ large desert animals ___ tiny forest animals
DRINK	___ consume a solid _X_ consume a liquid
FENCE	___ brick house _X_ wooden or metal barrier
EXPLAINED	_X_ made clear for understanding ___ confused with talking
HOTTEST	_X_ warmest ___ coldest
ICE	___ liquid water _X_ frozen water
LAUGHED	___ reacted to something sad _X_ reacted to something funny
OUTSIDE	_X_ not in a building ___ in a building
RETURNING	___ moving away _X_ coming back

The Great Barrier Reef

The world's largest coral reef system, the Great Barrier Reef, is a source of wonder for people around the world. Located off the coast of Australia, this ecosystem is home to many endangered species and is one of the most popular tourist attractions in Australia.

The Great Barrier Reef is around 2600 kilometers in length—it is so big that astronauts can see it from space! It is the largest living structure on the planet; it is about the same size as Japan!

There are so many animals that live there! Fish, sea turtles, giant clams, stingrays, octopuses, and jellyfish are only some of the different kinds of living things that can be found living in the Great Barrier Reef. There are also thirty species of whales and dolphins living there!

The Great Barrier Reef is made up of around 2900 individual reefs, which are made from over 400 species of coral. The hard coral exoskeletons are what actually forms the reef, slowly building up over time. The Great Barrier Reef has been forming for over 20,000 years! With so many animals depending on the Great Barrier Reef to live, it is very important we all help to care for it. Global warming, pollution, and overfishing are three threats to the health of the Great Barrier Reef. Oil spills and pesticides from farming are additional threats to its health. Be sure to do your part to help protect this amazing part of our Earth!

Choose the correct meaning:

CORAL	___ to gather and confine	
	_X_ a hard substance that forms reefs	
ECOSYSTEM	_X_ community of living things and their environment	
	___ money or pay	
GLOBAL	_X_ of the world	___ like a balloon
LARGEST	_X_ biggest	___loudest
LOCATED	_X_ where something is	___ who someone is
OVERFISHING	_X_ to deplete the stock of fish	___to pay too much
PESTICIDES	_X_ substance used to kill insects	___ plants or seeds
POLLUTION	___ fresh and clean substance	_X_ dirty or harmful substance

Down Under

Sandra's family was preparing for a huge adventure—they were traveling to Australia! She and her brother, Danny, were looking online to help plan which sites they wanted to visit once they arrived.

"Wow! Look at this," exclaimed Sandra. "The Sydney Opera House looks like the coolest building I have ever seen! We definitely need to go there!"

"Yes, I agree! I love how it is a building, but it looks like it has huge sails!" said Danny.

"We also definitely need to visit the Great Barrier Reef!" said Sandra. "It says on this website that we could go on a boat to see it up close!"

"That would be awesome!" agreed Danny. "I also want to make sure we see Uluru, also known as Ayers Rock. I have never seen a rock formation like that in the middle of a desert!"

Sandra looked at a picture of Uluru online and she agreed. They would add that to their list.

The siblings had fun finding many more places that they wanted to see while on their trip. They even found one website that taught them vocabulary words commonly used in Australia. They learned that Australia is called "Down Under" since it is in the Southern Hemisphere.

"I just can't wait to travel Down Under!" exclaimed Sandra happily.

desert	sails	Southern	boat
traveling	Ayers	brother	Siblings

Choose a word to complete the sentences.

1. Sandra's family was _traveling_ to Australia.
2. Danny is Sandra's _brother_.
3. Uluru is also known as _Ayers_ Rock.
4. You can take a _boat_ to see the Great Barrier Reef up close.
5. _Siblings_ are brothers and sisters.
6. Australia is in the _Southern_ Hemisphere.
7. The Sydney Opera House looks like it has _sails_.
8. Uluru is in the middle of a _desert_.

Exploring the Hemispheres

What is the weather like in December? The answer to this question can have very different answers, and it all depends upon which Hemisphere you live in!

A hemisphere is half of the Earth. Geographers, people who study the Earth, have divided our planet into two Hemispheres: Northern and Southern.

How did they divide the Earth? They used an imaginary line! The imaginary line that divides the Northern and Southern Hemispheres is called the Equator. It encircles the Earth's middle. Any place north of the Equator is considered part of the Northern Hemisphere, and any place south of the Equator is considered the Southern Hemisphere.

There are differences in the climates of the Northern and Southern Hemispheres because of the way the Earth is tilted toward and away from the sun. As our planet moves around the sun, the different Hemispheres do not get heated up equally. In the Northern Hemisphere, the warmer months are from June through September, and the colder months are October through May. In the Southern Hemisphere, the warmer months are October through May, and the colder months are June through September!

So, back to our original question: What is the weather like in December? If you live in the Northern Hemisphere, the weather in December is usually getting rather colder, as it is wintertime. If you live in the Southern Hemisphere, the weather in December is warming up, as it is summertime!

heated	Southern	Equator	Sun
Hemisphere	geographers	Northern	

Choose a word to complete the sentences.

1. A _Hemisphere_ is half of the Earth.
2. People who study the Earth are _geographers_.
3. Our planet moves around the _Sun_.
4. The _Equator_ is an imaginary line.
5. The _Northern_ Hemisphere is north of the Equator.
6. The Earth does not get _heated_ up equally.
7. The _Southern_ Hemisphere is south of the Equator.

Career Day

Frank's class was walking to the auditorium for a special event. The whole school was attending Career Day! They were going to learn all about different jobs that they could have when they were grown up.

When the auditorium was filled with all the students of the school, the principal, Mrs. Carpino, walked onto the stage and introduced the first speaker.

"I'd like you to meet Mr. Roger Delano!" she said.

Mr. Delano was a veterinarian. He spoke to the school about how he tended to many different types of animals. He said he had to go to school for many years to learn how to do his job. Frank thought it would be fun to spend his days taking care of animals!

Next Mrs. Carpino introduced a woman named Ms. Pluth. Her job was an airplane pilot. She said she was able to travel all around the world while working! It was exciting for Frank to imagine flying an airplane up high in the sky!

After Ms. Pluth, they heard from an architect, a florist, and a journalist. Then Mrs. Carpino introduced the final speaker of the day.

"I'd like you to meet Mr. Willis!" she said.

Mr. Willis was a geographer. Frank wasn't sure what a geographer did. Mr. Willis explained that geographers study the Earth. They learn about land formations, the environment, and the people who live in different places. He said that geographers can do many different types of projects to help the Earth function at its best. This career was Frank's favorite—maybe someday he would be a geographer!

Choose the correct meaning:

ENVIRONMENT	_X_ surrounding area	___ happy song
FINAL	___ the very first	_X_ the very last
FORMATIONS	_X_ shapes	___ flavors
FUNCTION	_X_ to work in a particular way	___ to have fun
GEOGRAPHER	_X_ one who studies the Earth	___ one who studies cars
IMAGINE	___ to remember	_X_ to dream or think about
PILOT	___ one who writes stories	_X_ one who flies airplanes
SPEAKER	_X_ one who talks to a group	___ one who dances
STAGE	_X_ raised floor or platform	___ raised ceiling or wall
VETERINARIAN	___ one who served in the military	_X_ animal doctor

The Milky Way

Our Earth is made up of many different countries and many different cultures. Sometimes it seems like we may not have anything in common with people who live in areas different from our own.

But there is something we all have in common with one another—we are all members of the Milky Way galaxy!

The Milky Way galaxy is one of many galaxies in the universe. It is home to our planet and Sun. In fact, it is so huge that in comparison our entire solar system seems tiny!

The Milky Way got its name because in the night sky it can have the appearance of spilled milk! There really is no spilled milk out there, the whitish band is actually billions of stars clustered together out in space.

At the center of the Milky Way is something quite strange—a black hole. Black holes are created when a giant star runs out of energy. The star implodes, causing an explosion called a supernova. Black holes can seem a bit frightening, as they suck up anything that cross their paths because their gravitational force is so strong! Scientists suspect that most galaxies have black holes at their centers.

The shape of the Milky Way is a spiral. Our Earth is situated in a part of the Milky Way most distant from its center—thankfully very far from the black hole!

So, the next time you are outside at night, look up and try to see our Milky Way—and know that together we are all part of this beautiful galaxy!

Choose the correct meaning:

GALAXY	_X_ Large group of stars	___ Large star
GIANT	___ Tiny	_X_ Very big
NAME	_X_ What something is called	___ What something does
NIGHT	___ Bright part of the day	_X_ Dark part of the day
SPILLED	___ Was put into a container	_X_ Fell out of its container
SPIRAL	_X_ Circular spinning pattern	___ Square grid pattern
STAR	___ Planet we live on	_X_ Bright burning lights in the night sky
UNIVERSE	___ A large city	_X_ All of outer space
DISTANT	_X_ Far away	___ Close
EXPLOSION	___ Gradual fading	_X_ Violent destruction

My Very Educated Mother

Every Friday at Rosie's school a guest speaker came to visit. Today the guest speaker was from the city's Lakeview Planetarium! This was exciting to Rosie because she was interested in space. After lunch, Mr. Krumdick, Rosie's teacher, introduced the guest speaker. "Class, I'd like you to meet Ms. Tibble. She is the Assistant Director of the Lakeview Planetarium!" said Mr. Krumdick. Ms. Tibble greeted the class, and took out a huge model of the solar system.

"Does anyone know the names of all the planets in our solar system?" she asked them.

Rosie raised her hand. Ms. Tibble asked her to come to the front of the class to demonstrate her knowledge. Suddenly Rosie felt nervous—what if she forgot one of the planet's names in front of the class? Then she would be embarrassed!

Rosie slowly began to name the planets. "Mercury...Venus...Earth...ummm..." Rosie started to blush. She couldn't remember the next planet's name!

"Oh, dear," said Rosie. "I cannot remember the rest!"

"That used to happen to me all the time," said Ms. Tibble kindly, "until I learned about My Very Educated Mother!"

"My Very Educated Mother?" asked Rosie.

"Here is a fun trick to remember the planets' names, just learn this funny sentence: My Very Educated Mother Just Served Us Noodles! Each word represents one of the planets!" explained Ms. Tibble. On the chalkboard she wrote:

My=Mercury Very=Venus Educated=Earth Mother=Mars Just=Jupiter
Served=Saturn Us=Uranus Noodles=Neptune

"Oh!" exclaimed Rosie. "That's a great way to help remember the planets' names!" She felt grateful to Ms. Tibble for teaching them this trick!

knowledge	chalkboard
remember	planet planetarium

Choose a word to complete the sentences.

1. I visited the p l a n e t a r i u m because I want to learn about stars.

2. My teacher writes on an old c h a l k b o a r d .

3. When you don't forget something, you r e m e m b e r it.

4. Venus is a p l a n e t .

5. When you learn something, you gain k n o w l e d g e .

Gentle Giants of the Sea

Can you imagine seeing the largest animal on the planet? You would be seeing the blue whale, which can be more than 100 feet (30 meters) long and 441,000 pounds (200,000 kilograms)!

The blue whale, scientifically known as Balaenoptera Musculus, is the largest animal ever known to have lived on the Earth. It is even bigger than any known dinosaur—the tongue alone of a blue whale weighs as much as an adult elephant! Blue whales hold another record too. They are the loudest animals on the planet! The call of the blue whale is louder than the sound of a jet engine. They can be heard by others up to 1000 miles (1600 kilometers) away!

Even though the blue whale lives in the water, it is not a fish. All whales are mammals. They breathe air, just like we humans do—except they breathe through a blowhole in the top of their heads!

Blue whales only eat tiny crustaceans called krill. They have never been seen hunting humans or other mammals; therefore, they have gained the nickname of Gentle Giants of the Sea. These giants also can live to be some of the oldest animals on the planet. Blue whales usually live to be 80-90 years old. The oldest one lived to be around 100! Blue whales are an endangered species, as there are not nearly as many blue whales left on the planet as there once were.

Hopefully we humans can help to protect them and we will see their magnificent species flourish once again!

blowhole	Mammals	protect	whale
Endangered	breathe	hunting	

Choose a word to complete the sentences.

1. M a m m a l s are animals that breathe air and produce milk.

2. E n d a n g e r e d animals may die out soon.

3. When you p r o t e c t something, you keep it from being harmed.

4. A w h a l e is a huge aquatic mammal.

5. To survive, humans must b r e a t h e with their mouths or noses.

6. When you try to kill an animal in the wild, you are h u n t i n g it.

7. Whales use a b l o w h o l e to breathe.

Megan's Big Surprise

The bus pulled up to the entrance of the aquarium, and Megan groaned. She wasn't looking forward to this field trip, and she thought that looking at fish all day would be boring. Mr. Jones, her teacher, announced, "Our field trip includes a viewing of the aquarium's newest addition, so when you enter, please go to the Aquatic Auditorium." "I bet we will just see more fish in there," thought Megan.

She entered the Aquatic Auditorium and was surprised that it wasn't just filled with fish tanks. Instead, there were rows of seats, all surrounding what looked like the biggest swimming pool Megan had ever seen! There was a woman standing at the edge of the pool. "Hello! My name is Diana, and I'd like you to meet a friend of mine," said the woman. Then she blew a whistle. Immediately, an enormous creature came swimming through the water, and stopped right next to Diana! The creature even popped its head up to let Diana pat it! "This is Bailey! Bailey is not a fish but a mammal. Bailey is a beluga whale!" explained Diana.

Megan could not believe what she saw—a whale!

Diana showed the class how intelligent Bailey was, as it was able to do all sorts of tricks. Megan was so captivated; she was disappointed when the show was over. Megan wished she could've stayed there longer! But soon, Mr. Jones was telling the class that it was time to get back onto the bus.

"How did you like the field trip?" Mr. Jones asked.

"I sure was wrong about the aquarium! It wasn't all fish—nor was it boring! Seeing a whale was a big surprise!" replied Megan.

Choose the correct meaning:

AQUARIUM	___ public place with land animals	
	_X_ public place with aquatic animals	
BELIEVE	___ think something is fake	_X_ think something is real
BORING	_X_ dull	___ interesting
CAPTIVATED	___ bored	_X_ interested
CREATURE	_X_ an unknown animal	___ a friendly plant
EDGE	_X_ outer side	___ very center
ENORMOUS	___ tiny	_X_ huge
INTELLIGENT	_X_ smart	___ strong
MAMMAL	_X_ animal that can breathe and make milk	___ animal that can fly

Rubik's Cubes

While simple in design, the Rubik's Cube has become one of the most popular toys of all time. Over 300 million cubes have been sold!
A standard Rubik's Cube, sometimes called a "3x3x3" cube, is a handheld cube with nine squares on each side. Each square on the cube has a colored sticker on it. There are 6 colors and 9 squares of each color. The goal is to get just one color on each side.
The cube will start with the colors all mixed up, so you will have to twist the rows of squares in a certain order so that the puzzle is solved. Most people will not get it on their first try, but there are certain patterns and strategies you can use to eventually solve the puzzle.
Some people have a passion for solving Rubik's Cubes quickly. These people are called "speedcubers". With practice, world-class speedcubers have been able to solve the puzzle in under five seconds!
To make things more interesting, some speedcubers have added challenges, such as solving the cubes with one hand, blindfolded, or with their feet! There are also competitions for solving larger, more complicated cubes.
If you get the chance, try out a Rubik's Cube yourself and see how long it takes you!

Choose the correct meaning:

COMPLICATED	___ simple _X_ complex
CUBES	___ shapes with six trianglular sides
	_X_ shapes with six square sides
EVENTUALLY	_X_ after a while ___ instantly
HANDHELD	___ able to be worn on your hand _X_ able to fit in your hand
INTERESTING	_X_ fascinating ___ boring
PASSION	_X_ enthusiasm ___ disgust
PUZZLE	_X_ a problem to solve ___ a session of physical labor
QUICKLY	___ slowly _X_ fast
SOLVING	_X_ completing a puzzle ___ creating a puzzle

Solving the Cube

It was Thomas's birthday, and he had just one gift left to open. The remaining present was a very small box, small enough to fit in your hand. What could this gift possibly be? Thomas started unwrapping it and soon recognized what it was: a Rubik's Cube! Thomas had read all about Rubik's Cubes and really wanted one. He was very happy with this present!
The next day, he started trying to solve the cube. He twisted the cube over and over again so that the colors would be all jumbled up. Then he began trying to make the colors match up!
The Rubik's Cube concept had seemed easy enough for Thomas, but actually trying to do it proved much more difficult than he'd expected. Getting a single color to match took him over 30 minutes, but he was eventually able to do this. He already had a headache, so he took a break.
After lunch, he went back to it, trying to get a second color to match up. This was even harder since he didn't want to mess up the side he had already completed. It took him almost all afternoon, but he was able to get two sides of the puzzle solved. Throughout the week, Thomas worked on his new puzzle. Some days, he would make lots of progress, and some days he was stumped. But he eventually solved the entire Rubik's Cube!
"Now," he said, "I want to be able to do it faster!"

| difficult | solved | twisted |
| color | stumped | headache | progress |

Choose a word to complete the sentences.

1. I made a lot of p r o g r e s s on my homework, answering twelve problems.
2. Dad's confusing riddle had me s t u m p e d !
3. Her favorite c o l o r is purple.
4. It is extremely _ d i f f i c u l t _ to climb Mt. Everest.
5. Together, my family s o l v e d the jigsaw puzzle.
6. I _ t w i s t e d _ off the cap of the bottle to open it.
7. The math problem gave me a h e a d a c h e .

Celebrating Holidays

A holiday is a festive day that occurs regularly, usually once a year. Different groups of people celebrate different holidays, and there are holidays celebrated with unique traditions in every country of the world!
Many holidays are religious, and people of the same religion often gather together to observe the special traditions of that day. Religious holidays can help strengthen people's religious faith. For example, Christmas is a holiday that celebrates the birth of Jesus. Most people who are Christians celebrate Christmas with traditions such as gift-giving and a midnight church service. Another popular religious holiday is Vesak, the celebration of the Buddha's birthday. Vesak is celebrated by Buddhists and Hindus and is a time of great joy and happiness.
Other holidays celebrate the seasons or special days of the year, such as New Year's Day. This is a day celebrating the new year and is observed on different days in various countries. Some New Year's traditions include setting off fireworks and gathering with friends and family members to wish each other good fortune for the new year ahead. Certain holidays are unique to one country, as they celebrate a particular historical event that happened there. For example, Independence Day, also known as the Fourth of July, is celebrated in the United States to commemorate the country's independence from England. Chulalongkorn Day is celebrated in Thailand every October 23rd to remember the contributions of King Chulalongkorn. No matter where you live in the world, there are holidays! These special days help to fill the year with joyful celebrations and time spent with family and friends!

Choose the correct meaning:

SPECIAL	___ normal _X_ unique
CELEBRATE	___ play a game _X_ have a party or ceremony
FESTIVE	_X_ joyful ___ somber
FIREWORKS	_X_ explosives used for fun ___ explosives used for warfare
FORTUNE	___ money _X_ luck
GATHER	_X_ assemble ___ break apart
INDEPENDENCE	_X_ being free from anyone's control
	___ being ruled by someone
TRADITIONS	___ personal routines _X_ cultural customs
VARIOUS	_X_ multiple, different ___ exactly one

Gracie's Favorite Holiday

"Grandma and Grandpa are here!" called Gracie happily as she watched them park their car. She had been watching for them to arrive and was so excited that they were finally here! Now they could start their Christmas Eve celebration!
Gracie ran to the door and opened it wide. Soon Grandma and Grandpa were coming up the steps, carrying lots of presents and a dish filled with Grandma's special casserole that she always made for holidays. Gracie helped them carry in their things and then gave them a big hug.
"I'm so glad you are here!" she said. "We are, too," said Grandpa. "It is a very special night—the night before Christmas!" Gracie's mom, dad, brothers, cousins, aunts, and uncles were all at her house too. They were preparing for a meal together, and then they would attend midnight mass at their church. It was an exciting time!
Gracie helped her mom set the table with their fancy dishes. Gracie's brother helped Grandma to place the gifts that they brought around the decorated Christmas tree. Soon the family ate the delicious meal. They now had time to play some games and sing Christmas carols! What fun!
Finally, it was time for mass. The family went to church and prayed together. While there, Gracie started feeling sleepy—she did not usually stay up this late!
As her dad carried her home after mass, Gracie saw the snow starting to fall through her sleepy eyes. She smiled and started to dream about Christmas morning, presents, and how this was her favorite holiday!

| presents | church | sleepy | cousins |
| celebration | decorated | delicious |

Choose a word to complete the sentences.

1. Father John, a priest, works at our c h u r c h .
2. Our family has a big _ c e l e b r a t i o n _ every year for Christmas.
3. You start to feel s l e e p y if you haven't been to bed in a while.
4. Fried chicken is a _ d e l i c i o u s _ food.
5. Children receive lots of p r e s e n t s on Christmas Day.
6. My aunt and uncle's children are my _ c o u s i n s _.
7. My family and I _ d e c o r a t e d _ the house for the holiday.

Flamenco Dancing

Flamenco dancing is a very popular activity for boys and girls in Spain. It is an old tradition that has been preserved by the people there. Seeing a Flamenco dance performed is something you will never forget!

Many Spanish children and adults take lessons to learn how to Flamenco dance. It is not easy! Flamenco dancing requires a lot of practice to get it just right. Usually, flamenco dancing is done to guitar music, singing, and the clapping of hands. Sometimes the dancer uses castanets while dancing. Castanets are small instruments held in each hand.

They sound like two sticks being tapped together loudly.

It is important for the Flamenco dancer to stomp his or her feet precisely to the beat! The dancers have to wear special shoes to help make the stomping sound even louder! The dancers have to hold their arms in certain positions. One arm is usually held up above the dancer's head.

The dancers also wear special dresses and suits. The dresses are very colorful and have many ruffles. The suits are usually dark-colored and have a matching jacket and pants. Even very young children have these fancy outfits for performing their Flamenco dancing!

Hopefully, you will be able to see Flamenco dancing performed in person. Until then, take a look on the Internet to see samples of this amazing type of dancing!

| feathers | glow | auditorium |
| travel | months | sounds | microphone |

Choose a word to complete the sentences.

INSTRUMENTS   ___ things you make food with
                X things you make music with
MATCHING   X with similar designs   ___ with different designs
PRECISELY   X exactly   ___ generally
PRESERVED   ___ forgotten   X kept alive
STOMP   ___ hit your hands together   X hit your foot on the ground
SUITS   X fancy outfits usually for men   ___ fancy outfits only for women

---

Dancing Around the World

Stephanie was so happy! Today she was going to her older sister's dance recital. Her sister, Janie, had been practicing for months with her dance class, and today was finally the big day! Stephanie and her parents arrived at the auditorium, and found great seats. The lights dimmed, and Stephanie knew that the recital was about to begin!

"Welcome!" said a man on the stage holding a microphone. "We hope you enjoy this very special recital. Our performers have worked hard learning three amazing dances from around the world! Travel to Brazil with our first dance—the Samba!" Suddenly music with a fast beat filled the air, and the light shining on the stage had a yellow glow. The dancers all came out dressed in brightly colored costumes and had feathers in their hair! The Samba was amazing! "Next, travel to Ireland for some traditional Irish Dancing!" said the man. This time the light shined a green glow, and fiddle music was played. The dancers had changed into new costumes and were all wearing curly-haired wigs! The Irish Dancing was great—the dancers' feet moved so quickly, while their upper bodies stayed still! "For our final dance, travel to Spain for some Flamenco Dancing!" announced the man. Guitar music filled the auditorium as the light on stage shined a red glow. The dancers came out wearing dresses with lots of ruffles and wore shoes that made loud sounds when they stomped to the beat. Stephanie felt so proud of Janie and all the dancers. She couldn't wait to sign up for a dance class herself!

| feathers | glow | auditorium |
| travel | months | sounds | microphone |

Choose a word to complete the sentences.

1. The campfire cast a bright orange _ glow _ on our faces.
2. The school play was held in the _auditorium_.
3. Clapping is one of the loudest sounds humans can make.
4. There are twelve months in a year.
5. You might speak into a microphone to make your voice louder.
6. Some people like to _travel_ in trains.
7. Birds are covered in _feathers_.

Hiccups

Have you ever been taken by surprise when a loud "HICCUP!" bursts right out of your mouth? How embarrassing! But do not worry, you are not alone. Hiccups happen to everyone. Hiccups happen when the diaphragm—the muscle beneath your lungs—suddenly contracts. And usually, when this happens, it continues to happen for several minutes.

Scientists are not sure why hiccups happen, and they do not seem to serve any purpose. All mammals can get hiccups, even cats, dogs, horses, and mice because they also have diaphragms! Birds, frogs, and snakes cannot hiccup because they do not have diaphragms.

You have probably heard lots of suggestions for how to get rid of hiccups. Maybe you have even tried a few! Holding your breath and counting to ten is one popular way some people can get rid of their hiccups.

Some people say putting sugar under your tongue might help, too. Other people say drinking water from the wrong side of a cup is the best way to get rid of hiccups. And the most popular way is to have someone try to scare you! Boo! Usually, hiccups go away all by themselves after a little while. Very rarely, people have hiccups for days or even years! The longest case of the hiccups lasted from 1922 to 1990! Mr. Charles Osbourne had a case of hiccups that for more than 60 years!

| suggestions | Counting | purpose |
| embarrassing | scare | alone |

Choose a word to complete the sentences.

1. My boss gave me suggestions on how to work faster.
2. People like to scare each other on Halloween.
3. I rarely go a day without eating lunch.
4. Shoes serve the purpose of protecting our feet.
5. Counting from 1 to 100 takes a long time.
6. Losing games can be _embarrassing_.
7. He lives alone in a small apartment.

Elliot's Embarrassing Moment

Every kid in the school dreaded the end-of-year presentations. Elliot was no different; he was not looking forward to the speech that he had to give in Mrs. Wilson's class.

"Be prepared to give your speech tomorrow," announced Mrs. Wilson. "It must be at least ten minutes long—and memorized."

Elliot's speech was about Galileo. Elliot practiced his speech many times that evening. He recited it to his mom, dad, sister, and even to his dog! Elliot felt prepared for his presentation, but he still was nervous!

The next morning Elliot woke up early and ate breakfast. He got dressed in his best clothes. He made sure to comb his hair so he would look sharp carefully.

Elliot arrived at school and waited at his desk. Soon Mrs. Wilson started calling students one by one to give their presentations. She called Sarah, who gave a presentation about Leonardo DaVinci. She called Danny, who gave a presentation about the Wright brothers. She called Oliver, who gave a presentation about Diego Rivera.

Then she called Elliot. Elliot nervously walked to the front of the class. His hands were shaking as he stood at the podium. He started his presentation when suddenly a loud "HICCUP!" jumped out of his mouth!

Everyone in the class began to giggle. Elliot blushed and felt very embarrassed.

"Don't worry, Elliot," said Mrs. Wilson kindly. "I get the hiccups all the time. In fact, I know a good trick to help get rid of them." She demonstrated how she drank water, but from the backside of the cup!

Elliot tried the trick, and it worked! Now he was able to successfully give his presentation. He felt so relieved when he was done!

Choose the correct meaning:

ARRIVED   X Got somewhere   ___ Left somewhere
BLUSHED   X Had a reddened face   ___ Hiccupped
BREAKFAST   ___ Last meal of the day   X First meal of the day
DEMONSTRATED   X Showed   ___ Learned
EARLY   X Before the typical time   ___ After the typical time
EMBARRASSED   ___ Happy and proud   X Self-conscious or ashamed
GIGGLE   ___ Laugh loudly   X Laugh quietly
NERVOUSLY   ___ Confidently   X Anxiously
PRACTICED   X Tried repeatedly to get better   ___ Forgot about
RELIEVED   X Glad that something's over   ___ Sad that something's over

Domes

There are many incredible buildings around the world that have a similar feature—they all have domes!

While there are many styles of domes, they all are similar in that they are constructed to be a hollow, upper half of a sphere. Architects, people who design buildings, have created some of the most famous domes atop churches, government buildings, and mausoleums.

In the United States, the Capitol Building in Washington DC has the nation's most important dome. There is a statue of a woman on top of the dome called the Statue of Freedom. The statue is 19.5 feet tall!

Another famous dome is in Malaysia. The Putra Mosque has a pink-colored dome, which had been constructed using rose-tinted granite, a very strong type of stone.

The Taj Mahal in India is easily recognizable because of its enormous dome. The dome, made of white marble, looks graceful on top of this huge mausoleum.

Lastly, the Pantheon in Rome is special in many ways. It was built in 120 AD and is still today the world's largest unsupported dome in the world! It has an oculus, a hole in the very top of the dome. This oculus lets in the light; it is called "the eye of the Pantheon" and is quite amazing to see!

There are many more domes in the world—and despite them all sharing certain qualities, each one has a style all its own!

dome	similar	Despite
enormous	constructed	Famous

Choose a word to complete the sentences.

1. The twins had s i m i l a r features, like their blue eyes and curly hair.

2. The elephant is so e n o r m o u s; it was the biggest animal in the zoo.

3. The workmen c o n s t r u c t e d a bridge over the wide river.

4. F a m o u s celebrities often live in huge mansions.

5. D e s p i t e their similar looks, the twins' personalities were very different.

6. At the University of Notre Dame, there is a famous golden d o m e atop one of the buildings.

Taj Mahal

India is a huge country with some very remarkable things—soaring mountains, a vast desert, and busy, crowded cities! If you were to travel there, it would be difficult to know what to look at first. Tourists' itineraries vary greatly, as it is the seventh-largest country in the world and there is so much to see!

But there is one place that every traveler to India is certain to visit: the Taj Mahal! The Taj Mahal is a famous mausoleum in Agra, India. It is considered to be one of the most beautiful buildings in the world!

Construction of the Taj Mahal took twenty-two years, beginning in 1631 and finishing in 1653—more than 20,000 people worked its construction. It is built of dazzling white marble, which was transported to the building site from many different countries by over 1000 elephants. The marble seems to change color at various times of day: in the morning, it appears pink, in the midday sun, it looks bright white, and in the moonlight, it appears golden!

The large dome is the central feature of the Taj Mahal. This type of dome is called an "onion dome" because its shape resembles an onion! The large onion dome is surrounded by four smaller onion domes.

So, if you decide to take a trip to India someday, be sure to schedule some time to see the famous Taj Mahal!

desert	Pink	decide	midday
tourists	resembles	mausoleum	

Choose a word to complete the sentences.

1. The d e s e r t is so dry, and the sand there is so hot!

2. A m a u s o l e u m is a building for tombs.

3. P i n k is the color of my favorite flower.

4. I need to d e c i d e what to eat for lunch, pizza or a sandwich.

5. We eat lunch at m i d d a y.

6. The t o u r i s t s took photographs while visiting the museum.

7. The little boy closely r e s e m b l e s his father—he looks just like him!

Skyscrapers

A skyscraper is a very tall building with many floors, also known as stories. These huge buildings stretch up into the clouds and soar high above the sidewalks below. Have you ever been up to the top of a skyscraper?

The first skyscraper built was in 1885 in Chicago, Illinois, in the United States. It was called the Home skyscraper, and it was ten stories tall. In those days, people could not believe that a building could be built that high!

Nowadays, there are skyscrapers that reach over 100 stories! The architects that build them use new technology and materials to make that possible. The tallest skyscraper in the world is called Burj Khalifa, and it is located in Dubai, a city in the country of the United Arab Emirates. It has 163 stories!

Some skyscrapers are known for their unusual designs. In the country of Azerbaijan, there are buildings known as the Flame Towers—and they actually look like huge flames rising up 770 feet out of the city! In Sweden, there is a skyscraper called the Turning Torso in which the top is twisted 90 degrees from the orientation of the ground level!

Be sure to check out more interesting skyscrapers, either in person or on the internet. There are many fascinating buildings to admire—and maybe you will be inspired to design a skyscraper of your own someday!

Choose the correct meaning:

ADMIRE ___ to purchase _X_ to appreciate

FASCINATING ___ dull or boring _X_ very interesting

HIGH _X_ up in the sky ___ low on the ground

SOAR ___ to feel pain _X_ to fly

DEGREES ___ to be dirty or sticky _X_ amounts

FLAMES ___ branches of trees _X_ tongues of fire

TALLEST _X_ the most vertical length ___ the most weight

TURNING _X_ to rotate ___ to talk with someone

UNUSUAL ___ same as the rest _X_ different from the rest

BUILDING _X_ a structure for people to go into ___ an imaginary structure

---

Uncle Ron's New House

Stanley loved visiting his Uncle Ron's apartment. It was so different than Stanley's house. His Uncle Ron lived in the city, where there was always something exciting going on! Music from street performers seemed to float in through the open windows, as did the delicious smells from the food vendors who were selling all kinds of tasty treats! Stanley never got bored looking out the windows where there were always interesting people walking by. The skyscrapers nearby were amazing to see! Stanley would look way up to try to see the tops of them.

Stanley was sure surprised when his mom told him the news that his Uncle Ron was moving to a new house!

"Why would Uncle Ron move?" asked Stanley. "His apartment is so cool!"

"Uncle Ron wants a bigger home," answered his mom. "He wants a yard to plant a garden in; he wants to move out of the city."

The next Saturday he and his mom went to visit Uncle Ron in his new house. When they arrived, his Uncle Ron was standing in his new yard.

"What do you think of my new house, Stanley?" asked his Uncle Ron.

The neighborhood around the new house was quiet—no exciting music. The air was fresh--no smells from food vendors. There were no people walking by, nor any skyscrapers to look up at. But one thing, the most important thing, was the same. It was his Uncle Ron's home, and Stanley realized that was all that mattered.

"I love it!" said Stanley as he gave his uncle a big hug.

apartment	tasty	realized
vendors	mattered	music

Choose a word to complete the sentences.

1. he a p a r t m e n t had two bedrooms.

2. I love tacos—they are so t a s t y!

3. The pianist played the most beautiful m u s i c I had ever heard.

4. Dad r e a l i z e d that he lost his wallet when he couldn't find it in his pocket.

5. The v e n d o r s sold many types of souvenirs, food, and clothing.

6. My teacher said that our attitudes m a t t e r e d more than our grades.

The Moon

Have you ever looked up at night and wondered about our moon? Why does it sometimes appear so big and round, and other times it looks like a thin fingernail with a crescent shape? How can the same object look so different? When the moon is visible in the night sky, it can appear as if it is shining like the sun. But this is not true! The moon does not actually give off any of its own light. It is only reflecting the light coming from the sun.

So, as the moon orbits the Earth, the sun lights up different parts of it, making it seem as if the moon is changing its shape from night to night. The truth is, it is just our view of the moon that is changing!

When the moon appears to be getting bigger, it's "waxing," and when it looks like it is getting smaller, it's "waning." When the moon looks its largest, and it is fully illuminated by the sun, it is called a "Full Moon."

As the moon moves around the Earth, and the portion facing us becomes hidden from the sun until we can hardly see it at all, it is called a "New Moon." It is fun to keep track of the moon's cycle, especially when there are no nighttime clouds to block our view!

wondered	hidden	Until	block
Actually	portion	illuminated	

Choose a word to complete the sentences.

1. Sally wondered where her lost book was.

2. A portion of my homework is done, but not all of it.

3. To block to the bright sun, she closed the curtains.

4. Until you eat your vegetables; you cannot have dessert.

5. Actually, I prefer to eat vegetables more than dessert!

6. The lamp illuminated the family room in the evening.

7. The moon was hidden behind some clouds last night.

Gordon and the Night Sky

The window in Gordon's bedroom was even better than the television. From it, he could see trees, a bird's nest, and even his neighbor Mrs. Mishkoff's garden. In the mornings, the sun would shine through the sheer curtains to wake Gordon up. But Gordon's favorite part about having a bedroom window was the view he had at night. Every time he went to bed, Gordon looked out and could see the moon. Gordon loved looking out and seeing the moon shining in the dark sky. Sometimes there were clouds covering his view of the moon, but Gordon didn't mind. He knew the moon was there behind them.

At school, Gordon learned about the lunar cycle, and he kept track of which phase the moon was going through every night. He loved the way the full moon seemed to fill the sky with such bright light, and he loved the way the crescent moon looked like his fingernail!

He wondered what it would be like to fly to the moon someday in a rocket ship. Gordon thought that maybe he would study to become an astronaut when he grew up so he could.

On Gordon's birthday, he was surprised by a special gift from his parents. They bought him a telescope. Together they set the telescope up in Gordon's bedroom. With the telescope, Gordon could see the features of the moon even more clearly. Gordon was so grateful to have the telescope, his window, and his amazing nightly view!

clouds	bright	moon	track
astronaut	telescope	window	

Choose a word to complete the sentences.

1. The gray clouds in the sky meant that it was going to rain.

2. I saw a cat in our yard when I looked out the window.

3. The moon orbits around the Earth.

4. To become an astronaut you need to go to college.

5. Looking through a telescope you can see stars more clearly.

6. The new lamp was so bright because it used two lightbulbs.

7. I kept track of how many days until vacation.

Petra

The world is filled with some amazing, magical places! One of those amazing places is called Petra!

What is so amazing about Petra? It is an ancient city, one of the oldest cities in the world. It was established in 312 BC! But what makes Petra so amazing is not just its age; it is also amazing because the city was built by being carved into enormous, rocky cliffs!

To see Petra for yourself, you would need to travel to the country of Jordan, which is located in Western Asia. It is located in the desert, which makes it even more interesting—how did the original inhabitants, so many years ago, get water and other resources needed to survive? How did they construct such an amazing city in the desert?

The people who built Petra were a tribe called the Nabataeans. The Nabataeans were excellent carvers, plumbers, and stonemasons—and ingenious water collectors! Not only did they build an elaborate city, but they somehow managed to grow lush gardens in the desert!

The city they built became a thriving and wealthy trading center. When it was at its peak, Petra was home to about 30,000 people. Sadly, in 363 AD, Petra was mostly destroyed by a gigantic earthquake. Many of the people had to leave the area, and the city was abandoned.

An explorer from Switzerland named Johann Ludwig Burckhardt discovered the remains of Petra in 1812. It is now protected as an important historical site, and many people visit it every year! Hopefully, you will get to see it for yourself someday!

Choose the correct meaning:

ANCIENT ___ extremely wealthy _X_ extremely old

BUILT _X_ created ___ destroyed with fire

ENORMOUS _X_ very large ___ very angry

ESTABLISHED _X_ began ___ ended

INGENIOUS _X_ clever ___ false

CLIFFS ___ a towering tree _X_ a steep rock face

DESTROYED _X_ made unusable ___ made colorful

ELABORATE ___ with no detail _X_ with lots of detail

DESERT _X_ dry, arid environment ___ a tasty sweet treat

EARTHQUAKE _X_ a natural disaster ___ a dessert with ice cream

Kelly Protects the World

One day in school, Kelly was learning about World Heritage sites. Her teacher, Mrs. Swanson, explained how a particular place could be chosen to be designated as a World Heritage site.

"World Heritage sites are special places that are being protected," she told the class. "These sites are cultural treasures and important natural habitats."

Kelly raised her hand as she had a question.

"Yes, Kelly?" said Mrs. Swanson.

"Where are all the World Heritage sites? And how many are there?" Kelly asked.

"World Heritage sites are all over the world! They are located in more than 160 different countries! Right now, there are over 1000 sites, and the list continues to grow!"

Kelly raised her hand again. "Yes, Kelly?" asked Mrs. Swanson.

"Why do these places need to be protected?" Kelly asked.

"There are various reasons these sites need protection. Sometimes important landmarks have gotten destroyed in wars; other times, natural disasters like floods have destroyed places. If a site has the World Heritage designation, great efforts will be made to help protect it or rebuild it, if necessary," explained Mrs. Swanson.

Kelly liked the idea of protecting special places on the Earth. After school, she looked online to view images of World Heritage sites. She saw amazing photos of faraway places: the Taj Mahal, the Great Barrier Reef, Petra, and Venice. She was surprised by how many beautiful places there were in the world. She dreamed of visiting them all someday!

Kelly was pleased that they would be protected by the World Heritage organization, and she promised to do her part to protect them too!

floods	faraway	destroyed
protection	organization	

Choose a word to complete the sentences.

1. When the floods came many people's homes filled with water.

2. It was sad to see that the fire destroyed the building.

3. Sometimes valuable things need extra protection from harm.

4. I dreamed of going to a magical castle in a faraway land.

5. An organization is a group of people working towards a common goal.

The Armadillo

The word "armadillo" means "little armored one," and if you take a look at one, you can see why! Armadillos are small mammals that have tough armor made of bony plates that protects them from enemies and other dangers.

No other type of animal has armor like this. The bony plates cover their backs, their legs, their heads, and their tails. The way the plates overlap one another adds even more protection.

The four legs of the armadillo are very strong, and they have big claws on their toes. The claws on their front toes are huge, and they are useful for digging. They live in holes in the ground, which they dig for themselves.

Insects, plants, and some fruits make up the diet of the armadillo. Sometimes they will eat small birds found on the ground. They have very poor eyesight, so they rely upon their strong sense of smell to find their food. They can smell things that are even 20 centimeters below the ground!

Armadillos live in the hot regions of Central and South America, and one species of them live in the southern United States. They do not have very much body fat to keep them warm, so they do not like cold weather!

The armadillo is a really interesting animal. They do not make good pets, as they prefer to live in the wild—and because they are nocturnal! They would keep you awake all night!

Choose the correct meaning:

AWAKE _____ sleeping _X_ not sleeping

SOMETIMES _____ every moment _X_ not always

RELY _X_ depend upon _____ to catch a ball

SPECIES _____ a special song _X_ a special type

BELOW _X_ underneath _____ on top of something

TOUGH _____ very soft and delicate _X_ hard and strong

CLAWS _X_ sharp nails on fingers or toes _____ a sharp stick

POOR _____ extremely strong _X_ very weak or insufficient

FRONT _X_ where something begins _____ where something ends

NOCTURNAL _____ awake during the day _X_ awake during the night

---

Unique Animal Week

On Monday, Rebecca's teacher announced that each student was to spend the week learning about a unique animal. The students would each have read about the animal, watch videos about the animal, write a report about the animal, and then give an oral presentation about the animal to the class on Friday.

At lunchtime, all the students were talking about the big assignment.

"What animal are you going to learn about?" asked Sarah, a girl in Rebecca's class.

"I don't know yet," answered Rebecca. "Do you?"

"I'm going to learn about the Mangalitsa pig! I saw a picture of one online, and I think they are cute!" said Sarah.

"I am going to learn about the armadillo," said Robert, a boy who was also in Rebecca's class. "I think they look amazing, like little four-legged knights!"

Rebecca started feeling worried, as she had no idea which unique animal she should learn about!

At home after school, her little sister Maggie was playing with her toys.

"Why do you look so sad, Rebecca?" asked Maggie.

"I can't think of what animal to learn about for my big school assignment," replied Rebecca.

"You can learn about unicorns," said Maggie as she handed Rebecca her toy unicorn doll. Unicorns were Maggie's favorite thing.

"No, I need to learn about a real animal. Unicorns are pretended," said Rebecca.

"I know," said Maggie,

"but narwhals are real! They are called the unicorns of the sea!"

Rebecca smiled and said, "You are right! I would love to learn more about narwhals! Maggie, you are so smart!"

favorite	Monday	Narwhals
unique	sea	smart	knights

Choose a word to complete the sentences.

1. _Monday_ is the first day of the school week.

2. _Narwhals_ are very unusual animals!

3. Every snowflake is _unique_; no two are alike!

4. Strawberry ice cream is good, but chocolate is my _favorite_!

5. Many kinds of fish live in the _sea_.

6. The student was so _smart_ that he won a special award.

7. The kingdom was protected by _knights_ many years ago.

Ants

You might not like ants when they are crawling in your kitchen, or on your picnic blanket, or on your peanut butter sandwich, but they are quite interesting insects!

Ants live in colonies. That means they live in a large group together. Each ant in the colony has a special job to do. The colony is very organized; the ants all know what to do to help the colony grow.

There is one queen ant, and she lays the eggs. The other ants are worker ants. They build the anthill and find food. They also act like soldier ants. Soldier ants protect the colony and sometimes attack other colonies.

Ants range in size from 2 to 25 millimeters, and they can be yellow, brown, red, or black depending on which species they belong to—and there are more than 10,000 different species!

The body of an ant is divided into three sections: the head, the thorax, and the abdomen. Two antennae are located on top of the ant's head, which are used for smelling or communicating with each other.

Ants are tiny animals but extremely strong! They can carry 20 times their own body weight as they deliver food and other items to different parts of the colony. That would be like you lifting a car and carrying it around the neighborhood!

colony	divided	communicating
soldier	queen	hill	lifting

Choose a word to complete the sentences.

1. Dad found a _colony_ of ants living in our backyard.

2. I _divided_ the cake into eight pieces.

3. The telephone is a great way for _communicating_ with one another.

4. She joined the army because she wanted to become a _soldier_.

5. The _queen_ ruled the kingdom with kindness.

6. Do you know that a _hill_ is like a very small mountain?

7. My arm was sore after _lifting_ the heavy piece of wood.

Picnic Pests

It was a beautiful sunny day, and Amelia's whole family was going on a picnic in the park. Amelia helped her mother to pack up the picnic basket with all kinds of delicious foods. "I love fried chicken!

I cannot wait to take a bite!" said Amelia as she put the fried chicken into the basket.

"It all sure smells good," said her dad as he walked into the kitchen.

"Are you ready to go?" "I think so," said her mom. "Is Billy ready?"

Billy was Amelia's younger brother.

Billy came running into the kitchen carrying a bag of candy. "Can I bring this old candy with me on the picnic?" he asked. "It is leftover from Halloween."

"Sure," said his mom. The family loaded up the car and drove to the park. Once they arrived, they spread a colorful blanket down on the ground. They took the picnic basket out and began enjoying the food.

Amelia noticed something small and black crawling on her piece of chicken.

"Oh no!" said Amelia. "An ant!"

Her dad said, "If there is one ant, there are probably more because ants live in colonies. These pests are rarely alone!"

Sure enough, her dad was right. Soon the whole blanket seemed to be covered with little black ants! "These ants are looking for something sweet to eat," said her mom. "Too bad they are eating our chicken."

"I have an idea," said Billy. Billy ran to the car and came back with his bag of candy. "The ants can eat this old candy!" he said. He spread the old candy out nearby the blanket. Sure enough, the ants preferred the old candy, and left the family alone to eat their delicious picnic!

fried	park	probably	Candy
picnic	pests	Nearby	blanket

Choose a word to complete the sentences.

1. _Candy_ is usually very sweet.

2. Having a _picnic_ is a fun way to spend the day.

3. My grandfather enjoyed eating _fried_ chicken on Sundays.

4. The swings and slide at the _park_ were being used by children.

5. I _probably_ will go to the movies tonight, but I'm not sure yet.

6. The mosquitos were being _pests_ to the fishermen.

7. _Nearby_ the school is the public library.

8. On cold winter nights I love to snuggle up with a _blanket_.

Niagara Falls

Did you know that there is an amazing natural wonder that can be viewed from two different countries? The Niagara Falls, a trio of three huge waterfalls, is located on the border of Canada and the United States. You can view it from whichever country you happen to be in!

Each of the trios of waterfalls has its own name: the American Falls, the Bridal Veil Falls, and the Horseshoe Falls. The three waterfalls together create the highest flow rate of any waterfall on Earth.

The waterfalls were created by glacier activity around 10,000 years ago. It is quite a remarkable sight, totally designed by nature! Scientists believe that Niagara Falls will be gone within 50,000 years due to erosion.

Many tourists visit the Niagara Falls every year, about 13 million! There are special boat rides that take you around the basin of the falls. If you decide to ride in one of them, prepare to get wet! The spray of the falling water gets everyone soaked! Some people have tried to go over the falls, even though it is illegal to do so. The very first person was a teacher named Annie Edson Taylor. In 1901 she traveled down the falls in a barrel! Luckily, she survived. Many who have tried to follow her example have not. So, if you are ever in Canada or the United States and you want to see an amazing sight be sure to put the Niagara Falls on your itinerary!

| barrel | soaked | prepare | illegal |
| created | countries | itinerary | |

Choose a word to complete the sentences.

1. My friend c r e a t e d a beautiful picture using colored pencils.

2. There are many c o u n t r i e s in the world.

3. To p r e p a r e for the math test I studied a lot.

4. We prepared an i t i n e r a r y for our vacation.

5. The big old b a r r e l was full of dirty water.

6. The rain came down so fast that we got s o a k e d.

7. The police arrested the man who had the i l l e g a l weapon.

The Best Vacation Ever

Linda and Geraldine walked home from school while talking excitedly about the vacation their family was planning. It was only two days away!

"I cannot wait to see the hotel!" said Linda. "Mom told me that it has a swimming pool!"

"I can't wait to ride on the boat! I read online that it takes you so close to the falls!" exclaimed Geraldine.

When the sisters arrived home, their third sister, Carol, was already there. She had stayed home from school because she was feeling a bit sick in the morning.

"Hi Carol," they both said to her. "How are you feeling?"

"Worse," Carol said sadly. "Mom said that I have a fever. If I don't get better, we will have to cancel the vacation!"

All three sisters felt worried that their vacation would be canceled.

"How can we help Carol to feel better?" asked Linda.

"Let's make her some chicken soup," said Geraldine. "That should help."

They made a pot of soup and brought it to Carol. She drank it and then went to sleep. In the morning, Linda and Geraldine rushed in to see Carol.

"How are you?" they asked. "Mom said I still have a fever!" Carol replied.

"Oh no! The vacation is only one day away!" said Linda.

"Let's make her some more soup," said Geraldine. They made more soup. Carol drank it and rested for the rest of the day. The next morning, Linda and Geraldine rushed in again to see Carol. But she wasn't in her bed! She was packing her suitcase!

"Mom said my fever is gone! We can go on vacation!" said Carol happily.

"This is going to be the best vacation ever!" they all said.

| worried | vacation | talking |
| suitcase | hotel | soup | fever |

Choose a word to complete the sentences.

1. The bowl of s o u p was very hot.

2. The h o t e l was near Niagara Falls.

3. Grandma w o r r i e d about her lost kitten.

4. My neighbor likes t a l k i n g with my parents.

5. A v a c a t i o n can be a special time for a family.

6. My s u i t c a s e was filled with clothes for the trip.

7. Your temperature goes up if you have a f e v e r.

Human Bones

How many bones are in the human body? Well, did you know that the answer to this question is not the same for babies as it is for adults?

At birth, the human skeleton is made up of around 300 bones. But by adulthood, some of those bones will have fused together, leaving you with 206 bones.

The size and shape of these bones are very different from one another, and so is their function. Some bones serve to protect delicate parts of the body, like the brain and heart. Other functions of bones are to support your body, to help with movement, and to produce blood cells.

The longest bone in your body is the femur bone, which is in the upper part of your leg, called the thigh. The smallest bone in your body is the stirrup bone, which is located in the ear—it is only 2.8 millimeters long!

The area of your body with the most bones is your hand, fingers, and wrist. There are 54 different bones there—all ready to help you write your name, pick up a sandwich, or throw a ball!

It is important to take good care of your bones by getting plenty of calcium in your diet. So, drink your milk and eat your cheese to keep your bones strong and healthy!

| strong | Babies | bone | blood |
| protect | longest | skeleton | |

Choose a word to complete the sentences.

1. B a b i e s are so tiny when they are born!

2. I wear a helmet to p r o t e c t my head while riding a bike.

3. My science teacher has a model s k e l e t o n in the classroom.

4. That girl has the l o n g e s t hair that I've ever seen!

5. I will be s t r o n g after exercising every day.

6. My brother broke a b o n e when he fell off the swing.

7. When I cut my finger a little bit of b l o o d came out.

The Halloween Parade

October 31 was Michael's favorite day of the year. It was Halloween! Halloween was a fun holiday that he celebrated with his friends and family. All the kids dressed up in costumes and went around the neighborhood to get candy!

This year his school, Glenwood Elementary School, was joining in the fun with a Halloween parade to take place at the end of the school day! All of the students were to bring their costumes in a bag, and then they would be allowed to put them on for the parade.

"Mom, I know what I want to dress up as this year," said Michael.

"I want to be a skeleton!"

"Oh my!" said his mom. "Are you sure that won't be too scary?"

Michael laughed and said, "It won't be!"

The next day he worked at making his costume. Michael gathered an old black shirt and some old black pants. He used white paint to create bones on the clothing. Then he found a black hat to put on his head. Now he was all ready for the big day!

October 31 arrived. Michael put his costume in a bag and brought it with him to school. As the day progressed, Michael watched the clock tick slowly—but finally, it was time for the parade!

Everyone loved Michael's skeleton costume, and he had such fun at the parade! Afterward, he and his brothers went around the neighborhood saying, "trick-or-treat!" They received a lot of candy as they wished his neighbors a "Happy Halloween!"

| holiday | costume | wished | parade |
| neighborhood | received | laughed | |

Choose a word to complete the sentences.

1. Which h o l i d a y do you prefer to celebrate most?

2. The princess c o s t u m e looked so cute on the little girl.

3. Dad l a u g h e d at all of my jokes.

4. The street was full of people as the p a r a d e went by.

5. Grandma r e c e i v e d the letter I sent to her.

6. There are 35 houses in our n e i g h b o r h o o d.

7. I w i s h e d my mom a happy birthday and gave her a gift.

Braille

Two hundred years ago, a French boy named Louis Braille became blind as a result of an accident he had. This means he could not see anymore. Being blind made many activities hard. Instead of giving up on these activities, Louis looked for ways to make them possible for blind people.

When he was only fifteen years old, he invented a way of writing for blind people. His invention, which is called Braille, has been used by many blind people all around the world.

Braille is a tactile alphabet. Tactile means using your sense of touch. Instead of ordinary letters, Braille uses dots that are raised on the page. Every letter of the alphabet has a special arrangement of dots to represent it. Using the tips of their fingers to feel the dots, a person can learn this alphabet just as they would one written in ink!

Entire books written in Braille have been created to assist blind people in reading. Additionally, many public signs include words in Braille, in order to help blind people be more independent when out of their homes. Special Braille typewriters have been created, allowing blind people to write on their own.

Louis Braille is honored every year on his birthday, January 4th.

This day is celebrated as "World Braille Day." This day spreads awareness about Braille and the importance of independence for people who are blind.

typewriters	assist	alphabet
independence	accident	blind

Choose a word to complete the sentences.

1. The car was in an a c c i d e n t and its window was broken.

2. The b l i n d man walked down the busy street using a cane and a trained dog to help him.

3. In English there are 26 letters in the a l p h a b e t.

4. The writers used t y p e w r i t e r s to compose their stories.

5. I can a s s i s t my grandma by helping her clean her house.

6. Many people take pride in their i n d e p e n d e n c e; they like to do things for themselves.

Scott's Special Cousin

Scott was nervous. He and his mom were going to visit with his aunt and cousin David, who lived many hours away.
He and David were the same age,
but that was where the similarities ended. David was blind.
Scott was nervous because he'd never spent time with a blind person before.
"Don't be nervous, Scott," said his mom. "You and David will have fun together!"
Scott didn't think that would be possible. What could David even do? How could they play together if he couldn't see?
When they arrived, David was waiting by the door.
"Hi, Scott," David said. "What do you want to do?"
"Umm, I don't know," said Scott. He didn't think David would be able to do anything!
"We could play games, listen to music, or get something to eat!" said David.
"I'd like something to eat," said Scott shyly.
"Me too!" said David. Using a cane to guide his steps, David showed Scott the way to the kitchen. He knew exactly where the cookies were kept.
"These are my favorite cookies!" exclaimed Scott, who was no longer feeling so shy.
"Mine too!" said David, munching on one. "Do you like Harry Potter?"
"I love those books and have read them all!
Did your mom read them to you?" asked Scott.
"No, I read them myself," said David. "I have Braille editions of Harry Potter." David showed Scott the books. Scott was interested in how the little dots felt and couldn't believe David knew how to read them!
When it was time to go, the boys made plans to visit again soon. Scott was so happy to discover that he had such a special cousin!

exactly	aunt	myself	boys
visit	waiting	munching	

Choose a word to complete the sentences.

1. My a u n t is my mom's sister.

2. Sometimes I like to go for walks by m y s e l f.

3. Do you ever v i s i t the Science Museum?

4. The bunny rabbit was m u n c h i n g a bright orange carrot.

5. My dad was w a i t i n g for my mom to finish getting ready.

6. The b o y s were playing video games all afternoon.

7. The identical twin brothers looked e x a c t l y alike!

Queen of the Adriatic

How would you like to live in a city where there are no cars, only boats? Where some of the streets are so narrow that two people are unable to walk side by side? Where most of the buildings are over 500 years old? If you would, you may like to live in Venice, Italy!

Venice is known to be one of the most beautiful, unusual cities in the world. It is actually a city built upon 118 islands separated by canals. These canals are connected by hundreds of bridges—over 400 of them!

This magnificent city is situated in a body of water called a lagoon, at the edge of the Adriatic Sea. Because it is completely built on the lagoon, roads for cars do not exist. Special boats called gondolas are used for getting from place to place through the canals, as well as other types of boats.

Venice is known to have a uniquely charming atmosphere and a very rich history. Some of the most famous places in Venice include the Rialto Bridge, the Doge's Palace, the Bridge of Sighs, and St. Mark's Basilica. Many tourists visit Venice every year to see these landmarks.

Venice has many nicknames: City of Bridges, City of Canals, Queen of the Adriatic, The Floating City, and City of Masks are just a few of them! Despite not being able to agree on a nickname, one thing most everyone can agree on—Venice is an extraordinary city!

atmosphere	landmarks	narrow
bridge	Canals	gondolas	Islands

Choose a word to complete the sentences.

1. The trail was so n a r r o w that we had to hike in a single file line.

2. I love to walk over the river on the b r i d g e.

3. C a n a l s are a type of waterway for boats to travel on.

4. While on vacation, we visited many historic l a n d m a r k s.

5. I s l a n d s are completely surrounded by water.

6. Riding in g o n d o l a s would be an exciting way to travel!

7. The a t m o s p h e r e at the surprise party was filled with excitement.

The Violinist of Venice

Little Antonio loved living near the water. He was born in Venice, Italy, which was surrounded by water. He loved the canals, the bridges, and the gondolas throughout the city.
But there was something he loved even more. He loved music!
Antonio's father played the violin, and he taught Antonio how to play too. The two of them would perform together for the people of Venice.
As Antonio grew up, he realized that he also loved his Catholic religion so much that he wanted to become a priest. So, he did! The people of Venice would recognize him and call him the "Red Priest" because he had bright red hair!
While Antonio was a priest, he still was able to continue playing his violin. He even taught music to children, particularly to girls who lived in an orphanage near his church.
Antonio became quite popular for also writing music. People would come from miles around to hear the beautiful music that he had written. He wrote over 500 pieces of music for not only violins, but for full orchestras!
Antonio lived from 1678-1741, but he is still very famous today for the beautiful music that he wrote. People still love to hear it and perform it—especially the people of Venice. Antonio Vivaldi is the much-loved violinist (and composer!) of Venice!

Orchestras	orphanage	perform
church	religion	written	taught

Choose a word to complete the sentences.

1. The actor liked to p e r f o r m on the theater stage.

2. An o r p h a n a g e is a special home for children who have no parents.

3. My grandfather t a u g h t me how to read.

4. People of the same r e l i g i o n often pray together.

5. Many books were w r i t t e n by J.K. Rowling.

6. O r c h e s t r a s are made up of different instruments.

7. A c h u r c h is often a very large building.

READING

COMPREHENSION FOR

3RD GRADE

100 ACTIVITIES - THIRD GRADE READING COMPREHENSION WORKBOOK

Patrick N. Peerson

Made in the USA
Monee, IL
18 October 2024

68247272R00072